GSD PLATFORM 5

Harvard University
Graduate School of Design

PREFACE
Constructing Imagination

MOHSEN MOSTAFAVI

Mostafavi is the Dean of the Harvard Graduate School of Design and the Alexander and Victoria Wiley Professor of Design.

Every year the Harvard Graduate School of Design faces the challenging task of choosing a series of projects, events, lectures, conversations, exhibitions, and publications for inclusion in the latest volume of *Platform*. This year is no exception. And as in previous years, the responsibility for selecting, editing, and formulating the overall context and concept of the book is undertaken by a faculty member together with a group of our students. I am grateful to Mariana Ibañez and the students as well as to others involved in the preparation of *Platform 5* for doing such an amazing job.

The material presented in this publication forms a small part of the incredible range and diversity of proposals and visions that our students and faculty have produced during the past academic year. This work is indicative of the School's commitment, as a global leader in the field, to exploring and articulating transformative ideas through the power of design. It is as important for us to share and communicate the outcome of our research and design investigations as it is to show the fertile circumstances and conditions for the making of these projects. For this reason, the book is organized according to a series of topics that run across disciplines and modes of practice.

The GSD has always recognized the indispensable importance and values of architecture, landscape architecture, urban planning, and urban design, yet has transcended their individual aspirations through intellectual cross-fertilization and collaboration. This year we celebrated the 75th anniversary of the founding of the GSD—an act conceived with the primary purpose of bringing a number of related but distinct fields of design under the same umbrella. It is of course imperative for us to acknowledge the contributions of fields such as architecture and landscape architecture prior to the creation of the School. But the obvious and yet radical proximity of the disciplines within the context of a graduate school has enabled the GSD, its students and faculty, to gain the benefits of being able to work and collaborate across the various design disciplines and beyond.

The more recent addition of research programs to our Masters in Design Studies and doctoral programs has greatly contributed to the intellectual vitality of the GSD as a leading site for the formation of design discourse. These programs propel the research activities of the GSD in a more distinctly projective direction. In the past year, the increasingly significant role of our research labs has done much to create a new and more porous environment for the intersection of research and design. At the core of the work shown in this book is the idea that design can and must have an impact on transforming and enhancing the daily lives of people everywhere.

It is crucial for this publication to make evident the deliberateness of this project by emphasizing the GSD's broader attention to the built environment as the primary domain of our thinking and actions. At the same time, we are cognizant of the fact that many of the imaginative constructs displayed in this book are at once part of the academy—the place of theoretical and disciplinary imaginings—and yet part of life.

INTRODUCTION

MARIANA IBAÑEZ
is Associate Professor of Architecture at the Harvard University Graduate School of Design. In 2007 she co-founded I/K Studio with Simon Kim.

We continue the tradition of Harvard University Graduate School of Design publications with the fifth in the series of *Platform*. With the directive to be a working curation of the environment of the School, the resulting volume is more than a compendium. It is designed as a multilayered document presenting various lenses to see the School in the past academic year, its present trajectories, and its future directions.

The table of contents unfolds the book into a single artifact, making explicit the prevailing themes that informed the production and debates in the School, and the overlaps that emerge among them. These overlaps, and perhaps unexpected adjacencies, reveal the complexities with which the design disciplines increasingly contend.

The volume's diverse material—drawn from studios, seminars, thesis research, events, and other activities—is organized in seven sections: Metrics, Matter, Activism, Discipline, Synthesis, Conjecture, and Format. These categories and the material within represent the broad spectrum of agendas, courses, initiatives, and collaborations that are established to explore design thinking and design production. This organization is introduced as a framework that intentionally differs from the departmental and course structure of the School, with the ambition to present a transversal reading of our programs that highlights both disciplinary concerns and shared explorations.

The first six sections are organized in a linear sequence, but can also be cross-referenced through the thematic markers that describe each project or event. The section on Format, however, is deconstructed and distributed throughout the book; it can be read in relation to the projects in each section or as a separate collection of documents. This "non-section"collects distinguished artifacts where the subject matter of the work is as important as its articulation.

The GSD is an exceptional environment of continuous debate and production. The agendas and pedagogical frameworks are complex and constantly evolving. Far from being a complete collection, *Platform 5* compiles the outcome of prominent work and exchanges that occurred during a year full of events, projects, symposia, and colloquia—both formal and improvised—that continually reinforced the dual importance of expertise and inquiry. The many people who came to the GSD as students, alumni, fellows, faculty, lecturers, conference participants—to discuss, to instruct—all arrived with their local knowledge and, within the School, created new relationships and ideas. This book is our attempt to share these concerns and discoveries with a larger audience.

METRICS

and their conditions of measure— their analytic and evaluative criteria—have produced a unique modular system for designers. The particular motivations of this system may be seen in synthetic and even artificial relationships among otherwise discrete orders. Metrics and indices, reified by powerful computational tools, have begun to imprint not only classifications and clusters but the very process of ordering and organizing. This promotes the idea of establishing large and complex sets of design elements while pairing or transforming those elements into new constructs and promising disciplinary possibilities.

This causal nature of evaluation can then be measured against the originating tables of meaning as well as the concluding transformations in performance and behavior. What is perceived, the techniques and tools required, and what is derived may form altogether new metric systems for the discipline and the academy.

Metrics are framed in this section as the underlying principle that systematizes formal organizations, programmatic affiliations, and their behaviors. Metrics may also be discovered in the production of form tied to social scenarios, new and alternative scales of investigation, and in the generative tools that organize geometric transformations.

George L. Legendre
Architecture Option Studio, Spring 2012

REAL AND IMAGINARY VARIABLES

Halfway between the socially responsive discourse of programmatic freedom and the alleged futility of parametric form-giving, this studio celebrated architecture's critical return to form. Our interest in the topic of form was neither aesthetic nor ideological. Contrary to the notion of shape (with which it is often confused), form is for us a syntactic, procedural, and (increasingly) technical proposition with a fair amount of disciplinary autonomy, like the study of language in the 1970s—or the more recent emergence of object-orientation in the software industry.

Building on the disciplinary ambition of the recently concluded high-rise design experiment conducted between 2007 and 2011 on sites ranging from Singapore to New York ("Rising Masses"1, 2, and 3), we explored the seminal thesis of architecture as a complex interplay of desire and automatic writing.

Architecture, in this view, depends on achieving a practical and theoretical balance between real and imaginary variables—real variables depend on empirical knowledge of a given type, site, and program; imaginary variables depend on the equally important though far less rational properties of indexical modeling. The two parts of the typological equation need one another to fulfill themselves: without the imaginary part, a type withers into predictability and repetition; without the real one, it is merely self-fulfilling and forfeits all relevance.

Beyond the single, monofunctional, and "semi-automatic" brief of high-rise dwelling, we opened up the real part of the typological equation to more types of drastically different scales and uses—some well-rounded, others less so—in the spirit of open exploration, and at the participants' discretion. In every other respect our objective remained the same: to figure out fresh ways in which a formal analytic model (otherwise known as a seed) might correlate to a building type's functional organization, programmatic uses and affinities, material structure, etc., and successfully integrate the type's real and imaginary parts.

ARTHUR LUI, NICHOLAS CROFT, WILLIAM QUATTLEBAUM

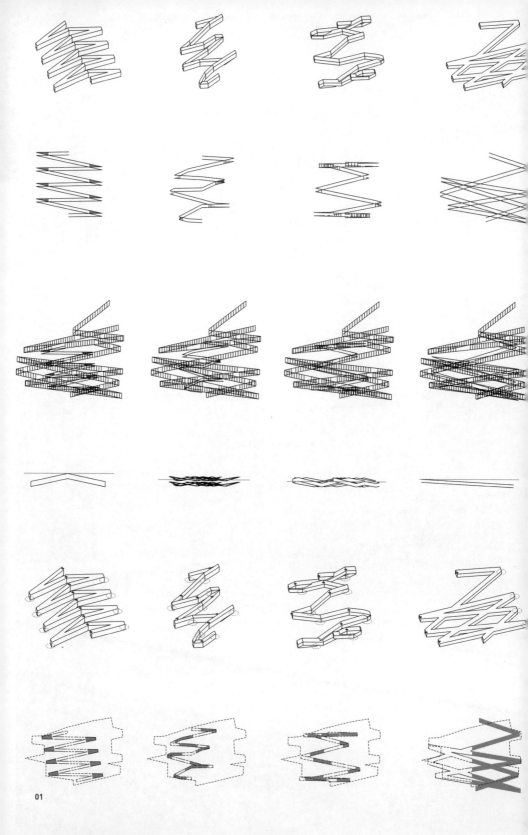

01

ALL IMAGES ROLA IDRIS

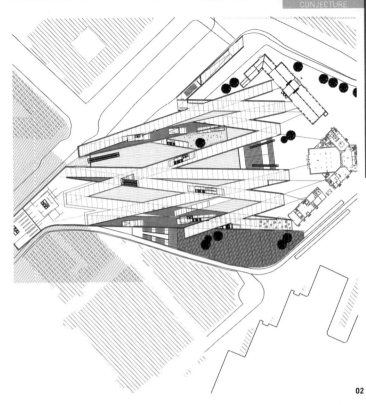

01 *Main Coiling Arcsine Surf, TM Analysis*

02 *Ground-floor plan*

03 *Model of Oslo Contemporary Museum of Art*

02

03

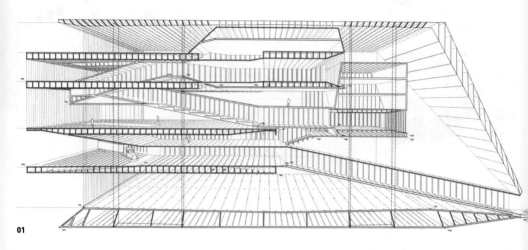

01

02

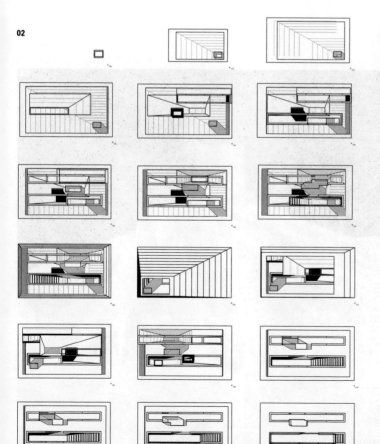

ELECTIVE SUPERFICIAL SPACES

In conjunction with the spring-term elective VIS-02404-00 Superficial Spaces, this studio will aim to produce sophisticated (if counterintuitive) new formal prototypes—incorporated into pragmatic urban and architectural proposals located in a variety of sites ordained by size and character in South Korea, Norway, and the United States.

ALL IMAGES ARTHUR LIU,
NICHOLAS CROFT,
WILLIAM QUATTLEBAUM

01 *Section perspective*

02 *Indexical transverse sections*

03-04 *Models*

03

04

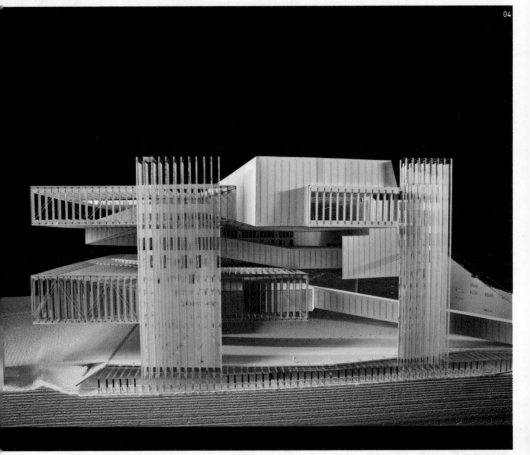

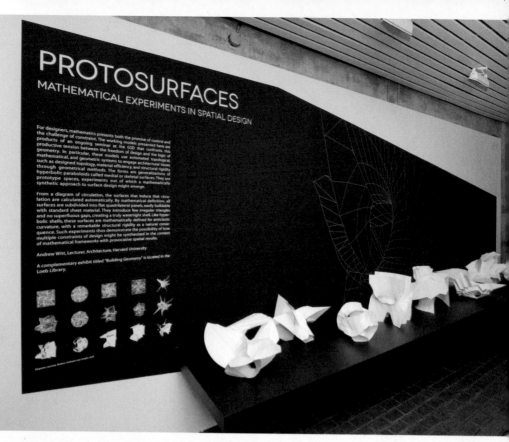

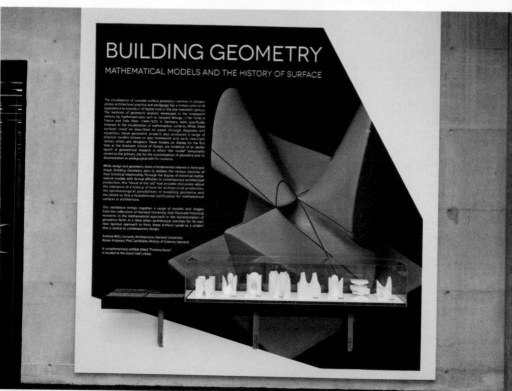

PROTOSURFACES
Mathematical Experiments in Spatial Design

Andrew Witt, Fall 2012

For designers, mathematics presents both the promise of control and the challenge of constraint. The working models presented here are products of an ongoing seminar at the GSD that confronts this productive tension between the freedom of design and the logic of geometry. In particular, these models use automated topological, mathematical, and geometric systems to engage architectural issues such as designed topology, material efficiency, and structural rigidity through geometrical methods. The forms are generalizations of hyperbolic paraboloids called medial or skeletal surfaces. They are prototype spaces, experiments out of which a mathematically synthetic approach to surface design might emerge.

DIGITAL MEDIA II *Andrew Witt also teaches the course Parametric and Generative Geometry Modeling.*

01 DOROTHY XU, KATHERINE CHIN

02 MAX WONG, RYU MATSUZAKI

03 JISOO YANG, YOUNG JAE KIM

04 RACHEL DAO, ELIZABETH ECKELS

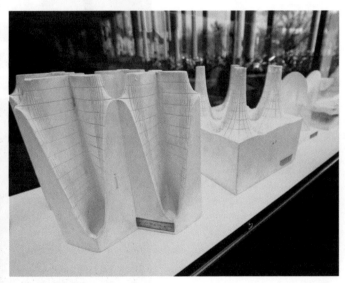

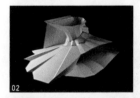

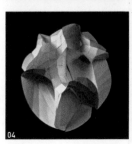

From a diagram of circulation, the surfaces that induce that circulation are calculated automatically. By mathematical definition, all surfaces are subdivided into flat quadrilateral panels, easily buildable with standard sheet material. They introduce few irregular triangles and no superfluous gaps, creating a truly watertight shell. Like hyperbolic shells, these surfaces are mathematically defined for anticlastic curvature, with a remarkable structural rigidity as a natural consequence. Such experiments thus demonstrate the possibility of how multiple constraints of design might be synthesized in the context of mathematical frameworks with provocative spatial results.

Preston Scott Cohen (Coordinator), Yael Erel,
Mariana Ibañez, Kiel Moe, Ingeborg Rocker,
Elizabeth Whittaker, Cameron Wu
Architecture Core Studio I, Spring 2012

LOCK PROJECT

The project was a study of movement in architecture. It was not about
bodily passage, virtual transformation, or implied structural forces, but
rather movement in time and space, actualized mechanically. It was a
project in which architecture becomes the geometrical inscription of
a series of actions and positions. As such, it kinetically redefined the
fundamental tenets of stasis and permanence.

The program was a building, parts of which were connected to and move
with the gate of a boat lock. The moving and static parts of the building
were to be interrelated in such a way that their movement had profound
consequences for the perceived and understood shape of the building
and its function. Among the mobile operations to be investigated were
folding, hinging, rolling, sliding, pivoting, and swinging.

The building was required to enable continuous pedestrian passage
across the lock when the gate is shut and nautical passage through the
lock when the gate is open. Each threshold, when open and functional,
prohibited passage through the other. As such, the project was about the
development of two crossing, mutually disruptive paths.

The building had to enclose two types of interior space: public areas for
assembly, accounting for 60 percent of the total area, and back-of-house
administrative or private spaces accounting for 40 percent. The two
types of spaces are distinguished in character by their scale and by their
ceremonial vs. perfunctory, functional character. Though some part of
the building had to be connected to the gate, its relationship to the banks
of the lock remained to be determined: hover above the two banks, sit on
top, be (partially) embedded, bridge between, or remain on one side. The
building had to be contained within a 20,000-square-foot rectangular site
area with a maximum height of 25 feet.

ANDREY YAKOLEV

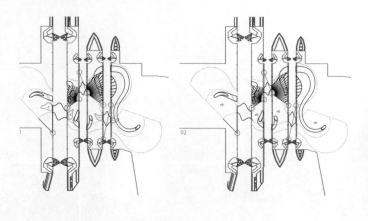

DEFINITION OF THE SITE:

The site was based on the study of one of the western pairs of half-gates of the three locks located between Boston's North End and Charlestown. Each student documented and analyzed the site of one pair of half-gates and developed a new site that contains a similar gate. The abstract site was designed to accommodate the addition of the partially kinetic building form and its various movements and positions. The site was assumed to be a fixed, existing condition or capable of being modified at any point during the design process. Like the building, it was a work in progress. In its final form, the abstract site and the proposed building combined allowed proper functional performance of the lock and gate.

01 BENJAMIN RUSWICK
Form/sequence derivation

02 JESSE WILCOX
Axonometric development

03-04 DUNCAN SCOVIL

BENJAMIN RUSWICK

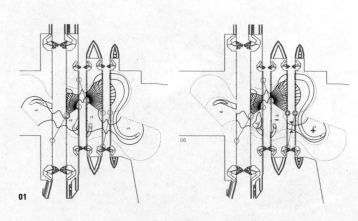

01

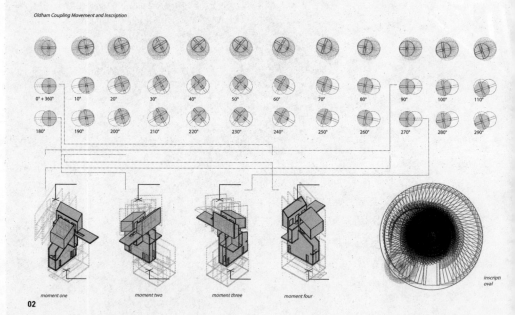

Oldham Coupling Movement and Inscription

0° + 360°   10°   20°   30°   40°   50°   60°   70°   80°   90°   100°   110°

180°   190°   200°   210°   220°   230°   240°   250°   260°   270°   280°   290°

moment one   moment two   moment three   moment four

inscripti oval

02

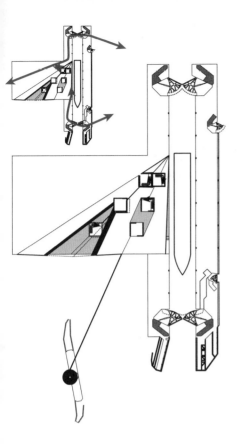 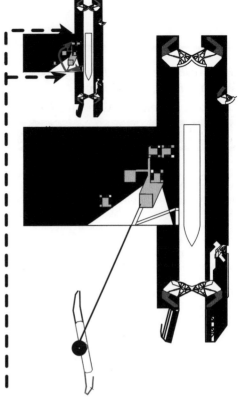

03

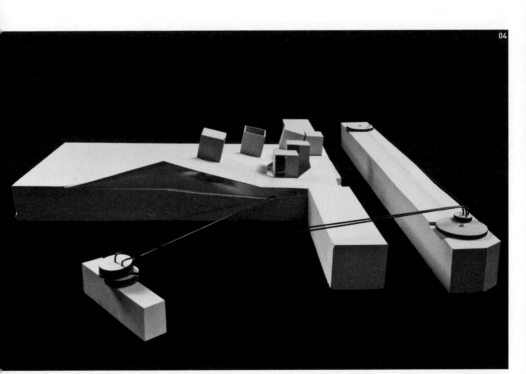

04

YAEL **EREL**, MARIANA **IBAÑEZ**, KIEL **MOE**, INGEBORG **ROCKER**, ELIZABETH **WHITTAKER**, CAMERON **WU**, PRESTON SCOTT **COHEN**   023

Gary Hilderbrand (Coordinator), Silvia Benedito,
Andrea Hansen, Jane Hutton
Landscape Architecture Core Studio I

URBAN PUBLIC GARDEN

This studio course introduced students to elements of landscape
architectural design at the scale of the public garden in an urban context.
As the first of a four-term sequence of design studios, the course aimed to
help students develop spatial literacy, critical design thinking, and skills
in the representation of landscape architecture.

The studio introduced and explored various issues of perennial concern
to landscape design through a typological reading of and intervention
in canonical projects from the history of the urban public landscape.
Topics included the examination of promenade and path, permeability
and pavement, ground cover and texture, spatial enclosure and bound,
threshold and limit, topographic complexity and sectional variation,
horizontal envelopment and canopy, prospect and refuge, among others.
Using a range of two- and three-dimensional media, both analog and
digital, members of the studio worked with orthographic, axonometric,
and perspective projection drawings as well as physical models.

Throughout the semester, students were exposed to and expected to
develop an iterative working method that translates conceptual thought
into models of spatial form through varying modes of representation; is
rooted in processes of conceptualization and elaboration parallel to those
of contemporary landscape architectural design; responds effectively to
criticism; and engages within a culture of productive peer review.

The studio examined the imponderable gaps between site, representation,
and built work, in the context of landscape design. Emphasis was placed
on the status and role of representation and the studio as a performative
venue for the production of landscape design.

TAKUYA IWAMURA

01

02

03

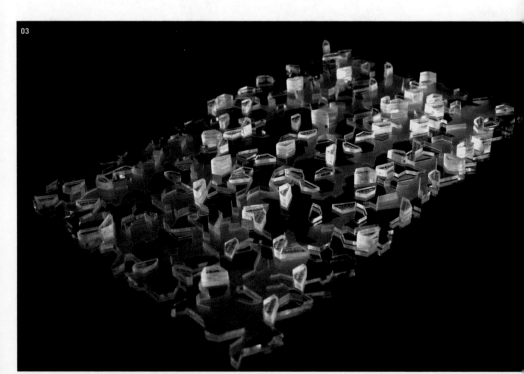

04

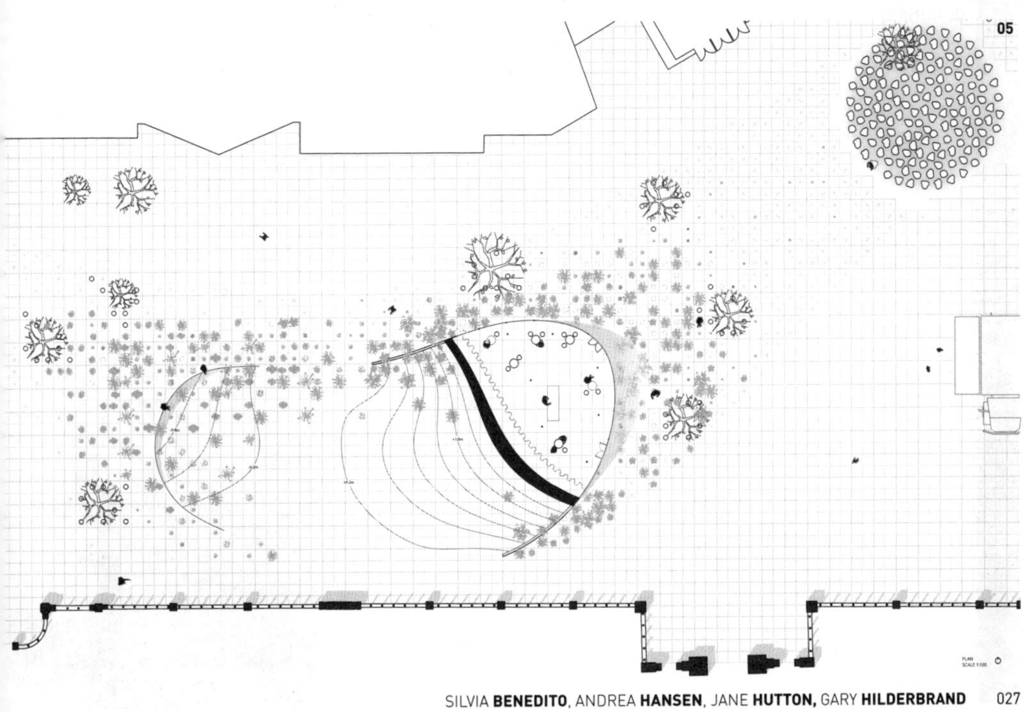

05

SILVIA **BENEDITO**, ANDREA **HANSEN**, JANE **HUTTON,** GARY **HILDERBRAND**   027

Christopher Lee
Architecture Option Studio, Fall 2011

DOMINANT TYPES AND THE IDEA OF THE CITY

This studio worked typologically. It recognized the city as a repository of architectural knowledge and potential. The city here was understood through its persistent architectures, its dominant types. To make a connection between type and the city is to establish a link between the works of architecture and the wider milieu in which the work is produced. For a type to be dominant, it has to persist and prevail. What is the most prevailing is also the most typical and what is the most typical is also common to all. And no other sphere is more common to all than the city itself. Thus dominant types can be understood as the typical elements that constitute the city and are the very embodiment of the common.

It is through this ideological and pedagogical premise that we approached the design topic for the year. The task was to rethink and design a communal housing project for 1,000 inhabitants in the city of Beijing. After more than a decade of surrendering the provision of housing to the market, the urgency to rethink and provide for affordable housing has resurfaced in China. Our task was framed by three preconditions. The first considered the typical dwelling unit as an irreducible space of coexistence in the city. The second considered the overall structure of this housing type as an artifact that embodies the idea of the city. And finally, the influence of the type had to act beyond its site boundaries as a dominant type for the city.

LUCAS CORREA-SEVILLA

ALL IMAGES SOPHIA CHANG

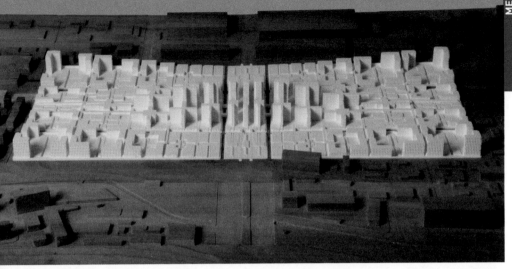

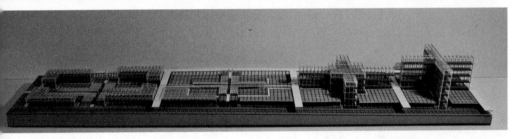

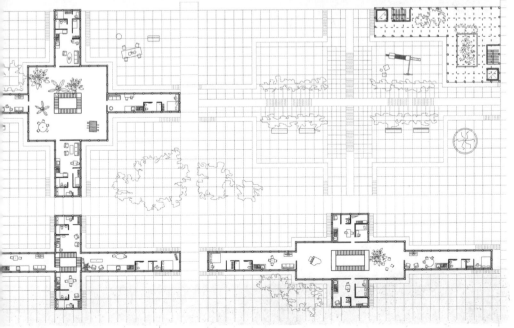

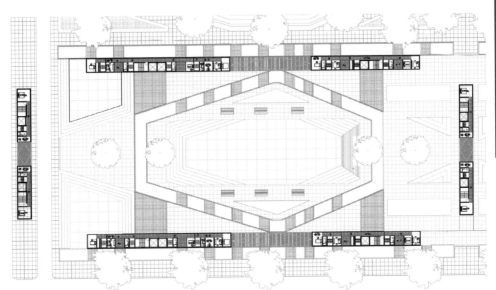

ALL IMAGES
LUCAS CORREA-SEVILLA

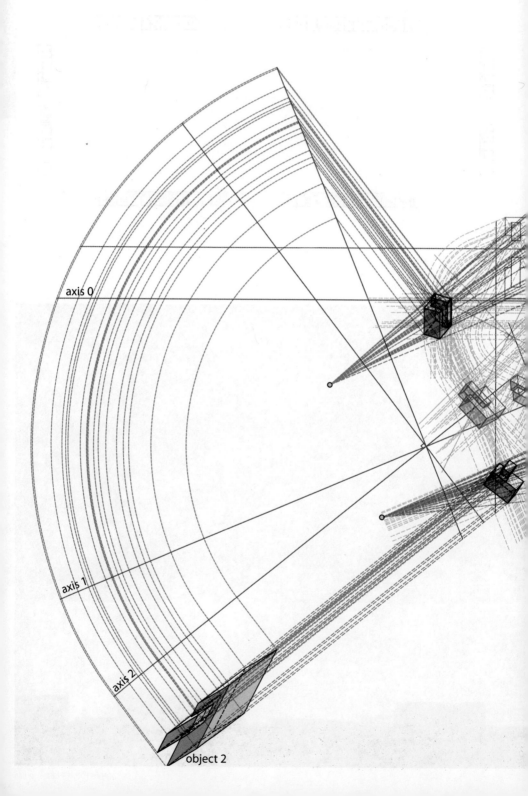

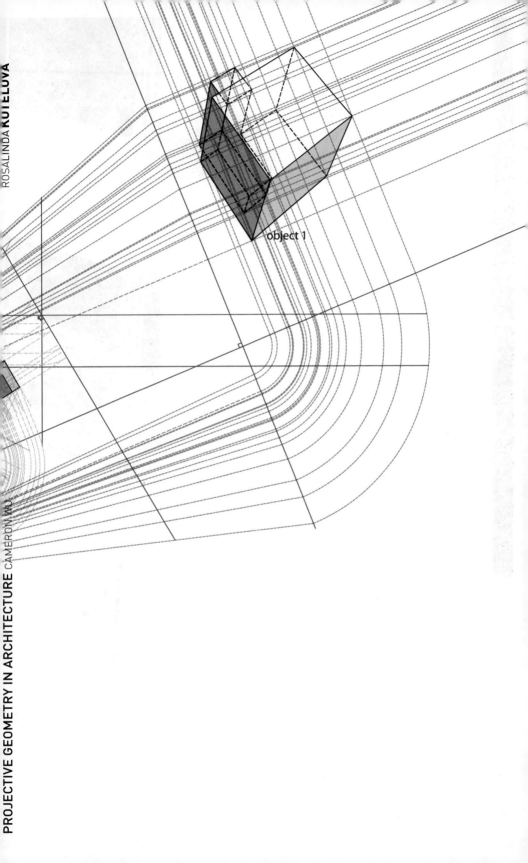

object 1

Joan Busquets
Urban Planning and Design Option Studio, Spring 2012

RETHINKING THE MANHATTAN GRID

Manhattan's development has been based on the Commissioners' Plan, which has just celebrated its second centenary. The precision of layout, the judicious definition of avenues and streets, and the geometry of the city blocks are still interesting and thought provoking. Many initiatives and projects have taken place on the island, gradually configuring the *forma urbis* of the central area of New York that can only be understood in terms of the forcefulness of the seminal grid project proposed at that time.

The hypothesis of the studio was to verify the capacity for transformation on the basis of the initial models, seeing them as layouts with the potential for constant reinterpretation that suggests multiple urban forms in keeping with the evolving demands of the program.

If twentieth-century Manhattan was a spectacular city thanks to its skyscrapers, the trends apparent in its transformation suggest that in the twenty-first century it could become the city of mixed or hybrid complexes that combine program and spatial composition by modulating the original grid at another scale, manipulating the initial modules. This, at least, was one of the working hypotheses for the studio.

The richness of the initial project lies in its open morphology that is capable of inspiring the design of other cities, following the regular grid layout seen in recent urbanistic history. To this end, the studio simulated the contribution of the Manhattan model to the construction of the global city, serving as a theoretical point of reference to enhance the experimental contents of the Studio, applied to New York but also to other large world cities.

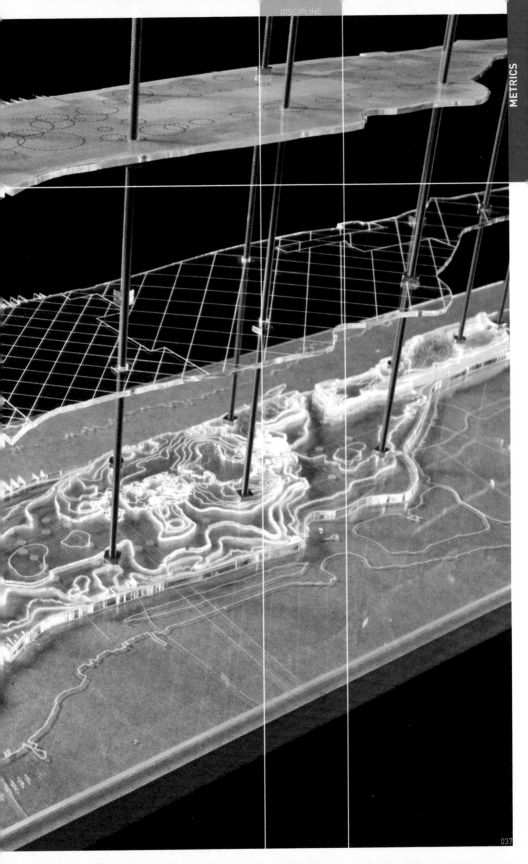

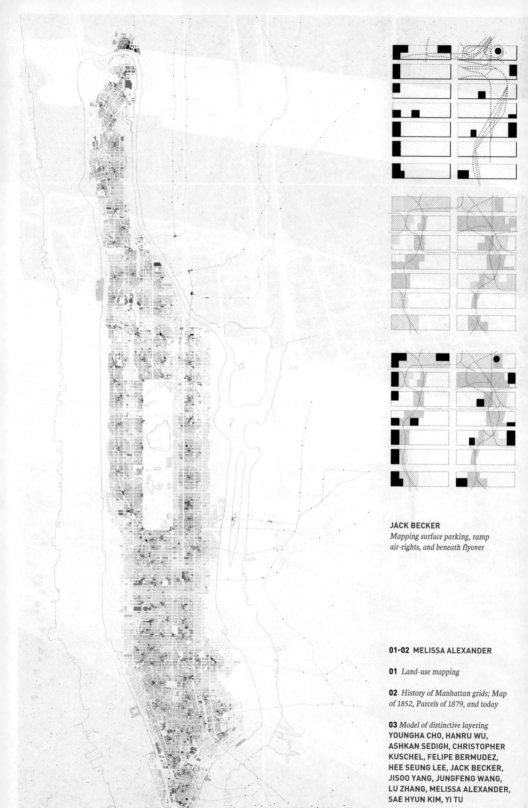

JACK BECKER
Mapping surface parking, ramp air-rights, and beneath flyover

01-02 MELISSA ALEXANDER

01 *Land-use mapping*

02 *History of Manhattan grids; Map of 1852, Parcels of 1879, and today*

03 *Model of distinctive layering*
YOUNGHA CHO, HANRU WU, ASHKAN SEDIGH, CHRISTOPHER KUSCHEL, FELIPE BERMUDEZ, HEE SEUNG LEE, JACK BECKER, JISOO YANG, JUNGFENG WANG, LU ZHANG, MELISSA ALEXANDER, SAE HYUN KIM, YI TU

01

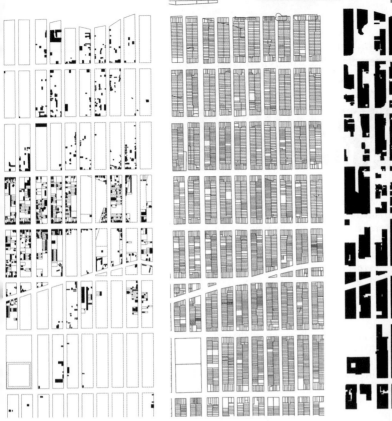

02

03

Alex Krieger and Kathy Spiegelman (coordinators), David Gamble, Ana Gelabert-Sanchez, Kathryn Madden, Janne Corneil, Daniel D'Oca, David Spillane, Anne Tate
Urban Planning Core, Fall 2011 and Spring 2012

URBAN PLANNING CORE I + II

The first semester core studio of the Master of Urban Planning program introduced students to the fundamental knowledge and technical skills used by urban planners to create, research, analyze, and implement plans and projects for the built environment. The studio will used the City of Boston as the students' planning laboratory and students were expected to understand the city through the lenses of planning elements such as demographics, economic attributes, market forces, and public and private stakeholder interests, all of which shape the city and inform decisions about land use, development, and infrastructure.

The second semester core planning studio expanded the topics and methodologies studied in the first semester core studio, aiming to prepare students for the mix of analytical and creative problem-solving needed to address planning issues at the advanced level of the options studios. The studio centered around a single large-scale planning problem with a regional, intermunicipal scope. The studio addressed the following concerns, all of which are currently central to planning: the pattern and development nature of settlement form; the visual and scenic impact of development either at the fringe or in built-up areas; accessibility, walkability, and the relationship between transit and autos; the location and utility of open space, particularly with respect to development; and, the respective roles of large-scale concepts (e.g., plans) versus regulation in shaping the built environment.

KELLY LYNAMA

CHURCH ST

FAR

6.0 — 7 stories

283 Longwood Ave
Hospital

6.5 — 22 stories

One Kenmore
Mixed Use

7.0

7.5 — 8 stories

Parkside Tower
Multi-Family Residential

8.0

8.5 — 17 stories

10 Buick Street
BU Dormitory

9.0 — 22 stories

International Village
NU Dormitory

9.5

9.6

10.0 — 19 stories

33 Harry Agganis Way
BU Dormitory

10.5 — 12 stories

65 Jimmy Fund Way
Hospital

11.0

11.5 — 24 stories

Back Bay Hilton
Hotel

12.0 — 21 stories

12.5

3 Blackfan Circle
Laboratory

13.0 — 16 stories

335 Massachusetts Ave
Multi-Family Residential

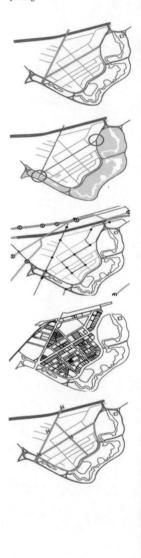

FABIANA MEACHAM
Diagrams of Fenway depicting implementation mechanisms for the proposed plan, including zoning and phasing.

01 ARED KATSEFF
Strengthening Boston's spine local density FAR

02-03 QINGNAN LIU
New Haven 2050 plan showing the implementation and phasing of Route 34.

1/4 mile

1/2 mile

1/4 mile

1/2 mile

Open Space

Non-Motorized

What Could Happen

02

PHASE 2: MEDICAL AREA

PHASE 3: UNION STATION

PHASE 4: WATERFRONT

03

$300M PRIVATE

$80M OTHER

$20M PUBLIC

GFA= 2.5M sqf
Avg FAR= 4

$150M PRIVATE

$40M OTHER

$10M PUBLIC

GFA= 1.6M sqf
Avg FAR= 4

$1.5B PRIVATE

$220M OTHER

$80M PUBLIC

GFA= 11M sqf
Avg FAR= 4

D. GAMBLE, A. GELABERT-SANCHEZ, K. MADDEN, J. CORNEIL, D. D'OCA, D. SPILLANE, A. TATE, A. KRIEGER, K. SPIEGELMAN   043

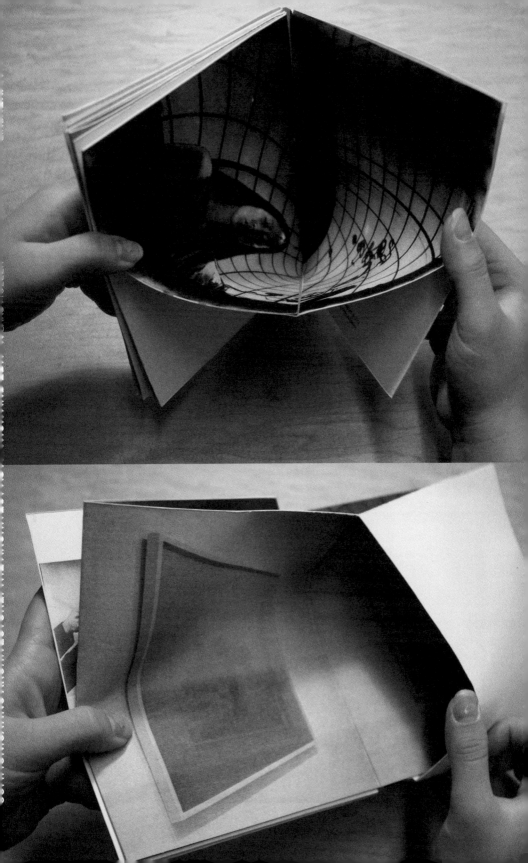

WEIGHTEDNESS

Thesis Advisor: Preston Scott Cohen

Matthew Waxman

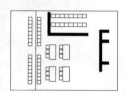
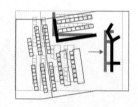

The Kritios Boy illustrates a moment in ancient Greek sculpture where there was a shift in the way the body was depicted. In the Kritios Boy, in leaning backward there is a change in the distribution of weight in the body —setting it in contrapposto. The way this weight shifts through the parts describes the body, in particular the relationships on the interior of the body between differences contingent upon one another. It is through a weightedness in a constraining of the parts that, by their very configuring and limiting of movement, enable the body to be seen to anticipate movement. Motion describes a relationship between interior and exterior. A building type is defined by narratives of function and use—conventions—that fix relationships between the parts. Like the animation of the body of the Kritios Boy, it is through these sustained narratives of use and function that the parts together as a whole become formally animate.

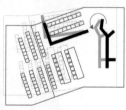
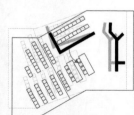
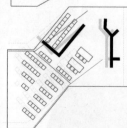

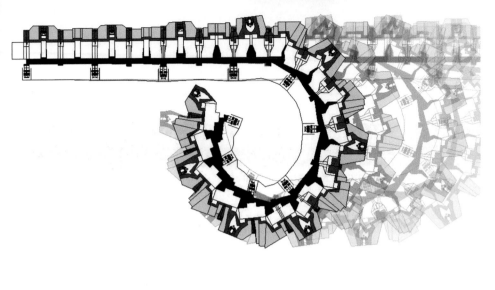

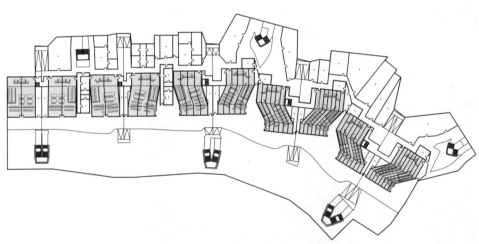

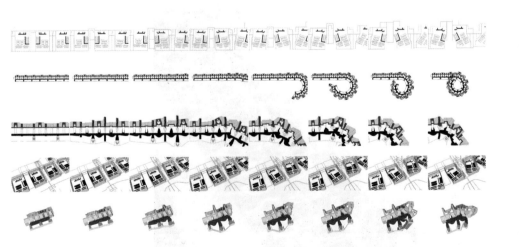

SPATIO-PHENOMENAL INTERVENTION
Sculpting the Ephemeral

Advisors: Sanford Kwinter, Krzysztof Wodiczko   *Melissa Kit Chow, Helena Solsar*

Spatio-phenomenal intervention (SPI) is work that is known to us through the senses rather than through thought or intuition, occurring and intervening in existing spaces or built into existing architecture. It consists of the work of artists, composers, musicians, and architects who utilize ephemeral media such as light, sound, and air to create atmospheric, sensory phenomena that enhance attention and direct focus.

PROJECTED FIELD, RAMP *is a light installation that creates a situation for the contemplation of existing spatial conditions. A digitally projected video negates gradients, and the materialization of colored planes challenges our perception of three-dimensional space. The piece effectively induces a dynamic, multistable perceptual field in which our expectations of space are placed into doubt, and sentient relationships between body and space are reinforced.*

SUSPENDED SOUND, STAIR *is a spatio-phenomenal intervention that challenges occupants' perception of a particularly reverberant stairwell by creating a gradient of sound absorption and accentuating color temperatures of existing light conditions through the accumulation of semi-transparent fabric.*

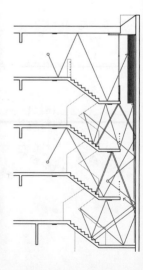

Wes Jones
Architecture Option Studio, Fall 2011

END(EAVORS) GAME

When the "age of the world picture"gave way to the "first machine age,"architecture went from being a book to being a machine, from representing to doing, from a concern with truth to an emphasis on function. With the dawning of the "information age," architecture was again asked to take account of a shift in paradigms. Many think of the digital as the epochal difference that must be answered, but in fact the digital itself has been enabled—driven—by a more fundamental, epistemological, and cultural shift toward an increasingly immersive engagement with a progressively more fluid "reality," where "doing"has become play and "function"has been supplanted by performance. This time, architecture, like everything else, is a game.

That doesn't make it any easier or less serious, however. This studio explored the game thesis through the design of a final resting place and display pavilion for the Space Shuttle *Endeavour* at the California Science Center at Exposition Park in Los Angeles. The shuttle has been called the "most complicated machine built in human history." The conclusion of the STS (Space Transportation System) program is not only the end of an era of manned space flight, it is also an acknowledgment of the probable limits of mechanical virtuosity—the loss of two out of the original four shuttles revealed the tragic genius of stuff at the tipping point between control and chaos. The design of an "Information Age"exhibition environment devoted to this apotheosis of the waning "Machine Age" (with its implicit curatorial opportunities and critical demands) provided an appropriate arena for gauging the disciplinary effects of the transition from "doing" to "playing."

DREW COWDREY

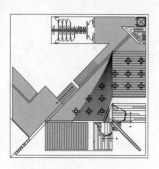
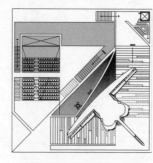
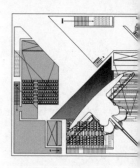
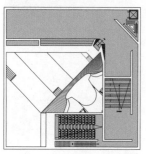

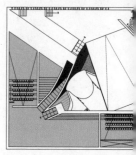

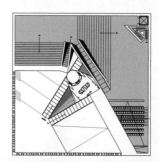

GAMES *are distinguished as much by their rules as by the play those rules enable or circumscribe. In architecture the more important rules are not inherited or legislated but discovered on the fly, in the feeling of rightness that settles over the project as it is refined during the course of design. A studio focused on game values will therefore not be a technique-driven studio, where "process" supplants thinking or stochastic dabbling yields inexplicable results. Instead, the game's natural regard for thinking and cleverness will be operationalized through willful, managed design that explicitly articulates relevant issues regarding the choice of games, their rule sets, and criteria for success (and modes of failure), as well as the strategies and tactics of play.*

LEFT PAGE TREY KIRK

THIS PAGE DREW COWDREY

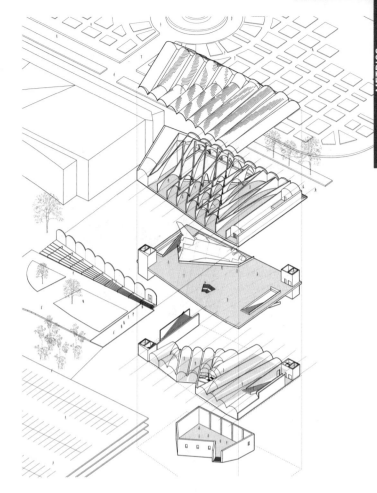

The House of Endeavour sits atop an old parking garage 6 miles south of downtown Los Angeles. It is made of twenty-five great towers—the radio tower with 100 receptors, the periscopes with rotating heads, the wind organs of ranging heights, the chimney stacks with exhaust fans, and the telescopes with spinning lenses. The garage is surrounded by a concrete moat filled with parked cars. To travel to the House, you have only the choice between

HOUSE OF ENDEAVOUR

James Templeton Kelley Prize

car and train, but since the train seldom runs and when it does, takes you in a meandering path around the city, most Endeavourists prefer to drive and park their cars directly below the House. The Endeavourist struggles to find the shuttle within the dark mechanical forest. He walks past several organ towers, and crater theaters, and suddenly the floor stops. There is a deep gorge in front of him extending down into complete darkness. On the other side of this narrow drop, a black wall. The Endeavourist slowly climbs the helical staircase that wraps around *Endeavour*. When he looks around, he sees several platforms extending out from the main walkway toward the shuttle. These are flying "chapels" located adjacent to the key elements of *Endeavour*. The last chapel looks into a window of the cockpit. The astronaut seats face upward against the direction of gravity. The nose floats. A weightless black ellipsoid in emptiness. So are you. There is nothing around you. The universe above. And that which takes you there. The Endeavourist touches… and prays.

ENDEAVOUR *is one of the retired orbiters of the space shuttle program of NASA, the space agency of the United States. Endeavour was the fifth and final spaceworthy NASA space shuttle to be built, constructed as a replacement for Challenger. Endeavour first flew in May 1992 on mission STS-49, and its last mission, STS-134, was in May 2011.*

01 *Flying chapel*

02 *Main entrance*

03 *Nave*

ENDEAVOUR'S MISSION:
Endeavour completed its final mission with a landing at the Kennedy Space Center at 06:34 UTC on June 1, 2011. Over its flight career, Endeavour flew 122,853,151 miles and spent 299 days in space. While flying Endeavour's last mission, the Russian spacecraft Soyuz TMA-20 departed from the International Space Station and paused at a distance of 200 meters. Italian astronaut Paolo Nespoli took a series of photographs and videos of the ISS with Endeavour docked. This was the second time a Shuttle had been photographed while docked and the first time since 1996. Commander Mark Kelly was the last astronaut off Endeavour after the landing, and the crew stayed on the landing strip long enough to sign autographs and pose for pictures.

02

TRANS-CODING

Thesis Advisor: Timothy Hyde

Jessica Vaughn

Preservation practice currently operates under the auspices of two polarized dogmas—those of image and authenticity. Adherents to the former insist on the prime importance of visuality (how a building looks), while disciples of the latter counter with arguments for historic purity (that the building must remain "untouched"). Framed in these binary terms the dilemma is unsolvable, and discourse has been unable to progress beyond infighting and oscillation between these two poles. Unfortunately, neither conception offers a satisfying purchase on methods for critical engagement with existing sites. Though frequently opposed in terms of recommended practice, both factions finally cast historic buildings as fetishized and inviolable objects—effectively undermining any attempt to confidently interact with the extant environment. This manipulation of norms will be tested on the "original" city office building —the Bank of England—thereby challenging both preservation convention and contemporary normativity, with the aspiration to subvert enervating discourses of parametric design, image, and authenticity through the instrumentality and qualitative capacity of re-appearance in code.

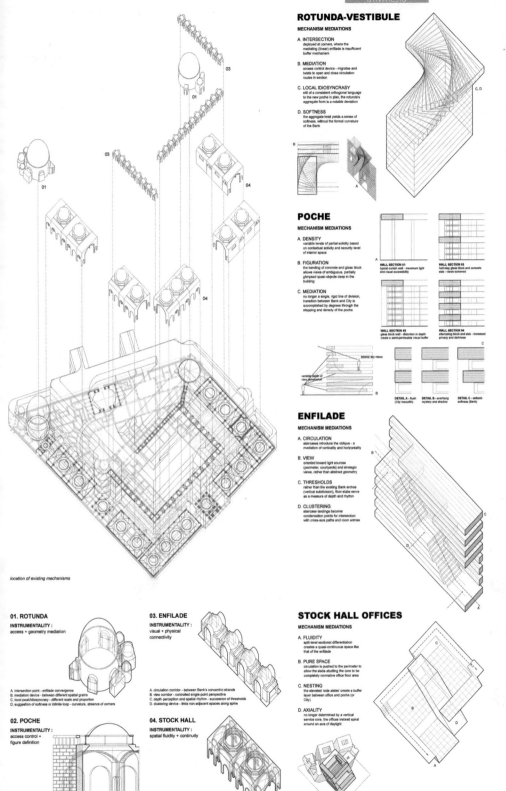

ROTUNDA-VESTIBULE

MECHANISM MEDIATIONS

A. INTERSECTION
deployed at corners, where the mediating (linear) enfilade is insufficient buffer mechanism

B. MEDIATION
access control device - migrates and twists to open and close circulation routes in section

C. LOCAL IDIOSYNCRASY
still of a consistent orthogonal language to the new poche in plan, the rotunda's aggregate form is a notable deviation

D. SOFTNESS
the aggregate twist yields a sense of softness, without the formal curvature of the Bank

POCHE

MECHANISM MEDIATIONS

A. DENSITY
variable levels of partial solidity based on contextual activity and security level of interior space

B. FIGURATION
the bending of concrete and glass block allows views of ambiguous, partially glimpsed quasi-objects deep in the building

C. MEDIATION
no longer a single, rigid line of division, transition between Bank and City is accomplished by degrees through the stepping and density of the poche

WALL SECTION 01
typical curtain wall - maximum light and visual accessibility

WALL SECTION 03
half-stag glass block and concrete slab - views screened

WALL SECTION 02
glass block wall - distortion in depth create a semi-permeable visual buffer

WALL SECTION 04
alternating block and slab - increased privacy and darkness

interior sky views

variable depth of view penetration

DETAIL A - flush (City monolith)

DETAIL B - overhang mystery and shadow

DETAIL C - setback softness (Bank)

ENFILADE

MECHANISM MEDIATIONS

A. CIRCULATION
staircases introduce the oblique - a mediation of verticality and horizontality

B. VIEW
oriented toward light sources (perimeter, courtyards) and strategic views, rather than abstract geometry

C. THRESHOLDS
rather than the existing Bank arches (vertical subdivision), floor slabs serve as a measure of depth and rhythm

D. CLUSTERING
staircase landings become condensation points for intersection with cross-axis paths and room entries

STOCK HALL OFFICES

MECHANISM MEDIATIONS

A. FLUIDITY
split-level sectional differentiation creates a quasi-continuous space like that of the enfilade

B. PURE SPACE
circulation is pushed to the perimeter to allow the slabs abutting the core to be completely normative office floor area

C. NESTING
the elevated 'side aisles' create a buffer layer between office and poche (or City)

D. AXIALITY
no longer determined by a vertical service core, the offices instead spiral around an axis of daylight

location of existing mechanisms

01. ROTUNDA

INSTRUMENTALITY :
access + geometry mediation

A. intersection point - enfilade convergence
B. mediation device - between different spatial grains
C. local idiosyncrasy - different scale and proportion
D. suggestion of softness or infinite loop - curvature, absence of corners

02. POCHE

INSTRUMENTALITY :
access control + figure definition

A. material density - perception of thickness and weight
B. spatial definition - sculpted to produce figural voids
C. mediation device - between Bank interior and City activity

03. ENFILADE

INSTRUMENTALITY :
visual + physical connectivity

A. circulation corridor - between Bank's concentric strands
B. view corridor - controlled single-point perspective
C. depth perception and spatial rhythm - succession of thresholds
D. clustering device - links non-adjacent spaces along spine

04. STOCK HALL

INSTRUMENTALITY :
spatial fluidity + continuity

A. quasi-continuous space - interlacing thresholds
B. pure office area - framed by circulatory side aisles
C. variation of cell proportion - non-uniform rhythm
D. perception of depth and axiality - aggregate length

Farshid Moussavi, Jonathan Scelsa
Architecture Option Studio, Spring 2012

THE FUNCTION OF TIME

This was the second in a series of research-based studios devoted to the spatial and temporal implications that contemporary art provokes for a museum today. In an effort to address different contemporary issues, artists have in the last two decades embraced different subject matters, scales, and media, resulting in an unprecedented range of artwork that has broken outside the white cube of modern museum design. To be a platform for contemporary art, the art museum needs to embody spatial diversity and it needs to accommodate continuous change. The Function of Time in a contemporary art museum addressed specifically the problem of unpredictability that is inherent in the condition of contemporary art.

Today countless museums, built before or during the early part of the twentieth century, house great collections of modern art. In the coming years, these museums will need to find ways to expand and adapt their current structures to accommodate contemporary art exhibitions. This studio focused on the Function of Time within such an existing art museum, approaching the need for flexibility and spatial variety. This studio investigated what could be a series of spatial forms—such as a shed, a house, a chapel, a lab, a garden, etc.—that could provide different contexts in a museum, thus fulfillin the diverse spatial needs of contemporary art. These spatial forms acted as the brief for the expansion of the existing museum.

Drawing from writings and conversations on contemporary art with Hans Ulrich Obrist, as well as other leading curators, the studio first produced a group survey of exhibitions before developing individual design projects for the expansion and revision of an existing art museum.

DREW COWDREY

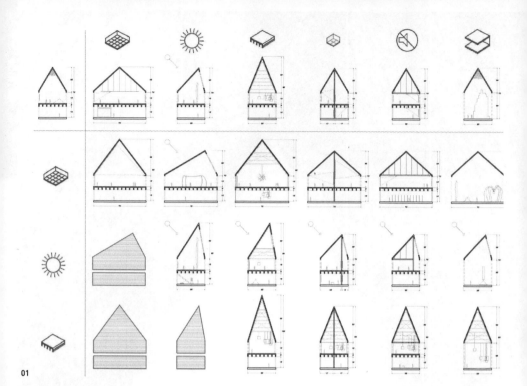

01

02

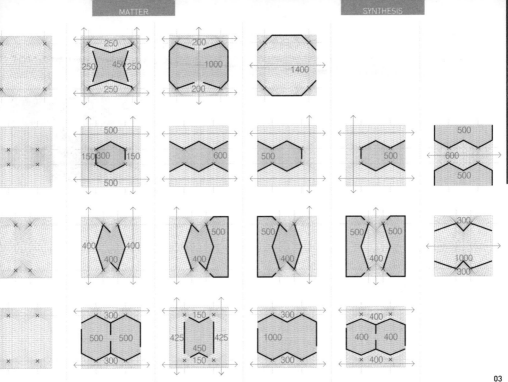

03

THE MUSEUM: NEW SPATIAL

FORMS *Much of contemporary art has emerged as a response to the museum building or the museum as an institution, such as Carsten Höller's Soma (2010), Urs Fischer's You (2003), Chu Yun's Constellation (2006) or Gregor Schneider's Totes Haus u r (2001).*

01 *This piece is a matrix that catalogs the variety of spatial types that are achieved in the art museum.*
DREW COWDREY

02 *Model*
DREW COWDREY

03 GEOMETRIC PLAN VARIATIONS
Interior spatial studies
PAXTON SHELDAHL

04 *Interior Rendering*
PAXTON SHELDAHL

04

LANDSCAPE INFRASTRUCTURE

Introduction: Pierre Bélanger

We are undertaking this symposium to explore the future of infrastructure itself, the glue of urbanization beyond the dogma of civil engineering and transportation planning. Discussions and lectures will focus on ways to address the predominate challenges facing urban economies today, which include climate dynamics, carbon and nitrogen wastes, population mobilities, and resource economies. These imperatives are inseparable. This is a key aspect to the work that we are involved in: they underpin the challenge of contemporary urbanization. That puts landscape architects in a privileged position to cut across a number of disciplines that have been dominant in shaping the discourse in the past.

As an outgrowth of the recovery of geography and the emergence of ecology over the past two decades, several new horizons have come into focus, positioning the field of landscape as both system and strategy for current infrastructural failures and spatial economic challenges. We're going to put into question the predominance of civil engineering on matters of infrastructure. That premise of civil engineers is based on federal funding, state planning, life-cycling of infrastructure, sustainability and resilience, and the pricing of infrastructure. Over the next thirty-six hours we're going to put those notions into question and propose, perhaps, alternative ways in which we can think about infrastructure. To do this, we'll develop a three-staged argument: historically, semiotically, and strategically, by looking at the redefinition, the representation, and the rebuilding of infrastructure through contemporary scholarship, research, and practice.

PIERRE BÉLANGER *is Associate Professor of Landscape Architecture at Harvard's GSD, where he teaches and coordinates graduate courses on the convergence of ecology, infrastructure, and urbanism in the interrelated fields of design, planning, and engineering. As a member of the internationally recognized Harvard Project on the City, led by architect and urbanist Rem Koolhaas, Bélanger completed graduate studies for the Masters in Landscape Architecture at the GSD, where he received the Janet Darling Webel and Norman T. Newton Prizes in design. Bélanger is professionally registered as a landscape architect and urban planner as well as certified in Canada as a surface miner, skilled in precision earthmoving and heavy equipment operations.*

Keynote: Rosalind Williams, "Infrastructure as Lived Experience"

I'd like to give a short introduction to the topic of infrastructure, first of all as a wording concept. I went to the dictionary. I'd assumed that "infrastructure" was an old word and that everyone else besides me understood what it meant. The more I looked at the word, the more it reminded me of the keyword "technology." Infrastructure, like technology, tends to be a recent term, a promiscuous term, one that has no clean definition and is very liable to reification. Words are emerging and taking on new meaning in response to historical phenomena that they purport to be describing. So infrastructure as a word and concept is very tricky.

ROSALIND WILLIAMS *is the Dibner Professor of the History of Science and Technology at MIT. In 2011, Williams received an honorary doctorate from the Technical University of Eindhoven in the Netherlands, where she has been appointed as Distinguished Visiting Professor. Williams studies the origins and effects from the evolution of large, constructed systems and the acceleration of technology for human life in a predominantly self-constructed world.*

Thomas Hughes, in *Networks of Power,* writes about technological style. He's expanding the definition from railroads, which you can see so clearly as tracks, to electrical networks, which have huge implications for the landscape but not always so directly. They're not like bridges, very visible in the landscape, but the fact is that infrastructure isn't always that visible.

Infrastructure is a rapidly changing term—there's not a clear definition, you're going to have to make it up as you go along—and in a sense I think that this conference is all about trying to define the word in the context of a rapidly changing world. In this world, it's not clear which authorities design, construct, pay for, and maintain infrastructure. Are they national, supernational, or something else? And how do citizens participate in these projects?

WATCH THE CONFERENCE "LANDSCAPE INFRASTRUCTURE" ON THE GSD YOUTUBE.COM CHANNEL
http://www.youtube.com / watch?v=OzoB5KAVHKQ

Christophe Girot, "Degrees of Precision: Understanding Landscape Infrastructure"

CHRISTOPHE GIROT *is Full Professor and Chair in Landscape Architecture at the Department of Architecture of the Swiss Federal Institute of Technology in Zurich (ETH Zurich). He directs the Institute of Landscape Architecture and the Landscape Visual and Modeling Lab, and is part of the ETH Future Cities Laboratory in Singapore. He earned a double Masters in Architecture and Landscape Architecture at the University of California, Berkeley. He practices as a landscape architect, focusing on large-scale projects involving dynamic topographic landscape modeling. Girot has taught at the GSD, the Royal School of Fine Arts Copenhagen, and many other institutions.*

At ETH Zurich we are working with equipment usually only given to the army corp of engineers, called Point Cloud technology, which we purchased with grant money to play around with in the Alps. We're actually a little bit more pretentious and less defensive than other speakers at this conference. We are saying: not only can we use the same kind of tools that engineers use, but we can probably show them how to use them differently than they currently do. The tools we've been developing in a way question all of the typical design tools of landscape architecture by introducing the third and fourth dimensions as basic tools of design.

Landscape architecture had adopted cartographic methods of graphic representation from other disciplines. We have digested and adapted the convention of the contour line, which comes from a marine tradition, but basically what we have accepted as a tool of representation is a crumpled handkerchief, an idealized cartographic map. What is extraordinary in these rendered cartographic drawings is that infrastructure is drawn to look ideal, very far from the experienced reality. The tools of the twenty-first century are going to radically change how we operate in our environment.

This image I present is not a film. It is actually a model, a physical model of the environment, showing accurate rock face in every minute detail. You can work your way in and out of the skin of a mountain. Every pixel you see is hanging on seven satellites. What is represented here is no longer material, but points of very highly precise information. God is in the data. We are rapidly entering a conceptual revolution that is necessarily going to effect the way we think about space and design space.

Peter Del Tredici, "Plants as Megastructure"

PETER DEL TREDICI *holds a Bachelors in Zoology from the University of California, Berkeley, a Masters in Biology from the University of Oregon, and a Ph.D. in Plant Ecology from Boston University. He is an Adjunct Associate Professor of Landscape Architecture at the GSD and a has worked as a Senior Research Scientist at the Arnold Arboretum for three decades. He recently authored Wild Urban Plants of the Northeast. His work challenges dialectics between native and exotic plants, and gives value to adaptive urban ecologies.*

WATCH "PLANTS AS MEGASTRUCTURE" + "DEGREES OF PRECISION" ON THE GSD YOUTUBE.COM CHANNEL
www.youtube.com/watch?v=OzoB5KA VHKQ&feature=relmfu

I want to talk about how infrastructure looks from the perspective of the plant. Primarily, I'll use the metaphor of disturbance. Disturbance is the great enemy of infrastructure, but also a prime factor driving ecological succession. If you look at the history of northeastern North America, the history of disturbance goes back at least 15,000 years, when most of the Northeast was covered in glaciers. You can still find the scouring of the landscape by the glaciers, and these kinds of disturbances are ongoing.

Landscape architects need to think about how plants interact with urban infrastructure. It is important to consider how we define what urbanization is. You can define urbanization by the extent of impervious surface, rather than the density of human population, because when you look at what plants are responding to, it's the former. I consider urbanization to be akin to glaciation; our heavy construction equipment is the urban glacier.

Little things that we don't pay much attention to can have a big impact. For example, road salt increases soil compaction, decreases water availability, and completely alters the soil biology. Yet we know that the minute a snowflake hits the ground, road crews are out spreading salt because no one wants to compromise public safety for the sake of a few plants. The chronic stress that urbanization and climate change place on native ecosystems, the impact of pollution on soil chemistry, and habitat fragmentation encouraging non-native species are ecology trends that will affect the urban landscape in the future. These forces drive vegetation patterns in urban areas. A whole new kind of ecology—an anthropogenic ecology—is forming before our eyes.

CATALYZING THE PARKWAY
Botanical l Aggravations in the Blue Ridge Mountains

Norman T. Newton Prize

Thesis Advisor: Charles Waldheim

Aisling O'Carrol

Located at the site of friction between an aggressive rhetoric of cultural heritage and the entropic nature of mountain landscapes, Catalyzing the Parkway considers the repercussions of the layered history of the Blue Ridge Mountains. The project engages both the inherent structure of the regional landscape and the established structure of the National Park Service through a landscape design strategy based on the botanical properties of the *Rhododendron maximum* and the *Cephalanthus oxidentalis*. Although the Blue Ridge Parkway and its ancillary landscape have become stagnated in a regime of nationalistic heritage

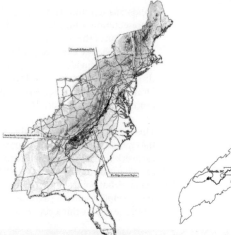

01

tourism, this project proposes an alternative to the 469-mile-long pastoral perspective. A newly engaged experience of the parkway and Blue Ridge Mountains is created by preserving the heritage parkway as a contemporary archeological ruin—acknowledging its history and revealing the controls, weaknesses, and frictions in the landscape—and simultaneously providing access and amenities for the contemporary visitor through the overlay of a new parkway system and reactivation of the landscape.

01 *National and regional maps*

02 *Landscape typologies: arrested landscapes, firebreak and edge habitats, harvest potential, irrigation zones*

03 *Model: firebreak and edge*

04 *Annotated rendering*

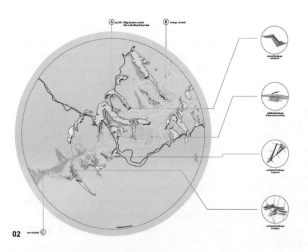

02

03

ACCELERATED LANDSCAPE

A. *Appalachian cove forest and mixed hardwood*
B. *Rhododendron maximum understory*
C. *Irrigation points and saturation zone*
D. *Berm - topographic interference*
E. *Soil - 1-3m depth in hollows*
F. *Weathered bedrock - 30-50cm depth*

ACCELERATED LANDSCAPE

A. *Appalachian mixed hardwood and spruce fir forest*
B. *Fog net - 30% capture of fog moisture*
C. *Stratocumulus clouds*
D. *Harvested water collection*
E. *Irrigation pipeline*
F. *Soil - 70-90cm depth in ridges*
G. *Weathered bedrock - 30-50cm depth*

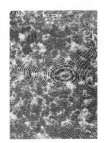
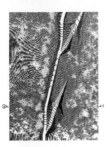

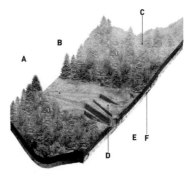

STABILIZED LANDSCAPE

A. *Appalachian mixed hardwood and spruce fir forest*
B. *6-8m vegetation break - firebreak*
C. *Firebreak path*
D. *Water diversion*
E. *Cephalanthus occidentalis propagation*
F. *Soil - 1-3cm depth*
G. *Weathered bedrock - 30-50cm depth*

ARRESTED LANDSCAPE

A. *Appalachian mixed hardwood and cover forest*
B. *Gabion basket retaining wall*
C. *Precarious slope*
D. *Woody vegetation growth*
E. *Soil - 1-3cm depth*
F. *Weathered bedrock - 30-50cm depth*

MATTER and material constitute the output and the physical manifestation of knowledge in our disciplines. With every project and its realized form and shape, each design department in the School communicates its expertise and knowledge to others. Additionally, designers experiment with materials to make explicit intrinsic properties and limitations, in order to gain tangible feedback from the material itself, beyond initial intellectual assumptions.

As a physical material, matter is bound in its given specificities— direction of grain, atomic and crystalline structure, mass, and phase state. It is also more than an inert object receptive to craft from the designer. There is an implicit testing and experimentation to find in which manner an idea is expressed in an object.

As designers work in new electronic media, the co-relations to physical matter remain present, as electronic objects or signals maintain their own domain of properties and behavior. There is also an additional graphic interface that mediates the experience, through which the transmission of perceived meaning and affect is still required.

Matter in both definitions is activated through a range of operations to rediscover existing building processes, such as rammed earth, and in particle or multi-agent systems that move beyond animations into robust digital simulations. Both have repercussions within their own materiality and properties to engage the design procedure itself. Stronger material systems are therefore manufactured and can be defined and scaled to serve other projects. This produces methods that transcend a small or local experiment to applications elsewhere and at larger scales.

The abundant experiments in craft and material that we conduct at the School are approached both as a manipulation of the natural and in the production of the synthetic. These experiments represent an important part of our curriculum. The questions they raise resonate with student and faculty projects both locally and abroad. The inverse is also true, as many tests and discoveries made abroad return to the School to inform academic work.

THE IRRATIONAL REAL
A Manual for Atomistic Architecture

Thesis Advisor: Timothy Hyde

Cara Liberatore

This project considered rationality both as a problematic construct and as fundamental tool for architectural reinvention. Since we construct reality as a kind of fiction rather than discover it in the world, the true Real only occurs in the moment in which rationality ceases to function. Counterintuitively, however, to produce any kind

01

of freedom from rationality, architecture must critically engage with rationality itself and attempt to dismantle rationality from within. As a second-order procedure, the Irrational Real has the potential to exist both as a technique of codification and as a form of architectural experimentation.

A manual for atomistic architecture provides the primary basis for an investigation of rationality as it pertains to architectural thinking and production. To achieve freedom from rationality, architecture must consider the world not as a set of a priori types or things, but simply as pure matter that is subject to codification. "Matter" can be defined as either an "event, affair, or circumstance," or as "physical objects, vaguely characterized." It is understood as both an influence on behavior or structure, and use or form. Matter continually oscillates between an event and a physical limit. If the rational real is a world of discrete constraints—building codes, geometric rules, zoning laws, and social conventions—then the Irrational Real might be achieved through the conflation of those rational systems. Seemingly disparate things, events, materials, behaviors, and rules—or, forms of matter—are now collapsed within a single, quantitative plane of code.

QUANTITATIVE PLANE OF CODE
The Irrational Real operates through the quantitative conflation of extensive and intensive constraints: extensive constraints being those restrictions on geometry, mass, measurement, or volume that pertain to a particular scale, while intensive constraints, such as limits on temperature, humidity, or duration, do not pertain to any particular scale at all.

TECTONIC OF IRRATIONAL REAL
Through an architecture of the Irrational Real, there is the potential to undo those normative structures of reality that surreptitiously structure daily life. If one presumes that architecture not only affects behavior but also dictates it, then one may argue that there exists a degree of causality between the production of formal or typological uncertainty and a new set of social or behavioral codes. Vagueness, fragmentation, and defamiliarity are all potential outcomes of an architecture that attempts to operate outside of normative preconceptions. The difficult tectonic that ultimately emerges from an architecture of the Irrational Real allows for the fragment, the contradiction, or the improvisational event, all of which enhance one's awareness and participation with architecture.

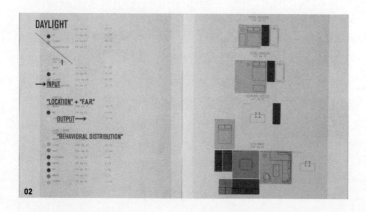

02

01 *Irrational Real rendering*

02 *Diagram of Irrational Real*

03 -04 *Itinerary floor-plan 5 and rendering*

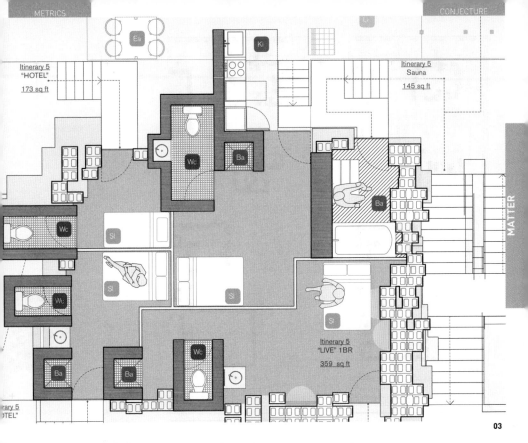

Itinerary 5
"HOTEL"
173 sq ft

Itinerary 5
Sauna
145 sq ft

Itinerary 5
"LIVE" 1BR
359 sq ft

03

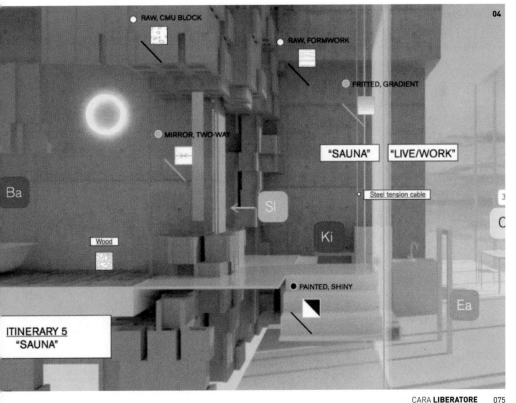

04

RAW, CMU BLOCK

RAW, FORMWORK

FRITTED, GRADIENT

MIRROR, TWO-WAY

"SAUNA" "LIVE/WORK"

Steel tension cable

Wood

PAINTED, SHINY

ITINERARY 5
"SAUNA"

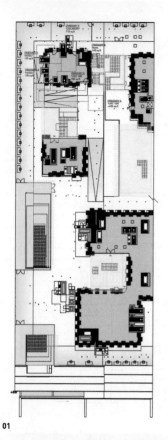

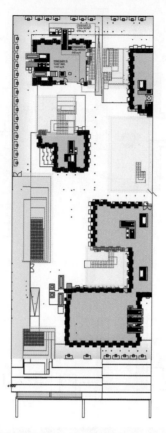

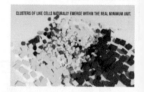

01 *Floor-plan 5 and 6*

02 *Movie still of occupancy size and program*

OPPOSITE *Model image*

01

02

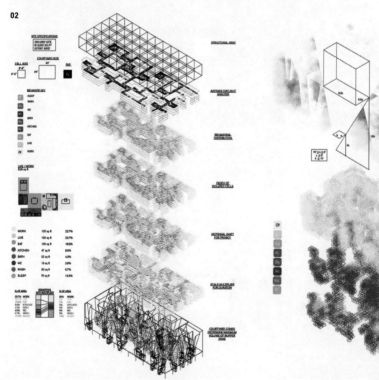

ARCHITECTURE THESIS THE IRRATIONAL REAL

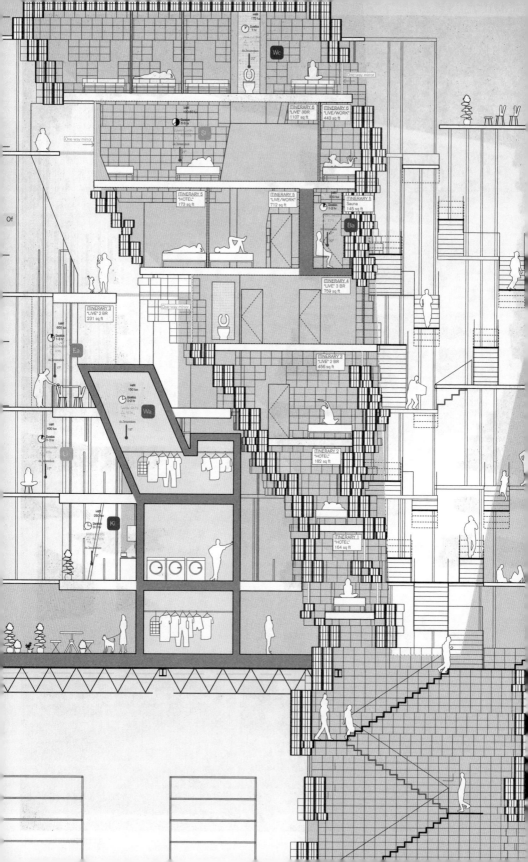

(RE)FABRICATING TECTONIC PROTOTYPES

Seminar, Spring 2012   *Leire Asensio-Villoria*

The course was framed by a general ambition to develop explorations in digital design, fabrication, and parametric tools that were informed and enriched by historical precedent while still maintaining a speculative and novel outlook. The primary focus of the course was the development of conceptual skills and techniques as well as technical understanding of the application of digital processes and tools in the development of tectonic and construction systems in architecture.

Students in this course completed projects that used a number of emerging and established digital techniques and processes to develop new prototypes for construction systems. These proposals took inspiration from and expanded on analysis of exemplary construction/tectonic systems. Existing system precedents were studied and reconsidered during the course to inform and inspire the development of each project. Students were encouraged to rethink existing systems to produce novel expression as well as performance.

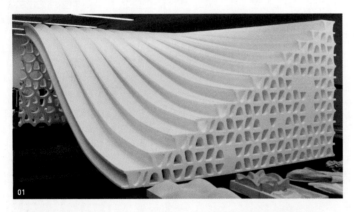

01

A period of analysis and documentation of existing systems and their associative geometric and material relationships initiated the development of a rigorous analytical understanding of specific construction and tectonic systems, as well as proficiency in applying this knowledge to construct associative/parametric digital models. These models constituted the tools to generate alternative variations of the analyzed systems. This informed a subsequent phase of prototyping using the fabrication laboratory's tools. The prototype fabrication exercise allowed students to gain knowledge in and explore the new potentials and capabilities of tools in the emerging field of digital fabrication. These digital design and parametric tools allow for the reconsideration and expansion of the potential applications of exemplary construction and tectonic systems today.

01 EDWARD GENTRY BECKER, STEVEN YING NIEN CHEN, ANIKA GRAMSEY WHITTLE HEDBERG, WEILUN XU

02-03 JILL M. DORAN, LAURA HAAK, ALEXANDER WILLIAM SHELLY, HALLEY WUERTZ

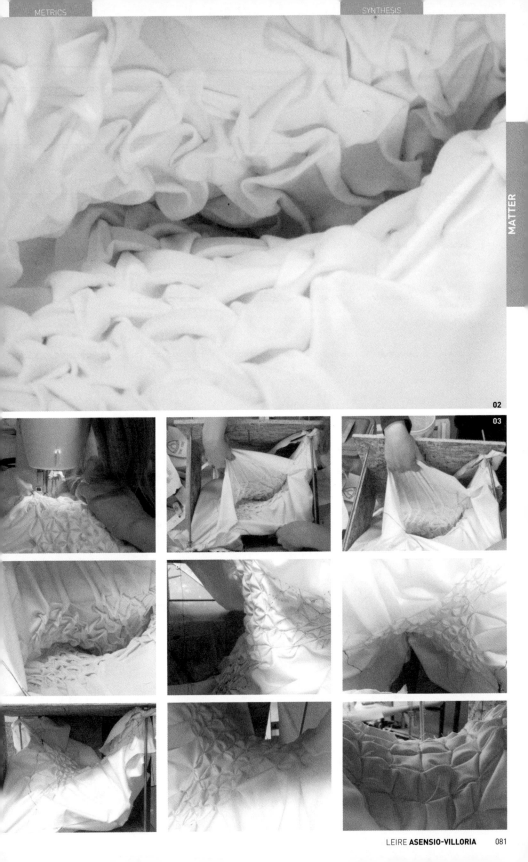

02

03

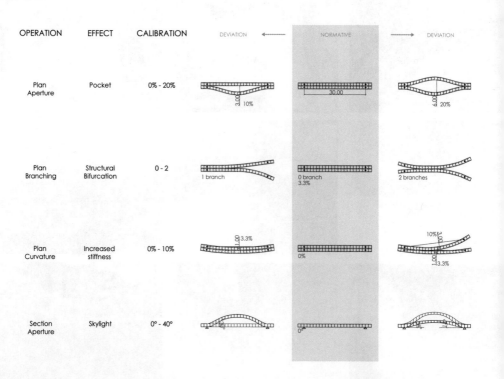

OPERATION	EFFECT	CALIBRATION	DEVIATION ←	NORMATIVE	→ DEVIATION
Span	Increased Space	6.00 - 30.00	6.00	3.00 / 24.00	30.00
Cantilever	Extended Space	1.50 - 9.00		1.30 / 6.00	9.00 / 6.00
Constant Deepening	Increased Stiffness	1.00 - 2.10	1.00	1.50	2.10
Variable Deepening	Material Optimization	0.70 - 2.10	1.00	1.50	0.30
Elevation Curvature	Adaptability	0° - 40°	BEAM	0°	VAULT
Plan Skewing	Adaptability	1 - 2	1.00 / 1.50	1.50 / 1.50	1.50 / 2.00

OPERATION	EFFECT	CALIBRATION	DEVIATION ←	NORMATIVE	→ DEVIATION
Plan Aperture	Pocket	0% - 20%	3.00 / 10%	30.00	20%
Plan Branching	Structural Bifurcation	0 - 2	1 branch	0 branch 3.3%	2 branches
Plan Curvature	Increased stiffness	0% - 10%	1.00 / 3.3%	0%	10% / 1.00 / 3.3%
Section Aperture	Skylight	0° - 40°		0°	

"BONES SERIES" REVISITED

The project revisited and updated the "Bones Series" (Huesos Varios) developed and tested by the eminent Spanish architect Miguel Fisac during the 1960s—an elegant and efficient structural system for long-span roofs. The "Bones Series" consists of a series of identical concrete sections that are post-tensioned to assemble long beams. The smart and meticulous design of their cross-section solve several structural and construction problems: the pieces are hollow, making them lighter while keeping a high moment of inertia; the asymmetric geometry creates openings for natural light and the valley collects and drains the rainwater.

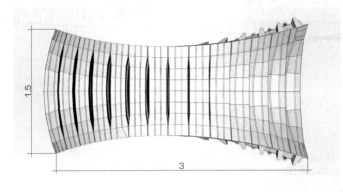

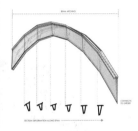

FISAC VARIATIONS

This project proposes an efficient and customizable structural system that takes advantage of contemporary technologies for the AEC industry. This system can adapt to a wide range of span-lengths and structural typologies, from flat slabs to compression-only structures to free-form surfaces. A central feature is its capacity for dealing with differentiated beam sections, which allows for fine-tuned control over natural lighting, acoustics, and water drainage.

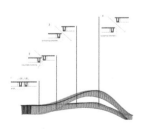

ALL IMAGES WILL CHOI, MATIAS IMBERN, FELIX RASPALL

CONCRETE MATTERS
Beyond Stillbirth Infrastructure

Thesis Advisor: Felipe Correa

Carlos Garciavelez

This thesis examined the physical and cultural dimensions of concrete in the city beyond purely utilitarian purposes. This thesis aimed at bringing back, through concrete explorations, the presence of the human subject in infrastructure by working through a series of scales that go from the intimacy of the body to the expansiveness of the freeway. If 122,000 cubic meters of concrete will be poured to construct

a double-decker system with the only purpose of moving vehicles, then the project is, from a humanist dimension, a stillbirth. The intervention takes the University City model as a device to rethink the nodes along the Periferico ring as mediators of space between the city inside the ring and the one beyond it, to shift this monofunctional infrastructure into a new, multi-layered organizational artifact at a metropolitan scale.

The design project focused on a specific node where these three lines of research are interwoven, creating a large urban artifact that functions as a catalyst for new relationships between the two urban edges defined by the Periferico ring. The new infrastructure project provides cultural, educational and recreational spaces within the leftover spaces of the Periferico peripheral, adding to the city a new set of scales that address the pedestrian.

PROGRAM: UNIVERSITY CITY
An expanded research on the University City in Latin America informed the selection of an academic campus as a program that could occupy the residual geometries between city and infrastructure. This program is specific to one of the nodes and part of a larger network of stops that each respond to specific needs through the specificity of program.

MEDIUM: CONCRETE
The third component of the research is concrete as a material and its possible uses beyond its role in heavy infrastructure, investigating the value of concrete from a cultural dimension, from the scale of interior furnishings to the scale of the city.

01 *Concept image*

02 *University campus in Mexico City*

03 - 04 *Infrastructure renderings*

03

04

BOTANICAL GARDENS

Cameron Wu (Coordinator), Jeffry Burchard, Yael Erel,
John Hong, James Khamsi, Jinhee Park
Architecture Core Studio II, Spring 2012

The new greenhouse facilities and its associated support programs serve three main purposes. First, it houses the expanded permanent (indoor) collection of the Wellesley College Botanic Gardens. Historically, Wellesley maintained one of the premiere botany departments in the country (before being subsumed by the biology department) and continues to host one of the most varied botanical collections in New England. The original greenhouse facilities, which actually pre-date even the original science building, Sage Hall (c.1925), are cramped, deteriorating, and in need of replacement. Tourists and visiting students often arrive in groups as large as sixty people.

Second, it consolidates the full-time and part-time faculty offices and staff of the expanding environmental studies (ES) department. Faculty and department resources were decentralized and scattered throughout the campus—most notably in the political science department. Because the ES department and curriculum serves as an interdisciplinary bridge between the natural sciences and other liberal arts departments at the college, this new facility is the most appropriate location for the department.

Finally, it serves as an iconic piece of architecture, whose physical presence embodies Wellesley's institutional commitment to preparing its students to address critical environmental issues of our time. The college has launched a fundraising campaign to endow the Wellesley Institute for Sustainability and the Environment (WISE). This institute will sponsor periodic lectures, grants, and seven visiting research scholars-in-residence annually. These scholars maintain offices and research facilities in the new facilities and interact with students and faculty on formal and informal levels. The greenhouse and its ancillary buildings function simultaneously as a museum, school, and research facility—each requiring its own size, programmatic needs, and pattern of use. Coupled with the college's desire to have this new facility perform as a new social and intellectual node of the campus, the architecture choreographs the collection and interaction of the various user groups as well as their subsequent dispersal into the different programmatic zones.

MATTHEW CONWAY

01 KEVIN MURRAY
Sampling, displacement, manipulation, and section perspective

02 MATTHEW CONWAY
Unfolded section showing linear movement through building with three oblique axonometric drawings emphasizing moments along the linear path including inhabitable poche, open green-house space, and rejuvenated atrium respectively

03 JOAN TOM
Section axonometric

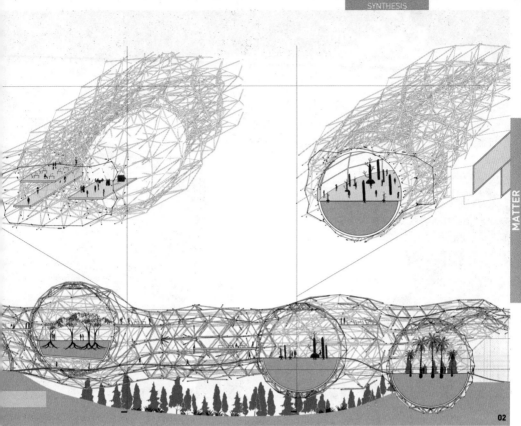

02

03

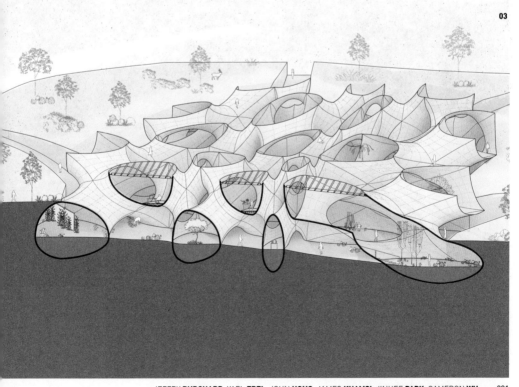

JEFFRY **BURCHARD,** YAEL **EREL,** JOHN **HONG,** JAMES **KHAMSI,** JINHEE **PARK,** CAMERON **WU**

WESLEY HO

JOSH SCHECTER

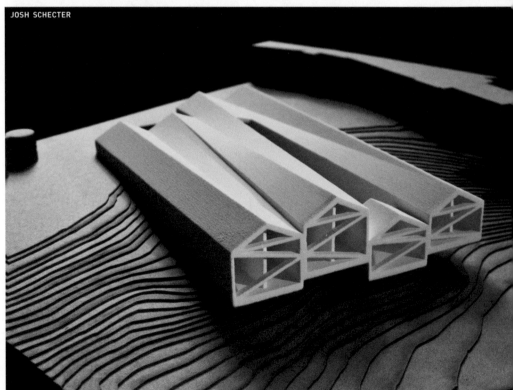

CHEN LU

JOAN TOM

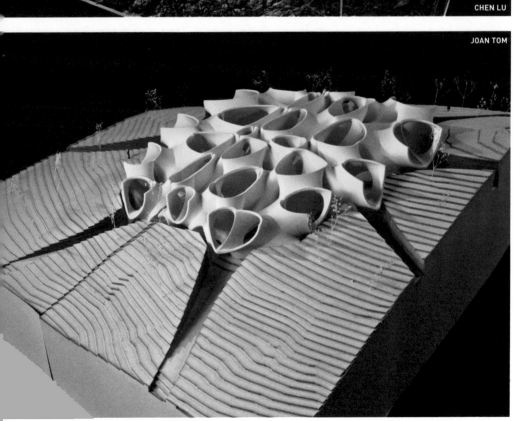

MUDWORKS
Rammed Earth and Sustainability

MudWorks was a design-build installation and exhibition demonstrating the potential of building with raw earth. Organized by the 2012 Loeb Fellows and led by Anna Heringer and rammed earth specialist Martin Rauch, the design and construction involved students, faculty, and the public.

ANNA HERINGER *is an architectural designer from Salzburg, Austria. Her work focuses on the use of local materials, skills, and energy sources to create buildings that are distinct and undeniably from their place. In 1998, Heringer lived in the village of Rudrapur, Bangladesh, as a volunteer for Dipshikha, a local nongovernmental organization. In that same town in 2005-2006, her diploma project, a school built from mud and bamboo, came to fruition. Following this success, in 2007-2008, she coordinated students from Bangladesh and Austria to build a vocational school and a pilot project on rural housing in Rudrapur. Her experience in Bangladesh taught her at a grassroots level that architecture is a tool to improve lives. Her projects aim to strengthen cultural identity, support local economies, and foster ecological balance through architecture.*

The exhibition within Gund Hall described eleven exemplary projects from five continents. Three techniques of earth construction were tested and were demonstrated here: rammed earth construction, formwork, and plaster lime. MudWorks demonstrates earth as a material central to architectural discourse for reclaiming cultural identity, providing tactile and human-scaled environments, and producing plentiful labor opportunities.

SEE ANNA SPEAK ABOUT THE EXHIBITION ON THE GSD YOUTUBE.COM CHANNEL
http://www.youtube.com/user/TheHarvardGSD

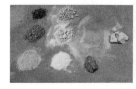

IMAGES ON LEFT PAGE
IWAN BAAN

SURFACE + DEPTH

Anita Berrizbeitia (Coordinator), Jill Desimini, Romy Hecht
Landscape Architecture Core Studio II, Spring 2012

This studio introduced the students to the challenges and opportunities of complex urban sites that have been designed and built many times over a long span of history. As a result, these sites bear a collection of traces of their previous histories—geological, material, programmatic, and, topographical—that are embedded within, and contribute to, the present condition of the space. In addition, the various contexts that surround the site have also been transformed. Street patterns, codes and regulations, demographic change, politics, economics, and time, have all had an effect on the urban landscape, causing it to continuously evolve. As landscape architect, one's first task is to seek an understanding— through various forms of research that include historical, social, material, spatial, and technical — of the processes that led to the site's current state. This research is critical because it forms the foundation of a project's argument and strategies. A basic assumption of the studio is that design is not a tabula rasa but a negotiation between past (e.g., visible traces, precedent, history, ecology) and future projections of the site.

Inherent in the GSD curriculum is the assumption that design is at the center of a landscape architectural education. The hands-on experience of the design studio is the synthetic act that brings together theory and technique in the making of landscapes. In this studio students applied the skills acquired through other courses to the design of landscapes.

ANDREW WISNIEWSKI

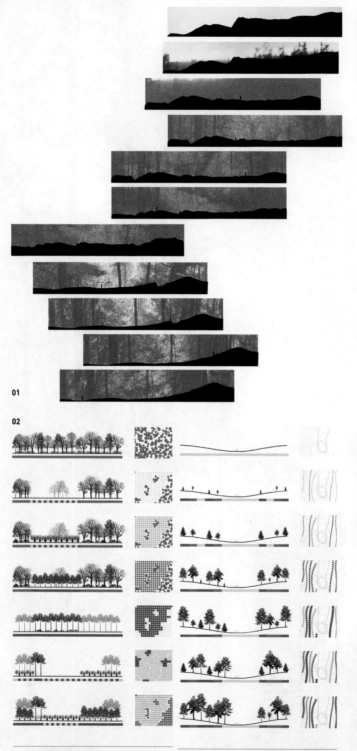

ARCHEOLOGICAL RECORD: TRACING GROUND THROUGH TIME

FOOTNOTE IMAGE *Contextual plan, archeological record of findings on site, polaroids shot on site, operational diagrams*

01 CARA WALSH *Sections*

03 CARA WALSH *Detail plan*

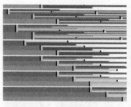

PATCH / FAIRWAY / URBAN EDGE / CONTOUR

FOOTNOTE IMAGE *Forest harvest timeline*

02 ANDREW WISNIEWSKI *Bear Den's Nursery*

04 ANDREW WISNIEWSKI *Silviculture strategies*

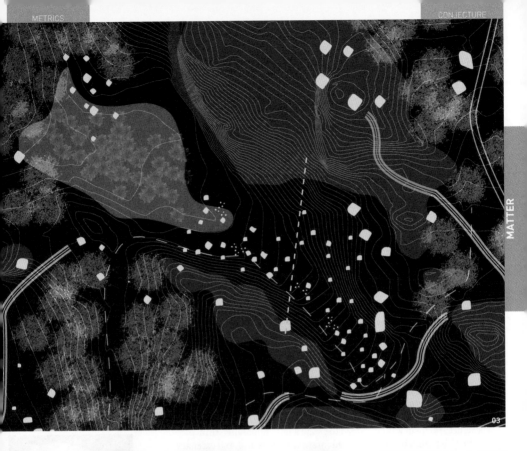

FABRICATING GROUNDS
Advanced Landscape as Digital Media

Seminar, Fall 2011

David M

The goal of Fabricating Grounds was to develop a system of rapidly deployable formwork for cold-weather conditions. The project combines the use of snow and ice as natural building materials with the process of parametric modeling and digital fabrication techniques for the construction of a thin-walled shelter. This project builds off of earlier research on pneumatic structures as form-finding and space-making devices.

The structure was intended to be used as a temporary shelter, which constrained many aspects of the project. The building materials needed to be readily available and easy to use. Since the shelter was intended to be used in cold environments, ice and snow were explored as traditional building materials for temporary structures for their excellent insulative properties and compressive strength. Instead of using traditional igloo construction, the proposed process could be self-forming under wet, frozen conditions. The formwork needed for this process had to be lightweight and packable to be carried in a large backpack.

A structural form was developed to create a self-supporting, thin-walled ice shell. This form utilized internal air pressure, and catenary diaphragms defined and controlled the desired inflated shape. The parametric modeling process allowed for sectional variability of the catenary structure to optimize multiple interior and exterior spaces. CNC tools were used to fabricate a set of plastic panels which could be joined to make the inflatable structure. While fabric reinforcement was used to strengthen and connect the catenary ribs, it was discovered that an ice shell of approximately half an inch was capable of supporting itself without further bracing.

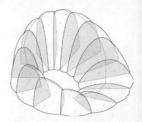

ARTICULATED RIBBED TORUS
This geometry allows for increased standing height, lower sleeping and storage heights, and sheltered accessible exterior space.

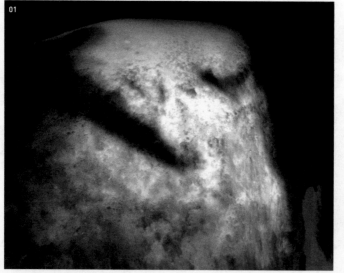

01

01 *Prototype photo*

02 *Prototype photo with structure diagrams*

ALL IMAGES CARL KOEPCKE AND MARSHALL PRADO

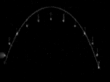 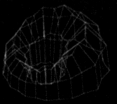  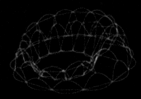

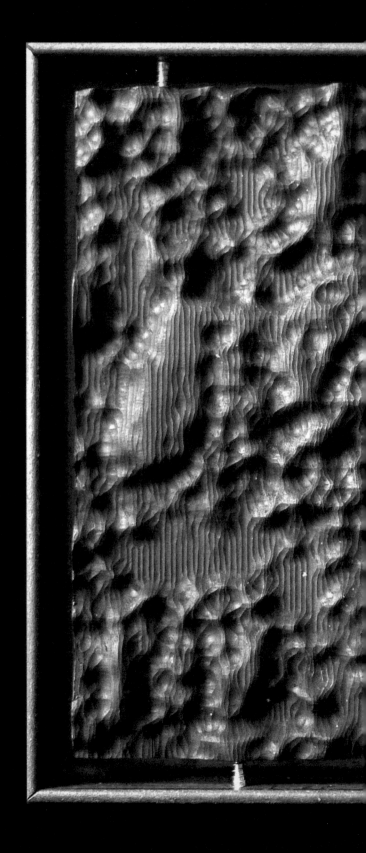

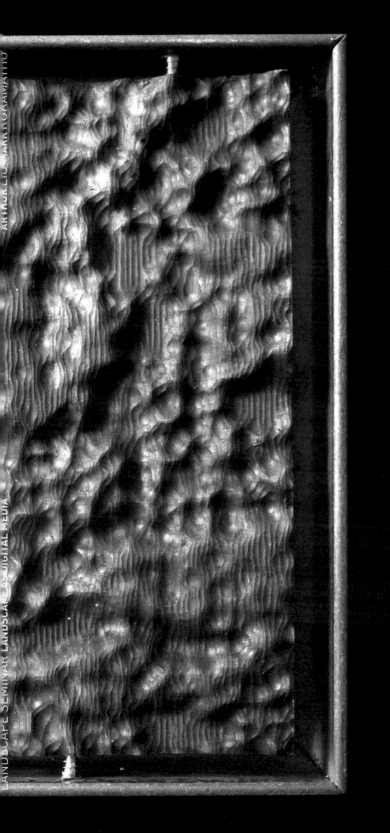

THE NEW COLOSSUS

Of Islands and Origins

Thesis Advisor: Hashim Sarkis

Andrew McGee

The island has long been the interface between the known and the unknown, the outpost on the edge of the frontier, the satellite stronghold that often operates just beyond the periphery of the rules and boundaries of the mainland. As such, the island becomes a staging ground for the visible and invisible machinations of empire. In this way, the island has often born witness to the evolution of Colossus.

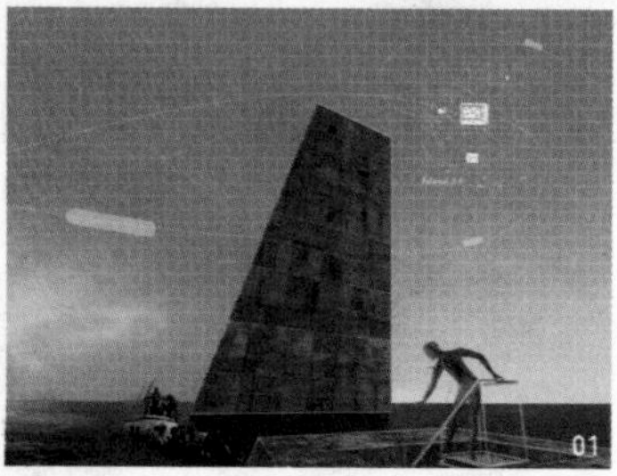

01

In particular, the Mediterranean Island, with its isolated interior yet still intimate connection to trade routes and shorelines of the inland sea, presents a hybrid typology that inhabits both ends of the spectrum of connectivity.

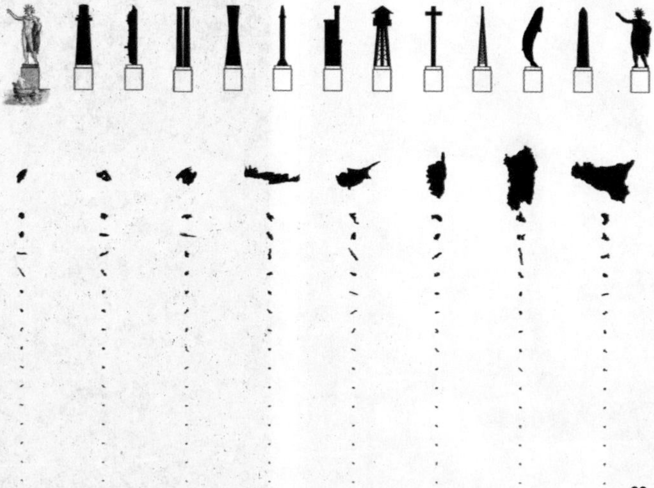

02

The origin of Colossus is constantly shifting, a hybrid of atmospheric and euclidian constructs that enriches its spatial condition and embeds in its edge a power to momentarily reveal the invisible. The New Colossus recalibrates the metrics of that liminal space between land and sea, territory and wilderness, isolation and connectivity, interior and exterior. The hybrid origin of the New Colossus must be harnessed and exploited to further augment architecture's ability to engage with these large-scale, latent conditions.

THE STRAIT OF SICILY

The Strait of Sicily, the divider between the two basins of the Mediterranean Sea, between religions and cultures of the East and West, and between economic disparities of the North and South, becomes the test site for a series of speculations on the form and function of the New Colossus, manifested through the figure of the island in a vast and often scaleless seascape. The new island Colossus is a half land-form, half architectural hybrid that engages in a contemporary debate about the scale of frameworks and contexts through which architecture is designed and thought.

THE FACES OF COLOSSUS

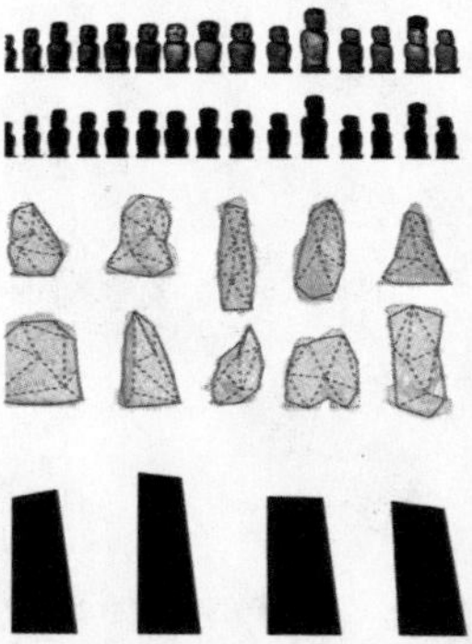

01 *Approach to each island Colossus*

02 *The faces of Colossus*

03 *How to make an island*

04 *Atmospheric site plan*

05 - 08 *Section drawings and section models*

choose a location

02. *define a boundary*

03. *pump out water*

lower in digging machines

05. *bore tunnels through seabed*

06. *excavate soil and sediment*

reinforce boundary

08. *mold island with excavated soil*

09. *house utilities in island core* **03**

04

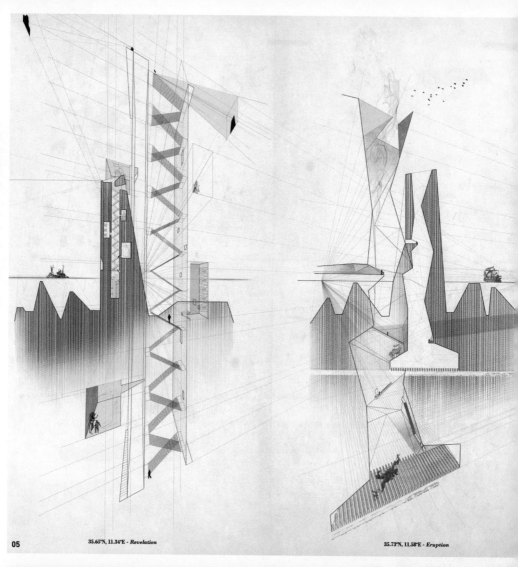

05   35.65°N, 11.34°E - *Revelation*   35.73°N, 11.58°E - *Eruption*

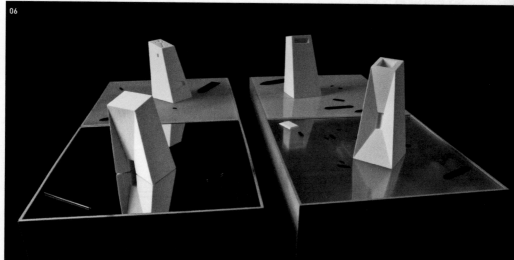

06

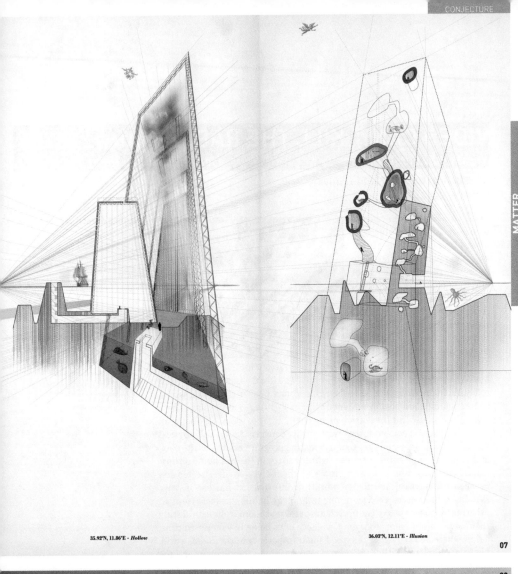

35.92°N, 11.86°E - *Hollow*

36.03°N, 12.11°E - *Illusion*

07

08

VIDEO CAN'T KILL THE RADIO STAR

Focus in the Future Library

James Templeton Kelley Thesis Prize

Thesis Advisor: Mariana Ibañez

Ben Brady

This thesis explored the tension prevalent in today's libraries from all scales. Video cannot kill the radio star. De- spite promises of obsolescence of one technology over an- other, we must realize that this is never the case. Video didn't kill radio. Photography didn't kill painting. Film didn't kill the theater and the age of digital

information will not kill the book and the library. "This" doesn't kill "that" but rather "that" may be redefined by "this." The library is at a unique place today, facing head-on the power, speed, and mobility of the digital world, while simultaneously being burdened by its own immense physicality. There are multiple causes for the tension prevalent in libraries today. One being an unproductive, sloppy, and forced relationship between digital and physical worlds of the library and the second being the program related to the book and to print media being forced to fight for space in its own home against extraneous programs that have attached themselves to it. The tension between the physical and digital worlds of information has left us with skeuomorphic objects, vestiges of one technology holding us back from an ushering into a new place. The prevalence of these skeuomorphs manifesting themselves in our media today are evidence of us being in a confused time, a time where we will call for the speed and transparency of the digital world, but at the same time still calling for a relationship to the slowness and the warmth commonly associated with libraries.

FUTURE DEPOSITORY

(Conceptual image to left) Currently Harvard University houses more than 9 million books 26 miles from its campus. Remote storage is an endemic problem to almost all large institutional libraries. This project speculates a rather pessimistic view of our society's future relationship with books. While in this future, the book cannot withstand the economic pressures, central to the city, it must remain in close proximity to the user. So, the future depository finds the cracks of the city. A 10-foot-wide, 750-foot-tall structure emerges in the spaces between tall buildings. With one small reference desk on the store front, the role of browsing changes drastically while the books, as a symbol of power and knowledge for a city, remain central and are physically and metaphorically lifted above the city.

SKEUOMORPHIC

01 *Exterior rendering of library*

02 *Skeuomorphic side table with site models*

03 - 04 *Exterior and interior renderings*

03

04

01

02

UNDER THE LIBRARY

Social program, digital public Space, wifi that is not Starbucks or McDonald's, street furniture

01 *Under the library*

02 *Wifi cold spot*

OPPOSITE *Plan and section*

WIFI COLD SPOT

The wifi cold spot is a full-scale room to actively remove yourself from the pressures of the digital world. From afar, it appears solid. As you approach you see plastic emerging from the interior, begging you to enter. And as you enter, a drastically different interior is revealed. You can only attempt to make sense of the space you are in and nothing more. You forget about the invisible pressures of the digital world. The interior is painted with a grounded, EMF-blocking black paint that blocks all radiation and signals in the space, rendering your wifi and your cell phone useless. This "anti-phone booth" exists in highly digitally charged public areas as a moment of pause and reflection.

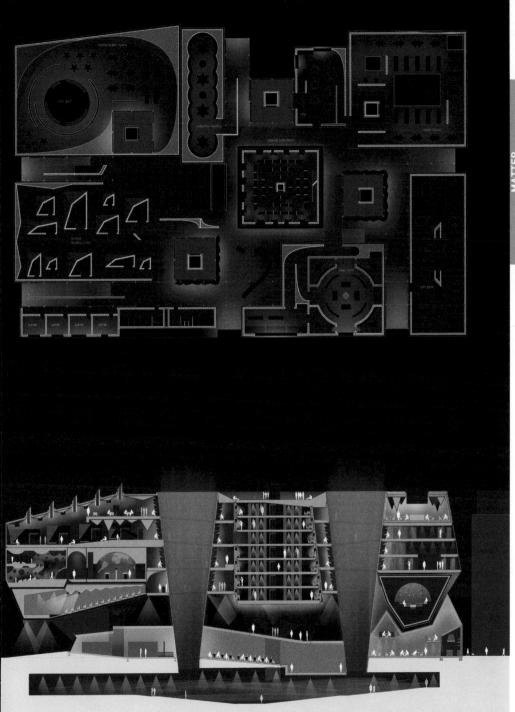

LIFECYCLE DESIGN

Seminar, Fall 2011   *Martin Bechthold*

The construction, maintenance, and operation of the built environment consumes significant resources in a world of rapidly depleting natural reserves. As our ability to design energy efficient buildings increases, buildings consume relatively fewer resources through their operation. Consequently the focus of sustainable design shifts increasingly toward the evaluation and thoughtful deployment of building materials themselves. Instead of using materials from primary resources, future buildings and other elements of the built environment will have to rely increasingly on the use of recycled materials.

This research seminar/workshop studied the broader issues of lifecycle design using recycled materials, with a special interest in components for the building envelope. In a workshop format, students were introduced to the fundamentals of lifecycle assessment, product development and prototyping, manufacturing processes, market research, and business aspects of product development, as well as design for production, assembly, and disassembly.

Case studies and readings complemented lectures and discussions. Working in small groups, students developed proposals and prototypes for building components based on recycled materials, and conducted initial studies on lifecycle assessments, design potential, assembly, and construction integration.

COLLABORATION AND FIELD TRIP
This course was taught in collaboration with Miniwiz, a Taiwan-based company focused on sustainable product development.

MANUFACTURING A TWIST
Inspiration for manufacturing the twist with the material constrains of cooling plastic came from pasta manufacturing patents.

ITERATIVE SHAPING STUDIES
Flow analysis studying speed through various shapes. Model images to the right—the hug tube and the tri-tube— have the optimal twist and curvature for facilitating photosynthesis for algae production.

FACADES + PLASTIC + ALGAE
Through the designed integration of these inputs, the collaborative system converts waste energy and off-gases into both energy and commercial commodities.

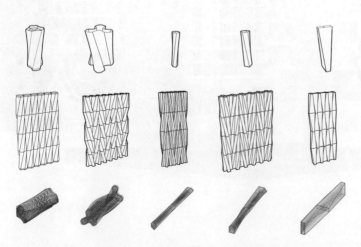

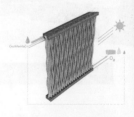

ALL IMAGES DASHA ORTENBERG, ALISON VON GLINOW, COREY WOWK, SENYA ARSENI ZAITSEV

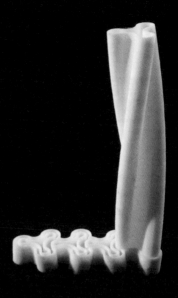

DESTRUCTIVE CREATION
Architectural Authorship through Material Removal

Thesis Advisor: Florian Idenburg   *Matthew Swaidan*

I think both of the criticisms in the footnote to the right are fair. Paired, I believe they suggest an opportunity for architecture to expand its set of tools. If architects have rendered themselves irrelevant in post-Fordist conditions by focusing solely on techniques of growth and development, it is time to explore alternatives. Not an architecture of addition, but subtraction.

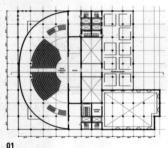 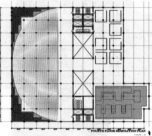

01

This thesis is an investigation of architectural authorship through the removal of material. The method I pursued was to select a site (the Crosley Building, a 1924 manufacturing facility in Cincinnati, Ohio), analyze the architectural logic of that building, develop formal techniques of removal based on the building's construction, and then test those techniques against a program that has a diversity of spatial requirements: a symphony hall.

KELLER EASTERLING
"Methods for demolishing, imploding, or otherwise subtracting building material are not among the essential skills imparted to architects in training. Believing building to be the primary constructive activity, the discipline has not institutionalized special studies of subtraction... The demolition plan, one of the first pages in a set of construction documents, provides instructions for the removal of building material, but only building material that presents an obstacle to more building material, the material of a new, superior design. Architectural authorship is measured by object building rather than by the admirable removal of material."

CHARLES WALDHEIM
"For the architectural profession, the city of Detroit in the 1990s entered a similar condition of meaninglessness precisely because it no longer required the techniques of growth and development that had become the modus operandi of the discipline. Absent the need for these tools, Detroit became a 'non-site' for the architect in the same sense that de Certeau's dead body ceased to operate as a site for the physician's attention."

DEMOLITION PLAN
Slab is cut around column capitals and allowed to rest on excess columns from the theater; restaurant first-floor demolition plan.

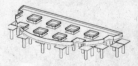

01 *Theater demolition plans*

02 *Model of building*

03 *Model of restaurant*

04 *Rendering of theater*

03

04

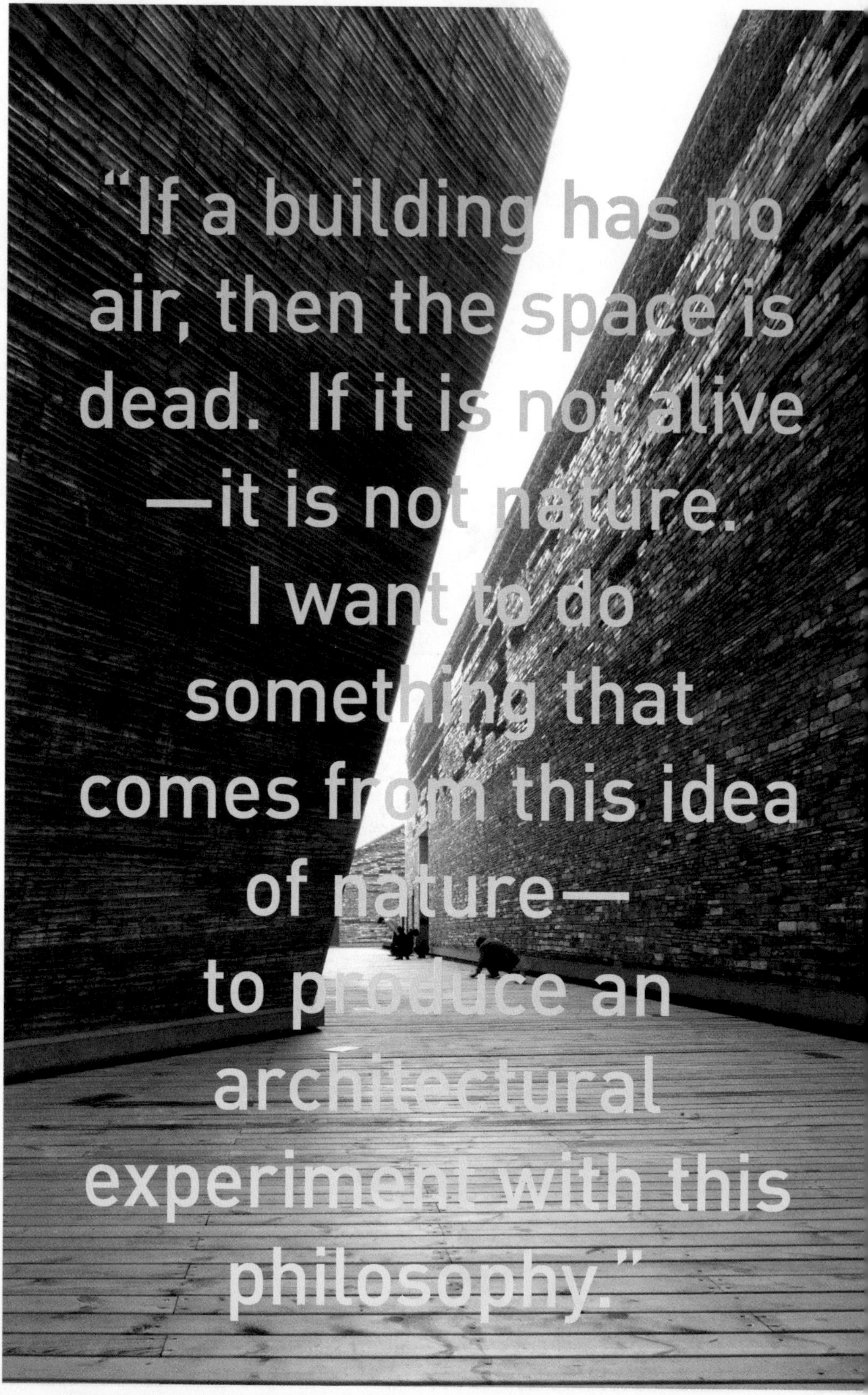

"If a building has no air, then the space is dead. If it is not alive —it is not nature. I want to do something that comes from this idea of nature— to produce an architectural experiment with this philosophy."

KENZO TANGE LECTURE: WANG SHU
Geometry and Narrative of Natural Form

I don't like to talk about China because China is a very new concept. It is a very nationalistic concept. It is a large area where many local cultures exist together. In China, many people do not believe in anything–they don't have a strong feeling about religion, for example. But landscape in China– to some–is almost a religion. Other people, they are just looking for change. They want new things, but they don't really know the meaning of "what is new." They just want to become new. They just want to become changed. In order to become new, architecture then produces buildings that gradually become higher and higher.

HARVARD UNIVERSITY
RADUATE SCHOOL OF DESIGN

WANG SHU
Principal of Amateur Architecture Studio and Head of the Architecture School, China Academy of Art. Amateur Architecture Studio was founded in 1998 by Wang Shu and Lu Wenyu in Hangzhou, China. Their approach is based around a critique of the architectural profession, which they view as complicit in the demolition of entire urban areas and the transformation of rural areas through excessive building. The practice first came to wider attention in Europe with their pavilion for the 10th Venice Architecture Biennale in 2006; a comment on the ongoing demolitions, their installation "Tiled Garden," was made from 66,000 recycled tiles salvaged from demolition sites.

I think we need another kind of architect. This is why I call my studio the Amateur Architecture Studio. My studio is a different type of system. It allows me to keep a certain distance, an independent position, so I can do some serious thinking in order to talk about Chinese culture as more than an abstract concept. Chinese culture comes from the earth, from the land, and from local traditions. What I am interested in is the relationship of the tradition of the Chinese landscape drawing system to the systems of architecture and urban planning. In the past, China had a landscape architecture system that covered the entire country. The system was not just about some gardens, or some landscape on the side of buildings, or about some park it was about the system.

Looking at landscape drawings, you can understand the meaning of cities through the landscape–it reveals a very large-scale vision of the area. These drawings express both what is in your mind and in your heart. It is a philosophy–a vision–where the landscape is the mix of artificial things and natural things together. This is a very typical Chinese philosophy. We call it the Tao system, where nature is the human's teacher. The Chinese believe we can create scenery with the land through a natural system. For me, this means architecture and urban planning can come from nature.

WANG SHU AWARDED THE 2012 PRITZKER PRIZE

Nature means that you should do everything analogous to living things. Living things have life–real life. If a building has no air, then the space is dead. If it is not alive–it is not nature. I want to do something that comes from this idea of nature–to produce an architectural experiment with this philosophy. The most important thing for my buildings are the conditions of atmosphere. People understand a clear concept about the form in my buildings, but the atmosphere inside also produces a strong sense of spatiality.

SEE ALSO *Landscape Wooden (Hill and Water) House studio taught by Wang Shu and Lu Wenyu.*

Sometimes I am not very sure about the future in China. But at other times, I still have some hope about the future, especially when I discuss it with the craftsman, with the farm worker–I find that they can understand my philosophy. They have great culture, great tradition, and they can understand these abstract things. It is a philosophy that not only artists and philosophers can understand. These craftsmen can create, together with you, things of high quality and produce incredible achievements with incredible force.

WATCH THE LECTURE ON THE GSD YOUTUBE.COM CHANNEL
http://www.youtube.com/user/TheHarvardGSD

IMAGE **LV HENGZHONG**
Ningbo History Museum.

LANDSCAPE WOODEN (HILL AND WATER) HOUSE

A NATURAL FORM OF ARCHITECTURAL NARRATION AND CONSTRUCTION

Architecture Option Studio, Fall 2011

Wang Shu and Lu Wenyu

In Chinese landscape painting, when "Hill and Water"paintings emerged, 1500 years ago, they represented the shift of attention from the subject to the view of the world, philosophically—social problems led to the transfer of interest to pure natural objects. Different from the landscape painting depicting only the natural landscape, houses began to emerge in "Hill and Water" paintings—creating a typology of "Hill and Water Wooden House." Distinct from the "Jie Hua"paintings that depict buildings, houses in "Hill and Water Wooden House"were not the dominant subject of the paintings. They were less important than the trees and stones depicted. I think this does not only illustrate the relationship between the building and the surrounding environment, but it is the content inside the painting that should be the subject that architecture discusses. The existence of buildings in the painting shows the desire for coexistence with nature. In my point of view, it also represents a humble attitude toward nature. How should a building nest between "Hill and Water" in a proper manner? It should perceive and learn the natural rules. By narrating and constructing the natural form, architecture mixes with the environment fully—humans live in it, feel it, wander around it, and judge it with a standard of whether it communicated the natural fascination. It is not about *formal architecture*, but an invitation to participate and feel the different philosophical and poetic experiences.

In traditional Chinese architecture, the most direct relationship to this philosophy is the construction of the garden. The garden is the means by which the "Hill and Water"paintings are constructed. It is interesting that the garden was often built in the city. To the over-artificial city, the garden is like an architectural critique, with nature as its reference. The proponents of the garden express their desire to rid urban. The garden usually shows the hidden status of villages within the hill. To build gardens in the city seems like being critical to the urban values. What interests the architecture designers is that in an empty site, where there are no trees, hills, or stones to make use of, how can we build a wider viewpoint, how can we curate and construct an arena conforming to the natural codes, and how can we make the building lose its central position in architecture, so that we are able to find a more sustainable means to construct?

LAP CHI KWONG

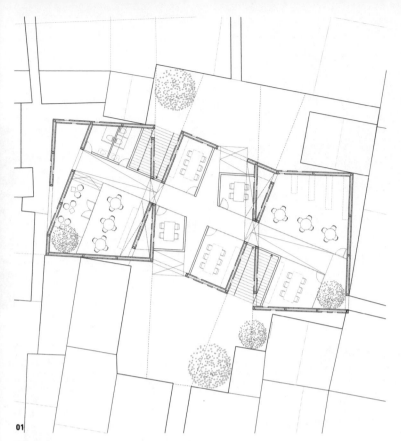

01

THE SITE: HANGZHOU, CHINA

The site is located near Hangzhou, China, along an ancient 2,000-year old canal. The ugly commercial development of residential buildings only an area of 25 meters wide by 4 meters long between the buildings a the canal. It calls for an architecture and landscape approach to remedy this renowned arena both in historic poetry and hill and water paintings.

01 *House: from the perimeter to wi all courtyards are connected throug continuous garden system.*

02 *Section of the commercial corrid with three private houses and connecting semi-private courtyard system.*

03 *Model of the enclosed urbanism of the homes through the wrapping the garden wall and interiorization micro-domesticity.*

04 *Model of entrance view to privat corridor balcony.*

ALL IMAGES ALISON VON GLIN

02

03

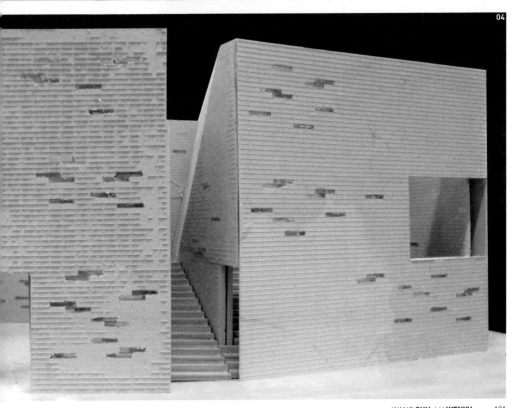

04

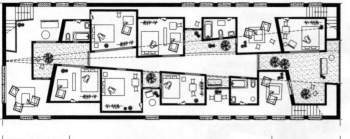

01 *Plan transformation*

02 *Interior study*

ALL IMAGES LAP CHI KWONG

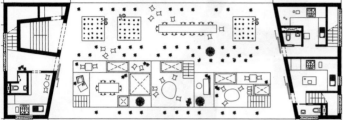

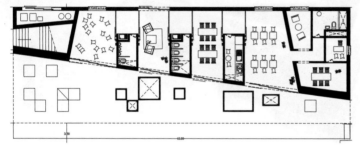

STUDIO TRIP SITE VISIT
The students took a trip to Suzhou and Hangzhou in China to observe and study Chinese gardens, as well as conduct an investigation on the site and traditional residential houses in Shaoxing.

LANDSCAPE WOODEN (TREE AND WATER) HOUSE WANG SHU, LU WENYU LAI CHI KWONG

ACTIVISM

126 127 128 129 130 131 132 133 134 135

150 151 152 153 154 155 156 157 158 159 160 161 162

ACTIVISM

positions design as an agent for social, political, and environmental change. In recent years, we have seen natural and man-made disasters increase in rate and severity. Climate change, resource scarcity, and underserved populations have made crisis a globalized and permanent condition. It is in the realm of design to develop strategies to produce effective change.

Some of these issues are current and pressing, and others are indicators of future conditions, yet all require design analysis and proposals. Therefore activism is framed as both responsive action and anticipatory practice.

The unstable nature of crisis requires designers to operate through flexible frameworks. While crisis and the manifestations of crisis signal multiple design problems, they also reveal design opportunities. Design knowledge is key in identifying and proposing alternative scenarios that can change the response as well as the response mechanism. The abilities of designers can become higher-order processes that move beyond built interventions to analysis, projections of long-term effect, and incremental growth.

Activism and the engagement of issues—within and outside of the School—that are pressing or latent may be extended to encompass a larger sense of change.

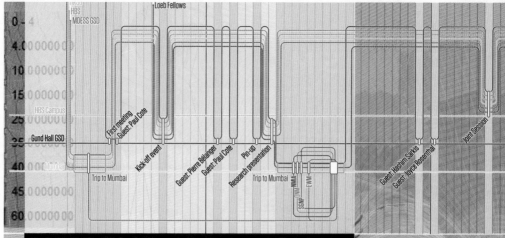

EXTREME URBANISM II

Urban Planning and Design Option Studio, Spring 2012
Rahul Mehrotra and Gareth Doherty

The studio engaged with the Mumbai Metropolitan Region (MMR) as
its site for inquiry, research, and design propositions. The pedagogical
thrust of the studio was to explore the potential for urban design and
planning as well as landscape, architecture, and real estate as instruments
for spatial imaginations at the metropolitan scale. This studio was the
first of a three-year thematic exploration of the Mumbai region, which
ranged from looking at infrastructure and ecology to questions of
housing, urban systems, and form. The studio researched and designed
components that focus on a menu of predetermined questions with
regional implications. Project formulation served as an important
component of the studio. The studio explored issues of extreme urbanism
in the form of social, cultural, and economic disparities and how these
manifest themselves in the MMR. Social interactions, public space,
and the broader issue of how design and planning can facilitate new
imaginations for the metropolitan region are central to the discussions.
The intent was to evolve new understandings of the contemporary
potential of the MMR and to position urban design and planning as well
as landscape, architecture, and real estate as instruments for a broader
strategy plan that is more nuanced in terms of the ecologies that it
recognizes and socially inclusive in its propositioned dimension.

VICTOR MUÑOZ SANZ (ABOVE)
CHRISTOPHER BUCCINO

130

Midterm

Joint Session

Final Review

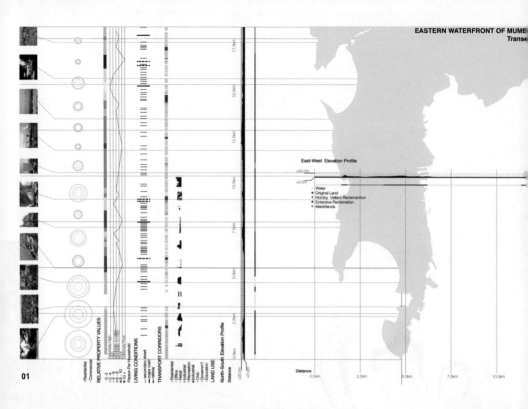

East-West Elevation Profile

+30.0m
+0.0m

● Water
● Original Land
● Hornby Vellard Reclamation
◆ Extensive Reclamation
● Marshlands

RELATIVE PROPERTY VALUES

LIVING CONDITIONS

—— secondary street
—— major road
—— railway

TRANSPORT CORRIDORS

LAND USE

North-South Elevation Profile

Distance

Distance

0.0km   2.5km   5.0km   7.5km   10.0km

01

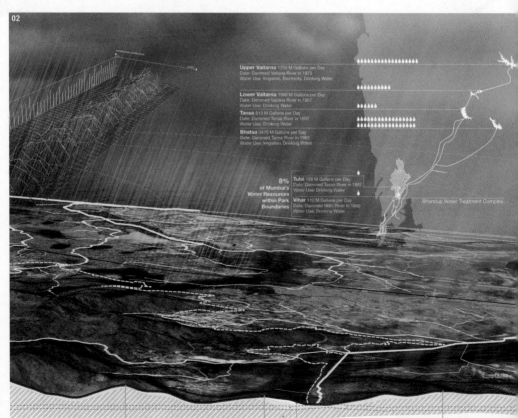

Upper Vaitarna 1755 M Gallons per Day
Date: Dammed Vaitarna River in 1973
Water Use: Irrigation, Electricity, Drinking Water

Lower Vaitarna 1068 M Gallons per Day
Date: Dammed Vaitarna River in 1957
Water Use: Drinking Water

Tansa 613 M Gallons per Day
Date: Dammed Tansa River in 1892
Water Use: Drinking Water

Bhatsa 3470 M Gallons per Day
Date: Dammed Tansa River in 1983
Water Use: Irrigation, Drinking Water

8%
of Mumbai's
Water Resources
within Park
Boundaries

Tulsi 128 M Gallons per Day
Date: Dammed Tasso River in 1897
Water Use: Drinking Water

Vihar 110 M Gallons per Day
Date: Dammed Mithi River in 1860
Water Use: Drinking Water

Bhandup Water Treatment Complex

02

The studio began with group research in four different sites within Mumbai.

01 JAMES WHITTEN, MONICA EARL, JAE MIN HA
Site: Eastern Waterfront of Mumbai

02 NICOLAS MAECKLE RIVARD, KATHARYN LEAH HURD, XINPENG YU
Site: Sanjay Gandhi National Park

03 ÓSCAR MALASPINA QUEVEDO, EINAT ROSENKRANTZ AMÓN, TOMAS FOLCH
Site: Quarries in Navi Mumbai

04 FARIDA HANY MAHMOUD FARAG, SONG E HAN, CHRISTOPHER MICHAEL BUCCINO
Site: Navi Mumbai International Airport

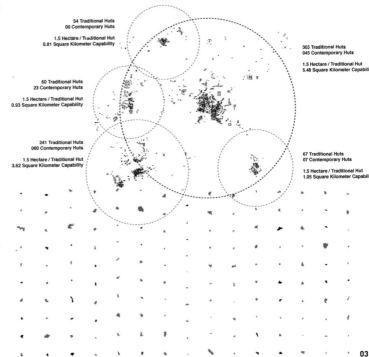

54 Traditional Huts
00 Contemporary Huts

1.5 Hectare / Traditional Hut
0.81 Square Kilometer Capability

065 Traditional Huts
045 Contemporary Huts

1.5 Hectare / Traditional Hut
5.48 Square Kilometer Capability

60 Traditional Huts
23 Contemporary Huts

1.5 Hectare / Traditional Hut
0.93 Square Kilometer Capability

241 Traditional Huts
060 Contemporary Huts

1.5 Hectare / Traditional Hut
3.62 Square Kilometer Capability

67 Traditional Huts
07 Contemporary Huts

1.5 Hectare / Traditional Hut
1.05 Square Kilometer Capability

03

ACTIVISM

04
QUA
Exc

EXCAVATION EDGE

EXCAVATION EDGE

Topography of Extraction _ 2001-2011

S07_2001-2011
S06_2001-2011
S05_2001-2011
S04_2001-2011
S03_2001-2011
S02_2001-2011
S01_2001-2011

S15_2001-2011
S14_2001-2011
S13_2001-2011
S12_2001-2011
S11_2001-2011
S10_2001-2011
S09_2001-2011
S08_2001-2011

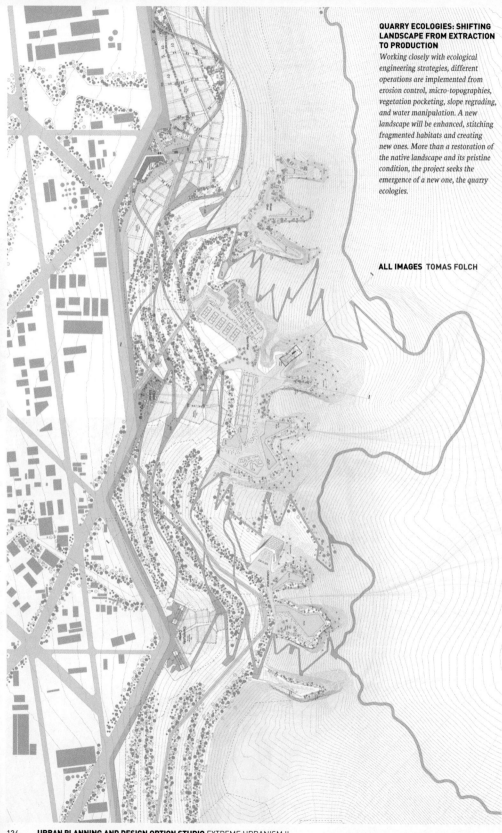

QUARRY ECOLOGIES: SHIFTING LANDSCAPE FROM EXTRACTION TO PRODUCTION

Working closely with ecological engineering strategies, different operations are implemented from erosion control, micro-topographies, vegetation pocketing, slope regrading, and water manipulation. A new landscape will be enhanced, stitching fragmented habitats and creating new ones. More than a restoration of the native landscape and its pristine condition, the project seeks the emergence of a new one, the quarry ecologies.

ALL IMAGES TOMAS FOLCH

COLLABORATIONS *The studio collaborated with the Loeb Fellowship and MDesS programs from the GSD as well as students and faculty from Harvard Business School, Harvard Kennedy School, and Harvard Law School.*

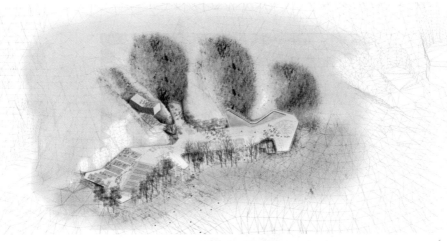

Urban expansion has typically taken precedence over claims for land as advances in technologies has made it easier for people to get their food goods from farther, faster. Globalization and industrial food production has ensured that most of us are able to be fed. However, growing health and environmental concerns have created a sort of backlash to this system and people are making more conscious choices about what they eat and from where it derives. As a result, the practices of the rural are now, more than ever, invading the urban.

More often than not, the produce we consume comes from processes far different from those used by the farmers who tilled and cultivated lands

URBAN CANOPY GARDEN

Thesis Advisors: Jacques Herzog and Pierre de Meuron   *Chris Masicampo*

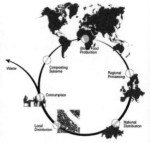

GLOBALLY VERSUS LOCALLY INTEGRATED FOOD SYSTEMS

The predominant model of the current global food system is the prime model by which food is produced and then ultimately arrives to our tables. The strategy of this design proposal aims to facilitate a more locally integrated system that scales down the steps associated with the current model. Inherent in the approach is a deliberate effort to eliminate the effect of food miles and create a more direct link to food sources.

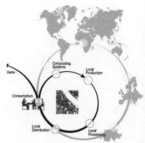

generations before us. We have long been able to replace the sun and now hydroponics has made it possible to make food without soil. The proposal of a garden canopy in Basel that hangs over the railways sought to take these technologies and reimagine how agriculture could be achieved in the city beyond the usual greening of existing surfaces. It came from a desire to reconnect and invigorate the city through the most commonly relatable and basic need of food.

FOOD AND CITIES *The flow of food has a fundamental impact on how urban territories expand and grow. Large distribution centers and transportation infrastructures are required to feed the evergrowing population of contemporary cities. Historically a city's growth was tied to its capacities to produce or import food from adjacent lands. With the advancement of transportation technologies, "foodsheds" became globalized and the geographic bonds between cities and their sources of food were broken.*

This research explored the food network of the Greater Boston area in relation to the larger food infrastructure of the United States. Food distribution, its historical context, and the impact of politics and culture were studied. The research revealed that in the dense urban fabric of Boston, much like its suburbs, the "big box" typology, which offers "one-stop shopping," is the thriving typology for food markets.

The thesis proposed to bring back the idea of market plazas in city centers, which are currently occupied by skyscrapers and shopping malls. Our civic centers, which symbolize our civic pride, should once again become a hub of interaction between the producers of food and its consumers. Community gardens and small farms can exist within these hubs to promote agritourism and provoke interest in how food is produced. Today, the Rose Kennedy Greenway, located above the buried Central Artery Highway, can provide an

FOOD IN BOSTON

Maria Galustian   *Thesis Advisors: Jacques Herzog and Pierre de Meuron*

ACTIVISM

opportunity for the city of Boston to not only revive such principles but go beyond them.

The thesis suggested layers of varied programs for this site that will bring public involvement to another level. The project defined a place of common ground for people to engage in the production of food as well as provide leisure and recreational activities. The public's involvement and a congestion of varied programs will define a new public space. Farms covering the highway ramps will reclaim the land for uses such as markets, bars, restaurants, and research centers. Such common ground will bring together people of different political and social backgrounds and will create a new understanding of physical togetherness.

This thesis constructed a new model of practice that uses making in a way that engages the public. The aim was to use the current condition within the profession as an opportunity for reinvention, to prove the discipline's relevance to the large demographic unserved by design. The ubiquitous streetscape was not just used

MAKE-TANK
Adventure in Small-Scale Urban Intervention
Thesis Advisor: Danielle Etzler

Julian Bushman-Copp

as the backdrop for architecture but as the social and cultural construct, which served as the site for this exploration. The method operated with the immediacy of small-scale interventions that can impact spatial conditions in the public realm. Architecture's relevance to those outside of the field will rely on how we shift the focus toward work of inclusion. The transition is integrally related to the values that it adopts during the time the field takes to rebound. The last century and a half has seen the establishment of an architectural profession, once the servants of royalty and aristocracy, that democratized practice to the extent that it became accessible to a larger public. However, the relationship between designer and client is in danger of reverting back to its origins and design is now viewed as a luxury only for the wealthy class.

URBAN TRENDS *It is projected that by 2030, over three-quarters of all countries will have over half of their population in urban areas. It is also projected that 95 percent of the world's urban growth in the next two decades will take place in cities of the developing world. In the cities of developing countries, three or four out of ten non-permanent houses are located in areas prone to natural disasters.*

There is always a "man-made" component to natural disasters. The number of natural disasters, the number of people reported affected by natural disasters, and the estimated damage caused by natural disasters has been increasing over the past century. These recent trends are closely linked to urbanization. Transitional shelters are rapid, post-disaster household shelters made from materials that can be upgraded or reused in more permanent structures, or that can be relocated from temporary sites to permanent locations. They are designed to facilitate the transition by affected populations to more durable shelters. A successful shelter must balance factors such as safety, lifespan, size, comfort, and privacy on one side and cost, timeliness, materials availability, maintenance and upgrade, cultural appropriateness, and construction skills on the other.

My project proposed an alternative solution to what is being used as disaster relief shelter today. By creating vertical multi-story units, my project was

TEMPORAL VERTICALITY
Disaster Relief Transitional Shelters for Haiti

Seung-Jin Ham   *Thesis Advisor: Jonathan Levi*

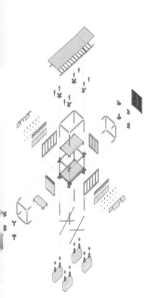

able to achieve high density while providing open space. The simple and intuitive joints and assembly system allowed for rapid deployment and implementation. The units can be disassembled and reassembled in a new location and because of its kit-of-parts nature, it is easy to replace or upgrade components as needed, making it an overall more sustainable system. Most of all, my project aimed to provide a spiritually uplifting living environment that will help restore human dignity to people who need it the most.

ACTIVISM

BURDEN OF DISASTER *While only 11 percent of the people exposed to natural hazards live in countries classified as low human development, they account for more than 53 percent of total recorded deaths. The burden of disaster is proportionally much higher in the poorest countries.*

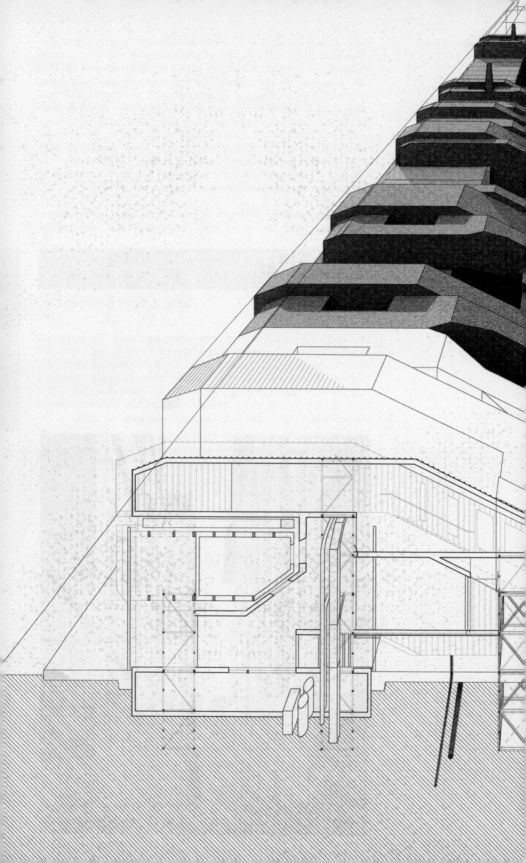

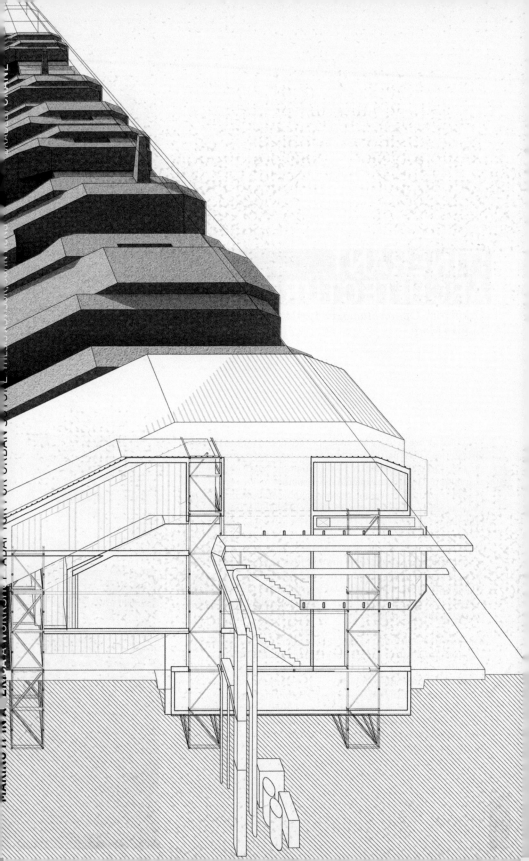

ITINERANT ARCHITECTURE

Architecture Option Studio, Fall 2011
Toshiko Mori

The world we live in today is complex, afflicted with various risks and instabilities. This is particularly true for underserved communities, whose situations are often overlooked by the reframing and repositioning role of architects. This studio explored the possibility for architecture to be itinerant, willing to travel and respond to some of the most desperate, underserved, and remote communities, by providing accessibility and bridging longer-term issues of security in fragile places.

These age-old predicaments of architectural reach can be seen through a contemporary lens to encourage the invention and innovation of a new architectural typology. It can be a new prototype or hybrid combination of multifunctional and traditional origin, balancing the parameters of resource scarcity, labor skill, material sourcing, and function against geometry, techniques, and technology.

This poses the potential for a simple yet elegant solution capable of translating sophisticated technology into accessible technique. The studio first analyzed global risks and crises, identifying six geographical locations and impending problems. To retain the focus on underserved communities, we analyzed the network of resilience at a local and grassroots scale. Following the current model of the Portable Concert Hall Project, we worked with world-renowned boat and sail fabricators of New England to explore the possibility of technology transfer through the itinerant nature of architecture.

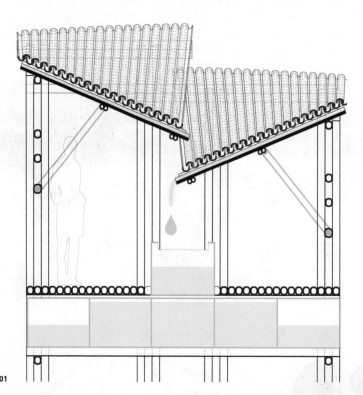

ROOF TRANSFORMATIONS

The rotation and direction of the roof changes based on seasonal variations.

01-02 JEUNG EUN LEE

03-04 JILL DORAN

01

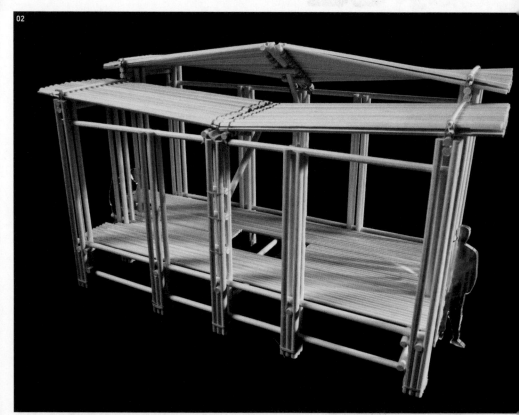

02

PARTICIPATION
EMPOWERMENT IN PRACTICE:

ANDRES LEPIK
MICHAEL HOOPER

*Traditionally, decisions about design
and planning have incorporated limited
public input. This top-down process has
been questioned at various times in the
twentieth century through alternative
participatory strategies, but the promise
of participation has not been realized at
a large scale. Now, at the beginning of
the twenty-first century, in a world of
rapid urbanization, expanding informal
settlements, and increasing debates
about the social relevance of the design
and planning professions, it seems
timely to take a new look at the possible
role of participation in planning and
design.*

03

04

There are extreme discrepancies between cultural and social ideas, dreams and realities. Architecture can negotiate these differences, mediate between extremes, offer resistance, and propose alternatives. This project is a critique of the United States prison system and the social, economic, and political conditions that have created and sustained it. The United States has the highest incarceration rate in the world, far higher than any other industrialized democracy, one of the highest throughout history. We imprison more of our ethnic minorities than South Africa at the height of Apartheid, and those imprisoned are disproportionately drawn from the most disadvantaged parts of society. This crisis is bleak and overwhelming and the architecture is stuck and stagnant, but with catastrophe comes an opportunity for change.

NOT A PRISON
There are many places in the world that make much more "humane" prisons, but my project is decidedly NOT a prison because what psychological studies like the Stanford Prison Experiment and Milgram Experiment have shown is that prisons create a power relationship that exacerbates conditions, inevitably lead to violence, and instill the very behavior that is supposedly being corrected.

BLOCK:2:BLOCK
Incarceration to Imagination

Thesis Advisor: Mack Scogin   *Annie Kountz*

This project is not about prison reform but an entire reworking, rethinking, and reinventing of the prison system. This is a new cooperative institution —a public, nonprofit, community organization. It is an entirely new kind of "Big House." It is not a prison but a sort of public university—a new hybrid of a community college, halfway house, and a public leisure center. This project is about the emancipation and empowerment of the individual through learning and play with the collective. It is an autonomous association of people who voluntarily cooperate for their mutual social, economic, and

MICROCOSM
This is a microcosm of a city, a cultural bricolage, a unique coexistence and celebration of various programs and people. Student-residents and patrons alike enjoy music, theater, sports, walking, gardens, wandering, or people watching. Of course, these things are already available to the public, but this is an intense architectural moment of inter-accessibility, inclusivity, and intermingling that allows for a creation and imagination of new activities and experiences. This attempts to promote a new way to assemble and interact.

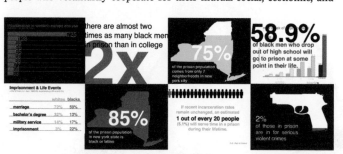

cultural benefit. It is a pedagogically oriented organization that acts like a summer camp or a study abroad program. It is an education-based self-help program that works on a semester system, but has no definite timetable. It is for anyone entangled within the criminal justice system who wants a way out. It is an alternative for people who would otherwise go to prison for non-violent offenses and a transitional facility for people coming out of prison. The aspiration is to provide opportunity to transform one's life by enjoying life and broadening one's mind. Testing their interests and creating their own curriculum gives them a sense of agency over their lives and their futures. The project gives back to an under-caste and attempts to instill a sense of agency, creativity, and imagination.

This project seeks to produce an intense space of convergence, of diversity, of connectivity, and of human potential.

Hospitals are a complex and unique form of architecture. In the United States they are public places and yet they incorporate the most private needs. They are predisposed to be emotional places for those who inhabit them, however they require efficient performance. They are simultaneously a manifestation of social conditions and scientific advancements. Few institutions have undergone the radical metamorphosis of

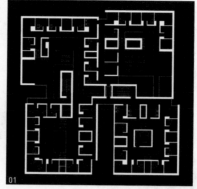

01

A LIVING CANCER CLINIC

Thesis Advisor: Ingeborg Rocker   *Jeff LaBoskey*

hospitals, which can be attributed to this unique combination of conceptual and architectural richness.

Nevertheless, when we think of hospitals, as Herzog & de Meuron have described, inevitably we think of architectural banality: "Endless corridors with inexpensive and sterile finishes flanked by countless doors to exam rooms, with elevators and small waiting rooms at the ends, repeated on as many floors as possible for maximum efficiency." The goal of my thesis project was to understand and challenge the current paradigm of the place in which we treat the sick and deliver health. By understanding the evolution of healthcare architecture, in relation to the forces that have shaped it, we can situate it in the context of our contemporary conditions and imagine another form.

The architecture challenges the dichotomy between sickness and health by collapsing the necessary components of treatment for those who are sick with spaces for the emerging activities associated with sustaining health. To accommodate this, the project was conceived as prototypical hybrid typology that can be proliferated and integrated into communities as part of the daily routine for the 3 million people who are diagnosed with cancer every year and those who are seeking activities for physical and mental well-being.

CONFIGURING THE PROTOTYPE SCHEME TO DAVIS SQUARE

This thesis project was investigated through two schemes; a prototypical condition, designed to fit on two generic suburban lots, and a site-specific scheme located in Davis Square. This dual investigation helped to clarify the crucial elements of the new prototype for healthcare and also further engage the transformational forces that ultimately define what a building wants to be. Therefore the resulting architecture is a manifestation of the a negotiation between desires, axioms, and constraints.

01 *Prototype plan*

02 *Prototype section*

03 *Project rendering as sited in Davis Square*

04 *Section and plan of implemented prototype in Davis Square site*

02

THINKING ABOUT "HOME-FOR-ALL"

Architecture Option Studio, Spring 2012
Toyo Ito

Over a year and a half has passed since the devastating earthquake and tsunami that hit Japan on March 11, 2011.

Various kinds of recovery actions have begun in all the affected areas. I have been paying frequent visits to the Sendai Mediatheque and other Tohoku Districts to assist reconstruction work. The project "Home-for-All" is one of the supportive activities. A number of people who have lost their homes are still being forced to live in cramped temporary housing. There is no place for them to enjoy meals or have a decent chat with their neighbors. The aim of the project was to provide a small but heart-warming public living room for them. I created communal places within the disaster areas, where people can gather to cook and eat, sit and talk around a wood stove, or read a book.

This is not simply a warm and reassuring place but will become a base for them to revive their community from zero and regenerate their towns for the future. It need not always be a newly designed piece of architecture, but could be the renovation of buildings that are partially destroyed. The "Home-for-All" project was not merely architectural design but was about raising the fundamental question of "What is architecture?" and reconsidering the existance of architecture from its very origin.

In this course, we visited a specific town in the Tohoku District and started by having a conversation with the local people. Then the individuals or groups were asked to explain their own proposal of "Home-for-All." The aim was for the proposals to reach a certain level of realization toward the end of the course. Lectures and reviews were given by representative Japanese architects during the running of the course.

ARIELLE ASSOULINE-LICHTEN,
JOHN TODD, HATTIE STROUD

GSD TALKS
"PARK BENCH STORIES"

MICHAEL JAKOB

"Small objects have sometimes complex functions. A bench in a garden is most of the time invisible. Once we pay attention to it (at least in certain gardens), it reveals its surprising semantic and narrative potential. In some important cases a seat becomes the center that organizes the scopic strategies of an entire site."

Michael Jakob is Professor in History and Theory of Landscape at Hepia and Professor of Comparative Literature (Chair) at Grenoble University. He is a Visiting Professor at the Harvard GSD. His teaching and research focus is on landscape theory, aesthetics, the history of vertigo, contemporary theories of perception, and the poetics of architecture.

ALL IMAGES JOHN TODD, ARIELLE ASSOULINE-LICHTEN, HATTIE STROUD

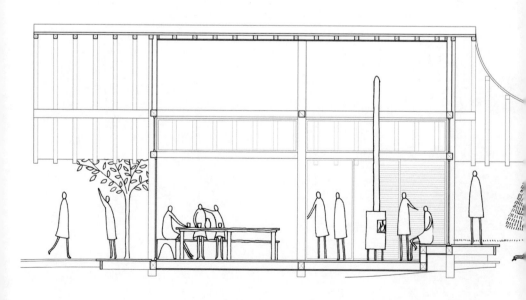

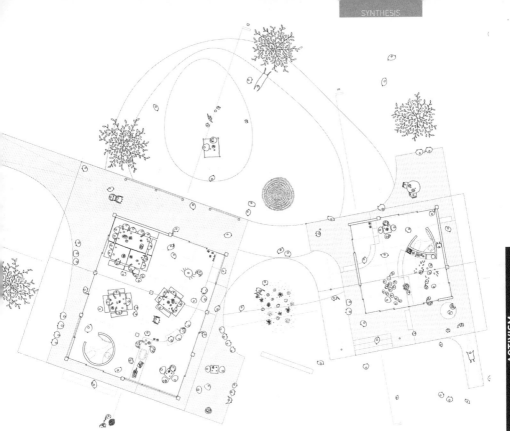

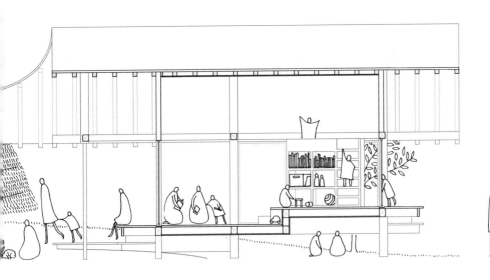

ALL IMAGES OSARUYI OGIEHON, MARK POMARICO, JUDITH RODGRIGUEZ

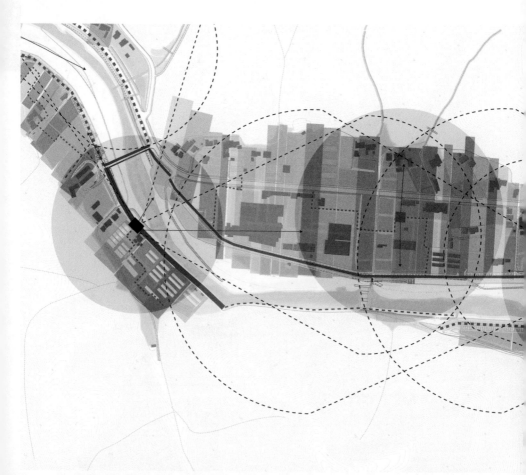

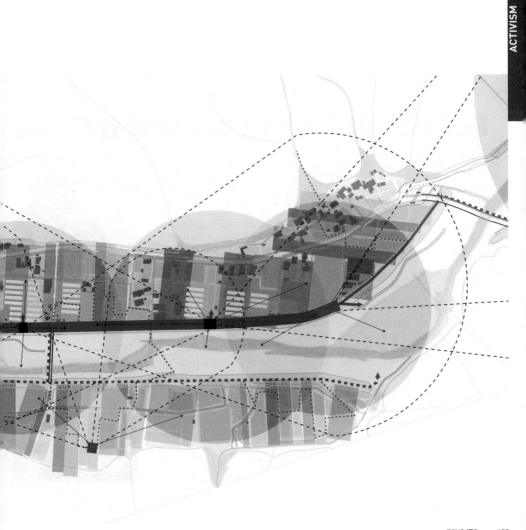

ETHICS OF THE URBAN

Introduction: Agonistic Urbanism

I want to talk about the title of this conference, because I think it is problematic. What is it that we can now call the urban? What is it that we speak of when we speak about urbanization? It is important for us, when we are speaking about cities, to acknowledge the degree to which the city itself is this site of contestation, of conflict.

When we talk about the city, we are referring to a kind of metropolitan condition that actually makes it possible for people to be, in the words of Georg Simmel, both an individual and hidden, in the context of the urban. We have also seen, especially in the last couple of years, the phenomenon of the use of public spaces in our cities as spaces of demonstration, as spaces being occupied. This is the phenomenon of encampment, of people constructing nomadic or temporary residence in the heart of the city. It references Jacques Rancière and the question of politics.

We are warned by certain philosophers, however, that we should not focus solely on the political and on politics, and that there should be, as Slavoj Žižek might say, a supplementary condition of the ethical that is always introducing some degree of normativity in relation to the political. At the same time, someone like Rancière would be critical of trying to focus all efforts and energies on ethical conditions, because you are then removing the possibility of concentrating on political rights and responsibilities. Therefore you do need to be more political and focus on the question of rights. Some of our colleagues here have used the word "just"or the concept of the "just city"as a way to try to introduce the ethical and political. During this conference, we will be speaking more about the tension between social structures, political structures, and properties of spaces specifically.

MOHSEN MOSTAFAVI
Mostafavi is the Dean of the Harvard Graduate School of Design and the Alexander and Victoria Wiley Professor of Design.

CONFERENCE SERIES
This is the third in a series of conferences organized by Mohsen Mostafavi, including Ecological Urbanism (2009) and In the Life of Cities (2011).

Below are extracts from the many presentations and discussions that took place at the conference. To view the complete conference, please see http://www.youtube.com/user/ TheHarvardGSD/videos?query=ethics+ of+the+urban

Public Space and Public Sphere

GB: If public life cannot be formal and heroic, it cannot exist at all. Yet publicness begins in the realities of everyday life. It could be that our participation in the public is barely intentional at all, and it is in coming to an awareness of our relations with others that our public lives take on the possibility of becoming political.

JK: In 2011, physical public space reclaimed status in the public sphere. From Tahrir Square to Zuccotti Park, public space asserted the centrality of conventional physicality in nurturing political protest and debate. The spaces I want to address have the legal obligation to be open for public use. But what public? What public uses? Who decides? Each public will have its own answer to that question and will assert its own legal frame for answering that question.

MODERATOR CHARLES WALDHEIM

PANELISTS ALEX KRIEGER, JEROLD KAYDEN, LIZABETH COHEN, GARY HILDERBRAND, GEORGE BAIRD

LC: Arab Spring exposed us to spaces that have had the potential of entertaining spontaneous political or democratic participation. These spaces were being reused; they were not designed for that one purpose of civic activity. Because of the access and comfort that people had in those spaces, they were able to use them for their own purposes.

AK: Hosting something in City Hall Plaza takes a lot of bureaucracy because it automatically becomes a political event. It is symbolically the place for all, but it also has to undergo some kind of control. We have to differentiate between the street, which is local as opposed to universal, and the plaza, which is a public realm.

CW: Does typology matter? Is there a typological residue in which a square is different and more able to be occupied than a traffic circle? Does typology ultimately matter vis-à-vis its publicness and as a subset of its publicness, its ability to be occupied for political speech?

Keynote Lecture: Immigrants and Citizens in the Global City

SASKIA SASSEN
Sassen is the Ralph Lewis Professor of Sociology, University of Chicago.

RESPONDENT HOMI BHABHA
Bhabha is the Anne F. Rothenberg Professor of English and American Literature and Language, and the Director of the Humanities Center at Harvard University.

Citizens are more anti-immigrant today than they were twenty years ago. There is on one hand a questions of inequality: when so many people are losing out, is the immigrant versus the citizens a viable vector through which to experience difference, conflict, or hatred? Second, when we have a global security apparatus, whom do they survey? We are the citizens, the ones who are to be protected, but we are under surveillance too. We are, by fiat, all suspects.

The citizen is an unstable subject, and so is the immigrant. This issue of destabilizing the formalized subject, citizens, is critical to gaining traction on the emergent urban landscapes. Citizenship is the most formalized concept or persona for membership. I think of citizenship as an incompletely theorized contract between the state and the subject. In that incompleteness lies the longevity of the institution, the possibility that it can incorporate new forms, formats, and contexts. In that instability lies all kinds of possibilities, both good and bad.

In the neoliberal moment we are living in, we have a formal subject that is the citizen and we have the immigrant subject. The undocumented immigrant is the most elusive subject because it does not exist. It becomes visible only when it intersects with the law. Yet both are incomplete subjects. In that incompleteness lies the possibility of unexpected futures.

What brings this all together is the notion of membership. When the excluded struggling for inclusion succeed, they actually expand the rights of everybody. The city is the space that helps us see something about membership, and makes it visible, in its conflicts and its accommodations.

Monuments and Memorials

MODERATOR ANTOINE PICON

INTRODUCTION NEIL BRENNER

PANELISTS ERIKA NAGINSKI, KRZYSZTOF WODICZKO, AND MICHAEL ARAD

AP: Why monuments and memorials? Because of the need to balance geography with history, and because it is among the places of struggle that are both de-assembled and re-assembled that we find collective memory. Today, more than ever, memory is a disputed and fragmented territory.

EN: In Paris in the 1790s, the representation of a newly formed body politic was about giving an image to the citizen, *le citoyen*; this made manifest some profound ambiguities, as effectively the citizen had not existed as something real before 1789. During the French Revolution, the execution of Louis XVI took place on what had been a royal square, which was re-dubbed for this occasion "Revolution Square"(now Place de la Concorde). The uncertainty of what the "Third Estate"would become translated into increased pressure to see citizenship in the public sphere—to make it visible, recognizable, and transparent.

MA: Cities carry the history of violence forward. Building the 9-11 Memorial was very much a product of the experience of being in the public realm and responding as a citizen. Public spaces are critical to our functioning as a society, as a democracy. We built half of the memorial and the other half is the public. We built a stage for the actors to go there every day together, to make it come to life and to meaning.

KW: War memorials dangerously consolidate the idea of service in war as our moral and sacred duty. Most important, they do nothing to end war. Aesthetically and symbolically, they negate any efforts to analyze and critically challenge such ideas, and to stop their perpetuation. We should be building a war-free civilization that demands the dismantling of war by exposing the false image of war and masking the process of making, staging, and commemorating, to confront our misguided willingness to join war and reveal the real toll of war—psychological, social, economic, environmental, and ethical.

THE SCHOOL OF THE YEAR 2030

Architecture | Urban Planning and Design Option Studio,
Spring 2012
Jorge Silvetti and Paul Nakazawa

In the context of the current efforts of Rio de Janeiro to reformulate
and develop public policies for strategic urban development and
renewal, this studio focused on relevant design issues associated with
the implementation of the city's novel policies that reconceive the
educational system of pre-school and elementary school environments,
while emphasizing their potential role as social agents for change.

Specifically the studio focused on the large favela "Complexo do Alemão"
as a test case of these policies, in order to provide urban and architectural
alternative designs that address not only the basic functional
requirements of contemporary educational systems but larger related
issues that touch on the multiplicity of urbanistic and architectural
aspects, potentials, and consequences of such interventions.

The studio addressed the following:

01 | The identification of strategic locations for these schools with
the aim to integrate the favelas with the rest of the city, reversing the
tendency to treat "improvements"on these informal settlements as
merely internalized interventions.

02 | The conception of school environments not only as exclusive
teaching spaces but as social hubs where larger community activities are
promoted.

03 | Pertinent issues of public transportation as an integral component
on the provision of school facilities.

04 | The proposed radical change to integrate in one locale both levels
of education (pre-school and elementary) that promotes a system that
profits from proximity and multiple experience of teachers.

CAROLINE SHANNON

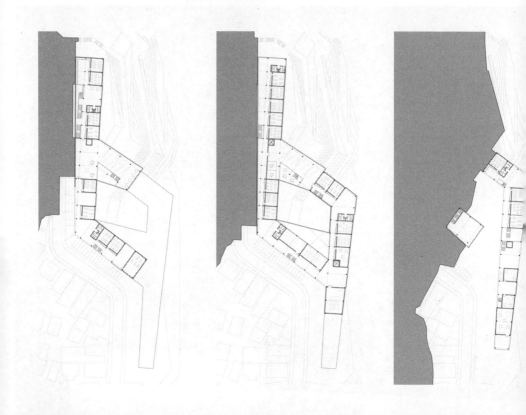

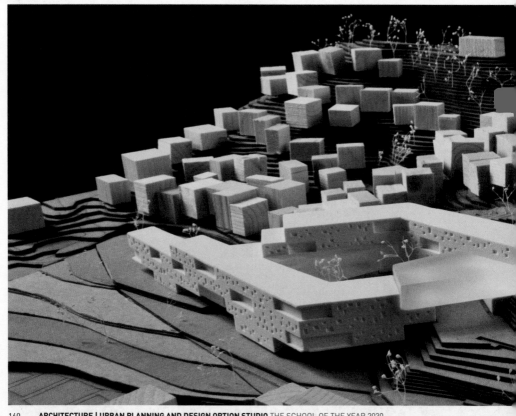

STUDIO TRIP TO RIO *The studio participated on a field trip to Rio de Janeiro from February 3 to February 11, 2012. Students traveled with Professor Jorge Silvetti and met the people in the favela that the studio was sited in.*

ALL IMAGES CAROLINE SHANNON

ACTIVISM

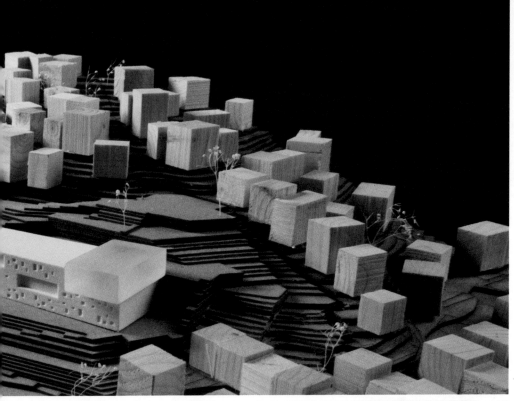

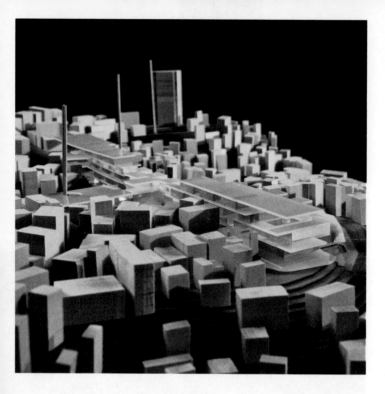

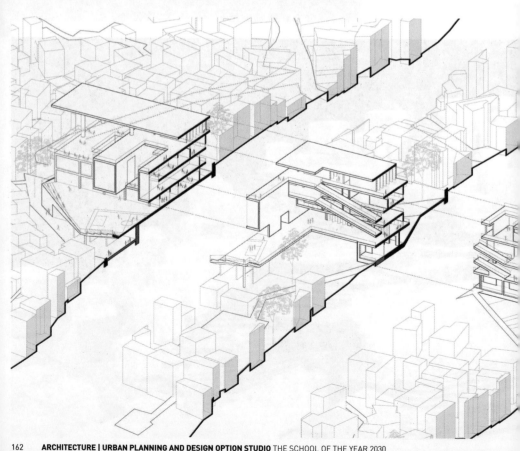

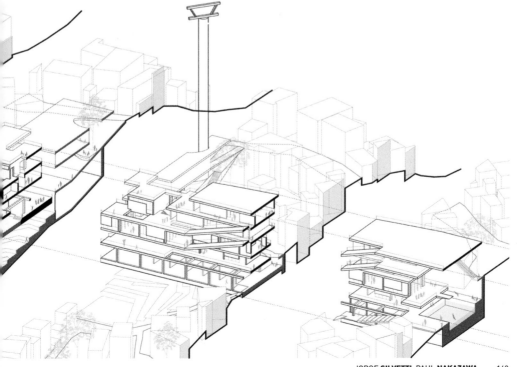

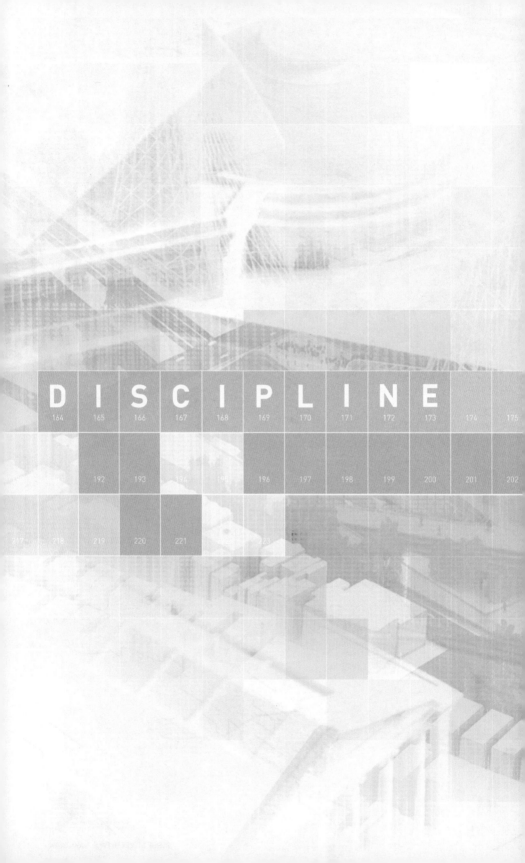

DISCIPLINE

DISCIPLINE is at the core of what we do as an academy and in the design professions. These are the bounded domains in which we place our objects of autonomy. These objects of knowledge, their conditions and circumstance, are common sets through which we apply our work and develop discourse. The boundaries may change as our methodologies and knowledge adapt, but within a measured and demarcated set. These demarcations may be blurred or overlapped so that shared traits among other disciplines may yield new knowledge sets, but with precision and order, so that scholars and designers can recognize the new and innovative when it emerges.

	Architectural Reckoning Preston Scott Cohen					Architecture Core III Site / Situation / System Eric Howeler					
	178	179	180	181	182	183	184	185	186	187	188	189

...vation	Urban Design Core Elements of Urban Design Felipe Correa						Lightfall Preston Scott Cohen	Discussions in Architecture Preston Scott Cohen + Guests		*My House is Better Than Your House*
204	205	206	207	208	209			212	213	216

In the work collected in this section, we look at projects and discussions that focus on how conventions, typologies, fundamental design tools, and established discourses are confronted. This section, more so than the others, looks at identifying critical relations between the traditions of the design disciplines, their contemporary manifestations, and their potential futures as emergent systems of knowledge.

This first project in the Architecture Core I semester was about the relationship between the plan of rooms, enveloping façade, and interior circulation of a building. The configuration of these three constituent elements proved to have the most profound consequences for the composition of the building as a whole. To study this topic, the project was designed in such a way that it required the resolution of tension between dueling organizational forms and systems.

The project served as a heuristic device for establishing a basis for the design and interpretation of fundamental architectural concepts. In addition, the combination of given elements and rules raised questions about the temporal definition of the building. The unfolded façade featured a repetitive fenestration pattern that served as the basic compositional structure. A façade vocabulary of other elements was integrated with the pattern as if to suggest that the façade was an existing condition. The vocabulary was based on the façade of one of several buildings at Harvard's campus.

PERIMETER PLAN

Preston Scott Cohen (Coordinator), Yael Erel, Mariana Ibañez, Kiel Moe, Elizabeth Whittaker, Cameron Wu Architecture Core Studio I, Fall 2011

Upon completion, the project represented hypothetically either a documentation of an existing building or an existing building enclosure of a subsequently redeveloped interior. In either historical hypothesis, the building is less the result of willful design than an account of an architectural anomaly.

Normally, we begin designing a building by dealing with existing conditions and constraints. In this case, to exercise the tensions inherent to the relationship between the plan, the enveloping façade and the internal circulation, we began with three givens: a maximum area requirement, an unrolled façade of fixed length that must be folded or curved to produce a closed figure in plan, and a staircase.

The subject of the inquiry was a dormitory. The maximum total building area was limited to approximately 68,000 square feet. The total linear dimension of the perimeter was 960 feet. The proportion and relative distribution of the windows was prescribed. The entrance and other informal common areas could be created by expanding the corridors. The building was composed of single rooms and double rooms. Every room had to have access to natural light.

CHAVAREE BUNYASIRI

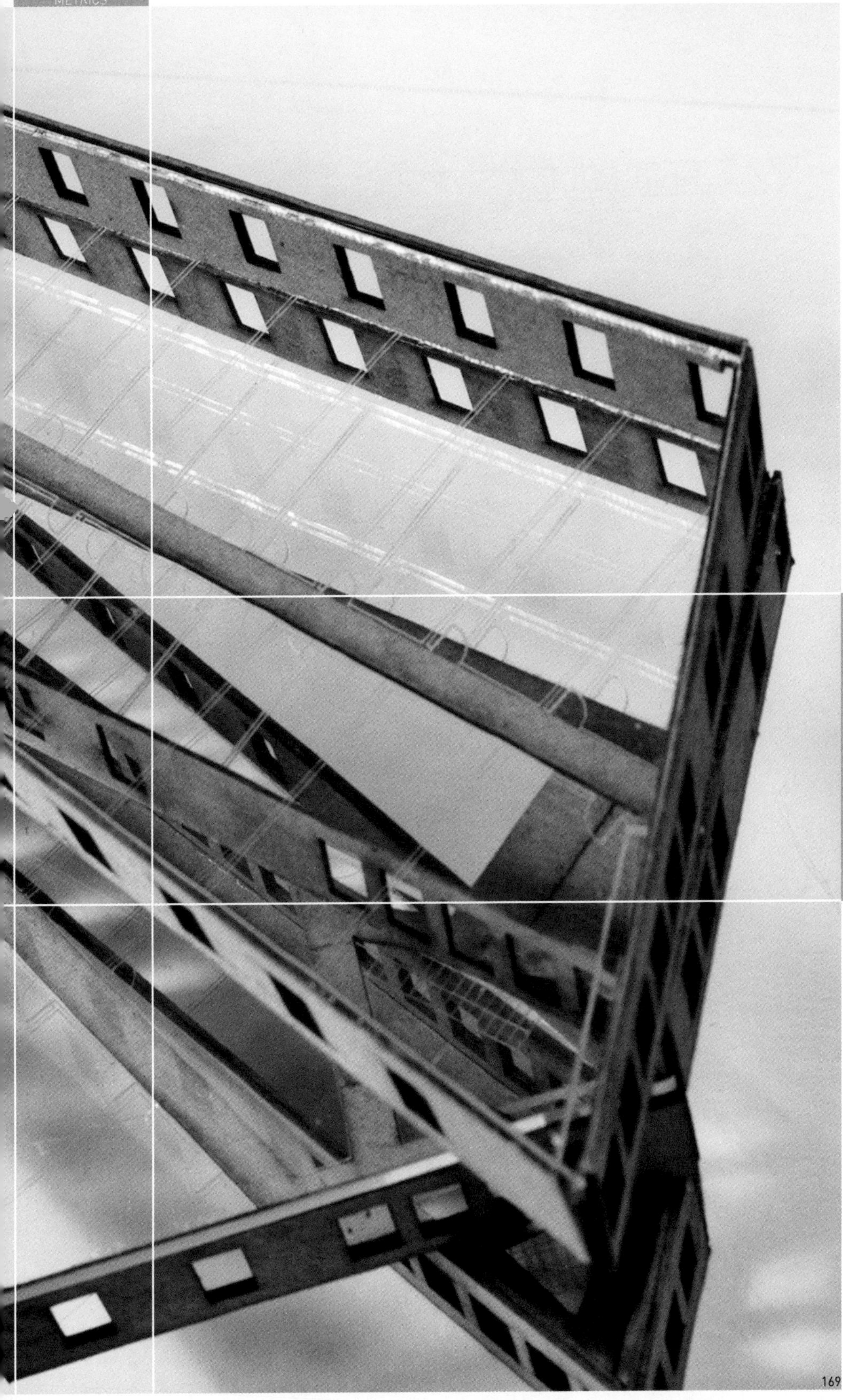

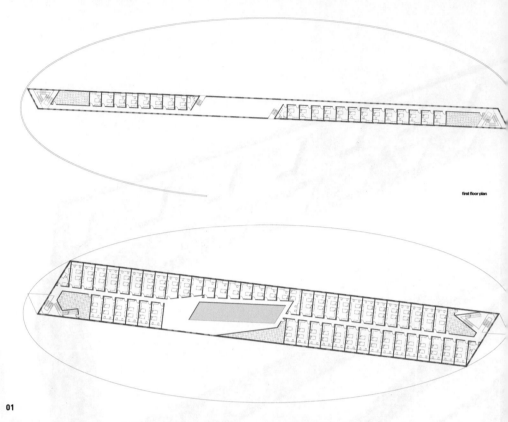

first floor plan

01

02

01-02 ELLIPSE STUDIES
CHAVAREE BUNYASIRI
Generative studies for footprint development

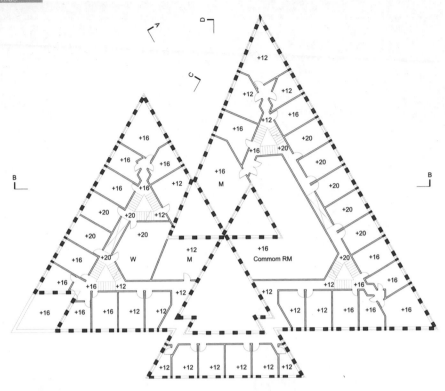

03

03-04 MODEL AND DRAWING
CHEN LU
*Alternate view showing the model
components exploded*

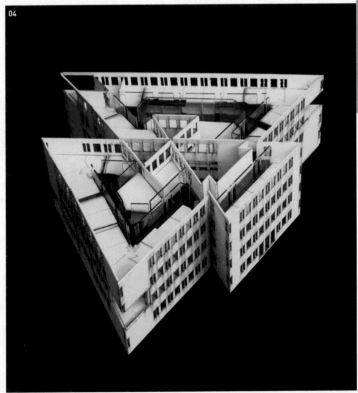

04

YAEL **EREL**, MARIANA **IBAÑEZ**, KIEL **MOE**, ELIZABETH **WHITTAKER**, CAMERON **WU**, PRESTON SCOTT **COHEN**   171

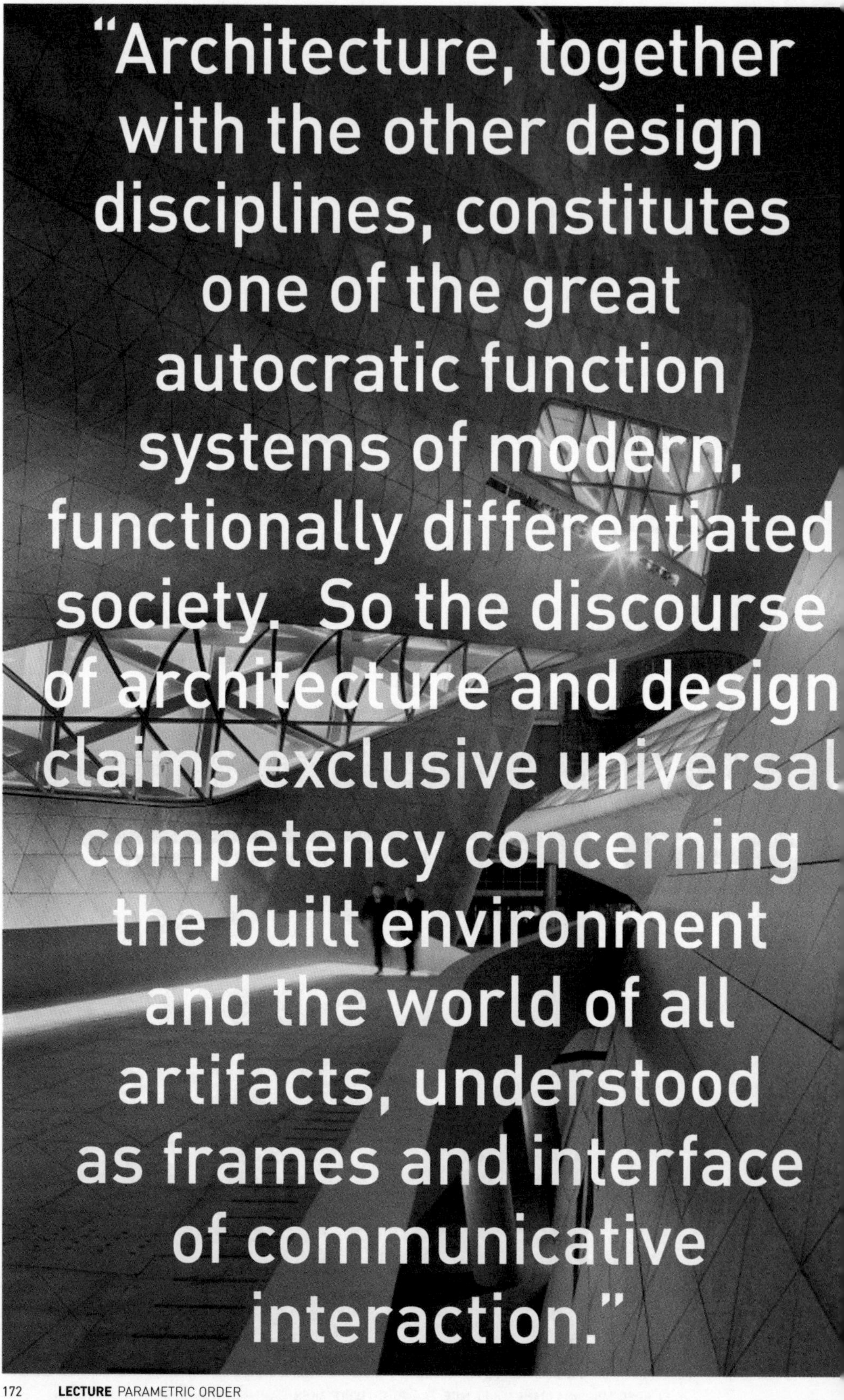

"Architecture, together with the other design disciplines, constitutes one of the great autocratic function systems of modern, functionally differentiated society. So the discourse of architecture and design claims exclusive universal competency concerning the built environment and the world of all artifacts, understood as frames and interface of communicative interaction."

What modernism did for the twentieth century, parametricism should be doing for the twenty-first century.

We are working on developing architecture as a coherent system of signification in abstraction and radical isolation from the kind of spontaneous semiotics and familiar sign systems of the built environment that are too fragmented and lacking informational density.

Since the crisis of modernism there have been thirty years of experimentation and confusion, but no real impact back on the built environment. My attempt with *Autopoiesis of Architecture* is to create a comprehensive and coherent theoretical edifice, a theory of architecture within the framework of communication theory.

What, for Marx, was the shift from feudalism to capitalism, in Niklas Luhmann's terms is a shift from stratification to functional differentiation. It no longer assumes that the economy is the basic driver of society, but that all aspects of society are equally relevant. So each of these functional systems has a particular key distinction, which structures the totality of the discourse. In architecture it is form versus function. It is about the beautiful versus the ugly as well as the useful versus the useless—what I call the double code of utility and beauty.

Parametricism is the epochal style after modernism. It is not only our work at the office of Zaha Hadid, it is an entire generation that has produced a new global discourse.

"I think that in terms of the global theory of society, what we need to realize is that the autonomous discourses are co-evolving and that they adapt to everybody else. If we do not adapt, we make ourselves irrelevant and disappear, and somebody else will step forth and pick up the mantle of architecture. So the death of architecture is always near. The discourse has the responsibility to keep itself relevant, to adapt, to understand, to make itself congenial to the rest of society, but in doing so must also remain autonomous."

Patrik Schumacher
THE AUTOPOIESIS OF ARCHITECTURE
A New Framework for Architecture

SEE ALSO The Autopoiesis of Architecture: Volume II, *published Spring 2011.*

PATRIK SCHUMACHER
Parametric Order: Twenty-first Century Architectural Order

DISCIPLINE

New computational processes have produced new design techniques that extend our capacities, but the microelectronic revolution has also advanced the economy, the financial system, the sciences. All subsystems of society have absorbed the computational revolution into their capacities.

In parametricism, all elements of architecture have become intricately related and malleable. It is an ontological shift from the use of primitives, which constitute all architectural compositions for the last 5,000 years, including modernism. Parametricism is something radically different. Our primitives are lines, blobs, nerves, particles, and scripts. Surfaces no longer constitute flat, rigid planes but register what is going on around them. They are reactive, pliant, and informed. Deformation becomes information. Instead of drawing them, we program these objects so they can establish relationships with each other—they resonate with each other and their context. These systems have multiple parameters that are dynamically controlled, systems that produce forms of intricate order.

Parametricism is a retrospective reflection on the crisis of modernism. There are no longer platonic primitives, repetition, or the kind of monotony that has been rejected in the real world. This was the agglomeration of pure difference; it was aestheticized and celebrated in postmodernism, and it happened all over the globe. I call it the garbage spill model of urban development. It generates a problematic kind of pluralism, where the lack of order produces visual chaos. It looks the same everywhere.

We are moving toward the intricacy of self-organizing natural models. These are complex variegated orders we find in nature, and now can be simulated as part of our design domain. All elements are open to become interconnected. Through these associative logics, the final aesthetic expression is one of intricate order that can only be generated through such laws of nature and the association of subsystems. These ideas are my invitation to the collective network of researchers and designers to test and go further within the same principles.

PATRIK SCHUMACHER *is partner at Zaha Hadid Architects. Schumacher studied philosophy and architecture in Bonn, London , and Stuttgart, where he received his Diploma in architecture in 1990. In 1999 he completed his Ph.D. at the Institute for Cultural Science, Klagenfurt University. He joined Zaha Hadid in 1988. In 1996, he founded the Design Research Laboratory with Brett Steele, at the Architectural Association in London, and continues to serve as one of its directors. Schumacher's contribution to the discourse of contemporary architecture is also evident in his published works, interviews, and projects which can be viewed at www.patrikschumacher.com and www.zaha-hadid.com.*

IMAGE HUFTON AND CROW
Guangzhou Opera House

BUILDING A NARRATIVE

Over the course of a narrative, a building may move through multiple diagrammatic configurations and typologies. In this manner, connections may be drawn between very diverse projects without relying on style or quotation. Instead, similar tensions and transformational tendencies may be mapped. In some cases, projects may even be made to evolve into one another.

This thesis sought to provide the tools for addressing the internal tensions that arise within two distinct types of buildings: the large civic hybrid, which internalizes multiple typologies within a single institutional wrapper, and the small fabric building, whose typology is disturbed by a competing demand or external pressure. The technique employed is a type of linearly developing formal analysis of implied transformation, which provides a means of accessing and discussing these conflicts.

WORKING BACKWARDS
Typological Narratives in Conflicted Buildings

Thesis Advisor: Preston Scott Cohen   *Carl D'Apolito-Dworkin*

These narrative analyses are not neutral or descriptive of a real genesis. Rather they are projective speculations, defined explicitly in opposition to the notion of a single architectural system capable of absorbing difference. They expose the inability of any parti to address all the imposed constraints and desires and demonstrate the way buildings negotiate misalignment, competing trajectories, and alien functions.

The readings are based upon the tendency of the human eye to perceive any configuration of more than elementary complexity as a composite object with a history. In addition, they assume that any architectural resolution is inherently incomplete, leaving some aspect demanding a new solution. Together, these two ideas allow a building to be destabilized and viewed, instead, as a step in an evolving diagram of responses to internal pressure.

HYBRIDIC BUILDING

The proposed building is a hybrid of a performing arts center and a school. It takes as a precedent narratives done from the Tel Aviv Museum of Art, the RISD College Building, and the City of Providence. Many hybrid buildings seek maximum interaction between all parts and produce a blur between two types. This building, preceding from Tel Aviv, argues that a central condition of the hybrid in tension is the demand that each type maintain a pretense to the whole. Preceding from the College Building, each of the two buildings attempts to totally hide or obscure the presence of the other, while at the same time being forced for pragmatic reasons to share certain functions and a common skin. The mismatch of scale, type, and organization (the arts center is centralized and composed of large spaces perceived sequentially; the school is linear and composed of small similar spaces in an array) causes a series of contortions and distortions.

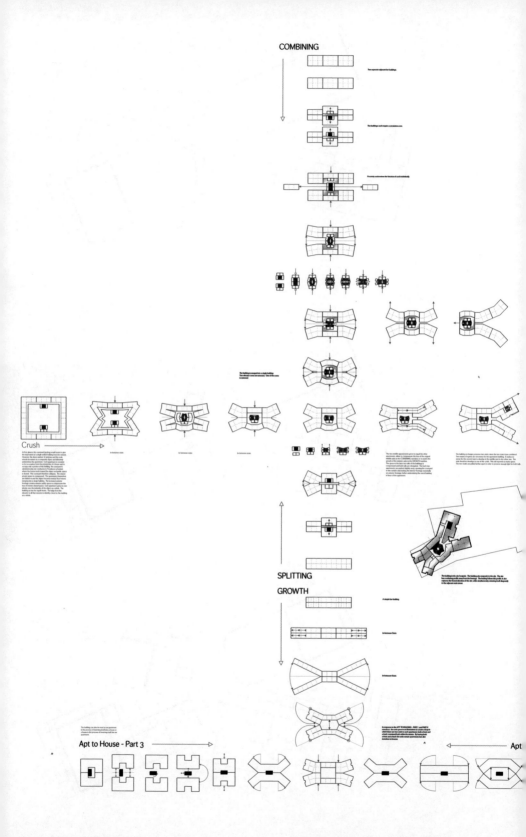

COMBINING

SPLITTING
GROWTH

Crush

Apt to House - Part 3

Apt

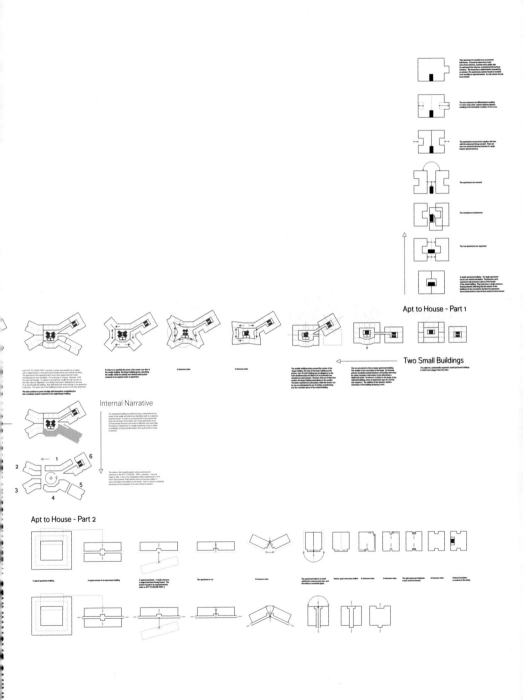

Apt to House - Part 1

Two Small Buildings

Internal Narrative

Apt to House - Part 2

The task of designing an addition to a highly respected building requires bringing judgments to bear perhaps more explicitly than in the case of any other type of project. Confronting this problem in no uncertain terms, this studio required making an addition to a particularly authoritative piece of architecture: a late nineteenth- or early twentieth-century classical museum or performing arts center. The addition to such a building either appears to extend the precedent, identify with the surrounding context and bring it into a new proximity with the existing building, or establishes an autonomous architecture that contests both the existing building and the context.

Among the goals of the studio was to define and exercise techniques for creating astonishingly rigorous types of reciprocity between buildings and their contexts. To do so, the "existing" conditions were invented. The approximately 200,000-square-foot classical building, derived from available drawings of precedents, looked as if it was authored by a disciple of a well-known architect such as McKim, Mead and White, Carrère and Hastings, Bertram Goodhue, or a less-known figure like Guy Lowell (architect of Boston's MFA). With all of its resolute authority and relative stability, it was placed in a semi-fictionalized site in one of several selected American cities.

ARCHITECTURAL RECKONING

Architecture Option Studio, Spring 2012
Preston Scott Cohen

The building/site relationship was be produced by transforming part of an actual found context. Existing buildings will be erased in order to create an open site. The existing building was sited to leave enough room for a "future" addition that doubled its size. Streets, surrounding buildings, and urban block patterns were modified such that the interrelationship between the site and the building exhibited a rare, though realistic, heightened degree of reciprocity.

To understand one of the types of reciprocity to be established between the invented existing building and the surrounding city, it was useful to imagine a physically heavy model of a large, classical building sitting on a somewhat elastic table cloth to which elements were attached that belonged to the surrounding city. The model of the building turned or translated in one direction, which stretched and tore the table cloth. The surrounding streets and block patterns adjusted by stretching, shearing, shifting, and regrouping, ultimately settling in such a way that they seemed to constitute a plausible, albeit exceptional, existing condition.

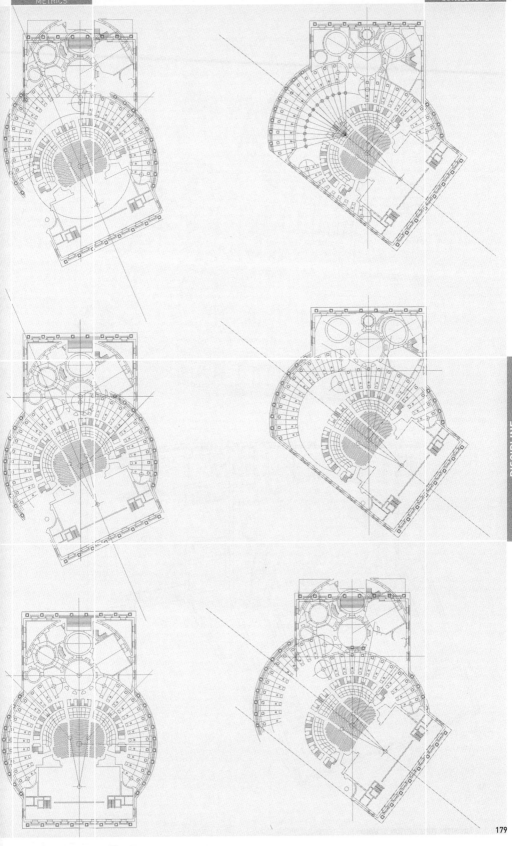

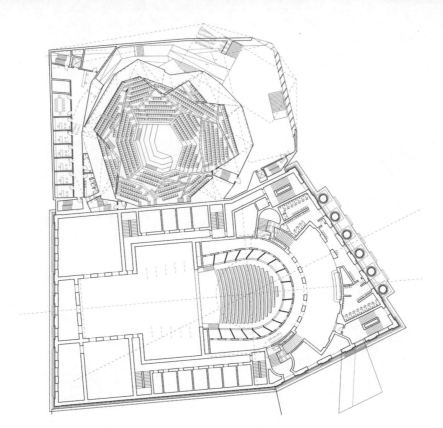

01

02

01 ANTHONY SULLIVAN

02 MICHAEL JEN

03 ALEXIS COIR

EXISTING VS. ADDITION

One of the most difficult challenges posed by the addition was that it had to rob the existing building of one of the most fundamental aspects of its symbolic authority: namely, its role in providing the primary entrance to the cultural institution that it houses. By accommodating contemporary programmatic demands, the addition gained the upper hand in shaping interior spatial sequences despite being similar in size to the more historically significant original building. In addition, the addition fostered new types of cultural production not supported by the older building. Thus the consequences of the addition were perhaps most profoundly evident in the structure, sequence, and formal language of interior spaces, all of which was thoroughly developed, was were the exteriors.

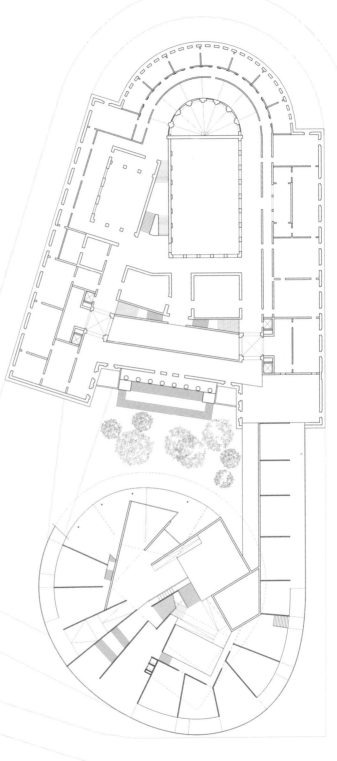

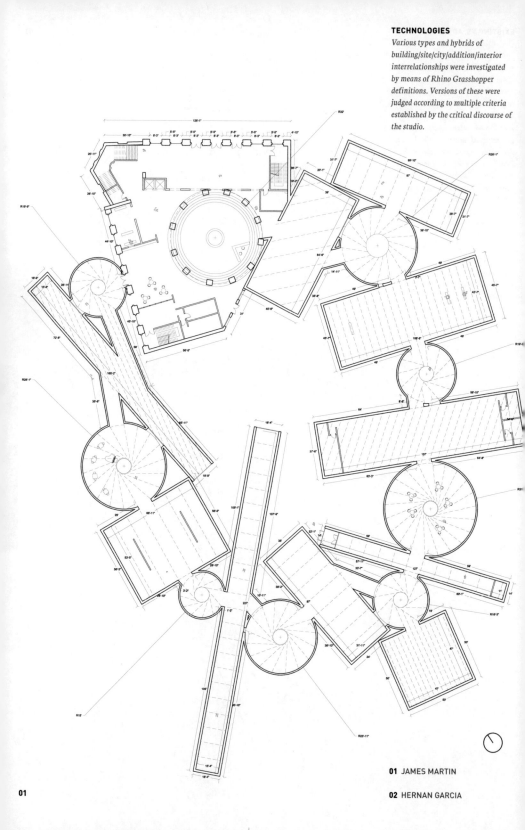

TECHNOLOGIES

Various types and hybrids of building/site/city/addition/interior interrelationships were investigated by means of Rhino Grasshopper definitions. Versions of these were judged according to multiple criteria established by the critical discourse of the studio.

01 JAMES MARTIN

02 HERNAN GARCIA

01

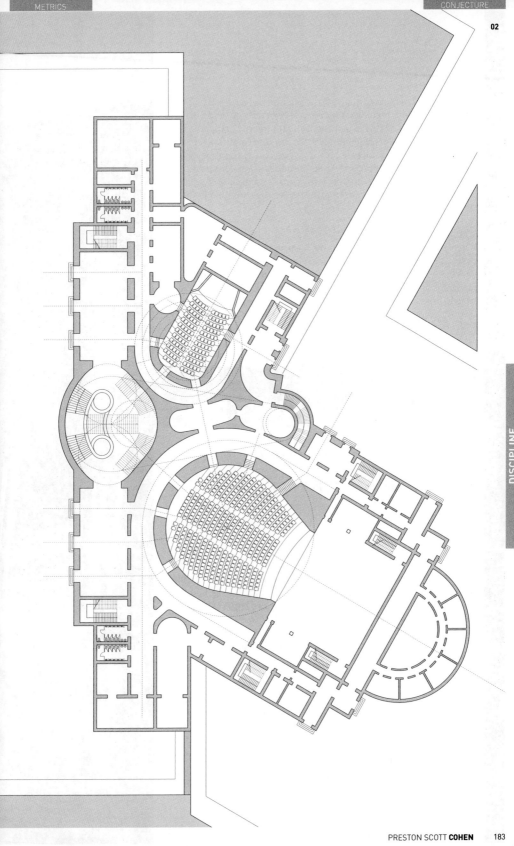

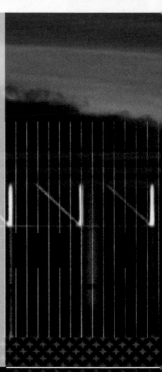

SITE

Often assumed to be fixed or given, the site is in fact a variably defined and extensive context for design. The definition of site may be productively expanded to include the legal limits of a property (boundaries, easements, and setbacks), the physical conditions of the site (topography, existing structure), as well as perceptual and atmospheric conditions (climate, exposures, views, and adjacencies). This studio investigated the site of an existing but incomplete building designed by Paul Rudolph in 1962—the Government Services Building on Cambridge Street in Boston.

SITUATION

Whereas "site" is understood to define the place of architecture, geographically, "situation" may define it temporally. Situation may also refer to its larger cultural or political context. A site may have particular significance or importance based on its value (as prime real estate), its political or symbolic importance (as the one-time residence of Paul Revere), its environmental status (more or less contaminated by PCBs), or the events that occur on or near it (as the temporary home of the Big Apple Circus).

SITE |
SITUATION | SYSTEMS

*Eric Höweler (Coordinator), Vincent Bandy,
Danielle Etzler, Florian Idenburg, Jonathan Levi,
Maryann Thompson
Architecture Core Studio III, Fall 2011*

SYSTEMS

Construction involves the management and disposition of thousands of building components, materials and systems organized by building trades. The proper integration of each system into a larger whole ensures that the building performs the way it is intended. Consideration of each allows for a synthetic structure capable of accommodating the internal forces of program and situation, as well as the external forces of site and context.

PROJECT

This semester focused on the primary forces that shape an architectural project—site, situation, and systems—to develop an architectural project as a comprehensive design, from concept to constructability. The third semester focused on the building as a material and cultural artifact, with an emphasis on tectonics, materiality, structure, envelopes, urban, and site-specific concerns, as well as performance criteria such as acoustics, day lighting, and energy performance.

WAQAS JAWAID

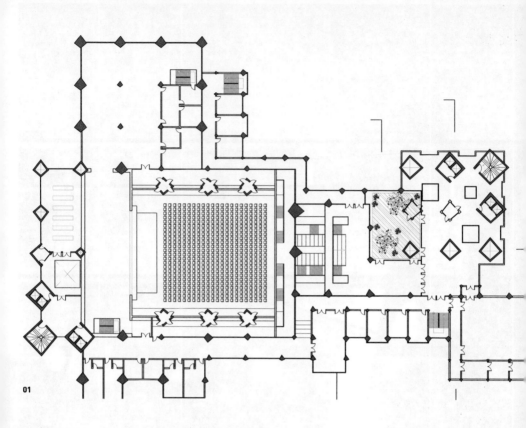

01

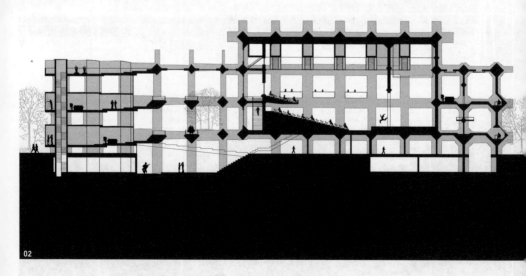

02

01-02 DAVID THIESZ

03-04 WAQAS JAWAID

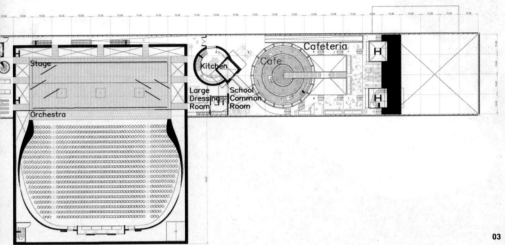

03

DISCIPLINE

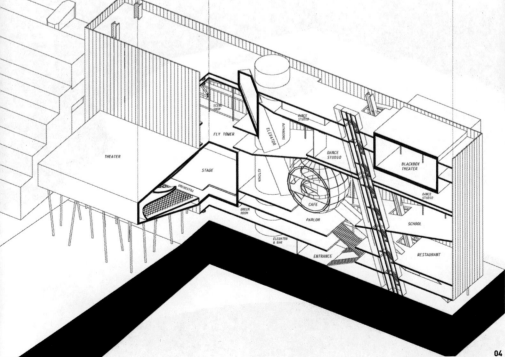

04

VINCENT **BANDY**, DANIELLE **ETZLER**, FLORIAN **IDENBURG**, JONATHAN **LEVI**, MARYANN **THOMPSON**, ERIC **HÖWELER** 187

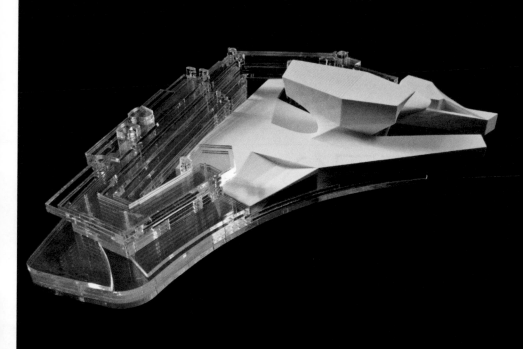
WILLIAM ROBB

JENNIFER LY
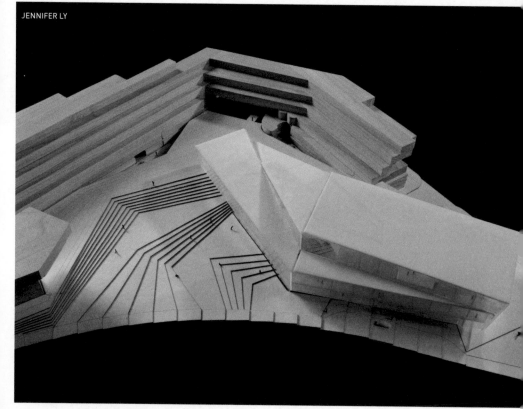

DAVID THIESZ

JENNY HONG

VINCENT **BANDY**, DANIELLE **ETZLER**, FLORIAN **IDENBURG**, JONATHAN **LEVI**, MARYANN **THOMPSON**, ERIC **HÖWELER**

LAUREN GERDEMAN

VINCENT **BANDY**, DANIELLE **ETZLER**, FLORIAN **IDENBURG**, JONATHAN **LEVI**, MARYANN **THOMPSON**, ERIC **HÖWELER**   193

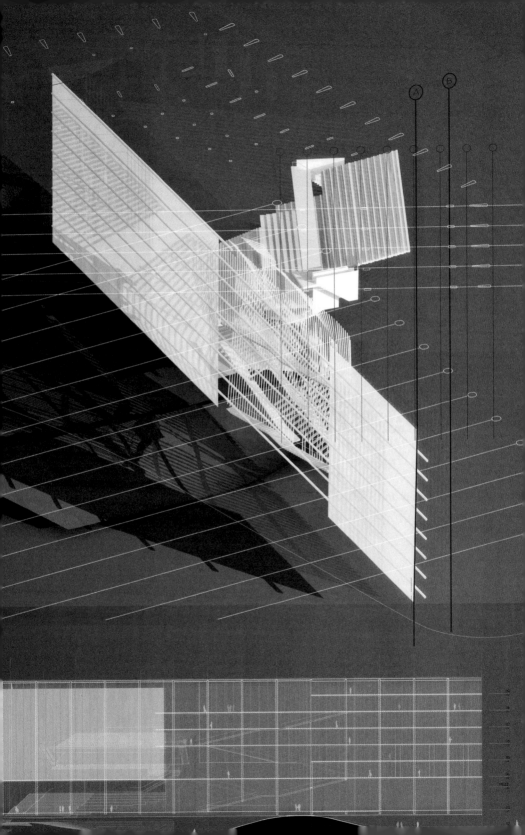

Biased toward expediting movement and inherently resistant to supporting other forms of inhabitation, transportation infrastructure is an archaic monument to monofunctional use. With ever increasing levels of urban density throughout the world, infrastructure in the city is an underworked territory that must sustain a larger agenda.

At a time when the scale of architectural commissions has grown to nearly infrastructural proportions, new models are necessary to work at this very large scale. The intersection of city, water, bridge, tunnel, on and off ramps constitutes a distinct condition. This studio tested the potential of an evolutionary, inhabitable, and hybrid form of infrastructure—a new mega form.

The legacy of infrastructural utopias is realized in the northern tip of Manhattan where the George Washington Bridge enters Manhattan, forming an elevated highway that crosses the city and incorporates Nervi's revolutionary bus station and a series of housing towers. This unfinished modernist project terminates abruptly at the eastern edge of Manhattan, where the highway crosses the Harlem River and carves through the Bronx with a remnant wake of on and off ramps.

EVOLUTIONARY INFRASTRUCTURE
THE NEW MEGA FORM

Architecture | Urban Planning and Design Option Studio,
Fall 2011
Marion Weiss and Michael Manfredi

Completing this utopian project raised new questions: how can this dynamic but unfinished hybrid be reconsidered as a new mega form, where a new reciprocity between the precision of architectural expression and the systemic logics of ecology, landscape, and infrastructure can generate a contemporary paradigm?

The studio was initiated with a three-week research project, that investigated the utopian legacy of the mega project, inflected to engage current ecological, social, and cultural agendas. The studio then tested, through a series of proposals, the potential of a new paradigm for the mega form; a live/work complex simultaneously engaged with the infrastructure and the latent ecologies of the site.

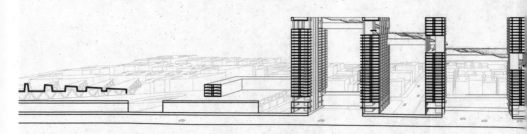

EVOLUTIONARY INFRASTRUCTURE

INTRODUCTION BY PRESTON SCOTT COHEN

Their work, as many of you know, is well known for its integration of architecture, art, infrastructure, and landscape design, for which they have received many of the highest honors in the design field. What is most remarkable is not only their genuine interdisciplinarity but the fact that it is a synthesis that is bracketed very clearly within architecture itself. By this, I mean that they are not only committed to a new model of practice, which integrates all of the fields, but a unity which at the same time activates a decidedly architectural perspective: meaning, they work in a very tectonic way, they work with the magnificent play or behavior, I should say, of light and materials molded to architectural shapes and elements, lines, planes, and volumes composed according to the spatial tropes of interior and exterior, the sequences and hierarchies entailed in these kind of spaces that we know to be architecture, even often as they are set into the landscape.

ALL IMAGES CERI EDMUNDS

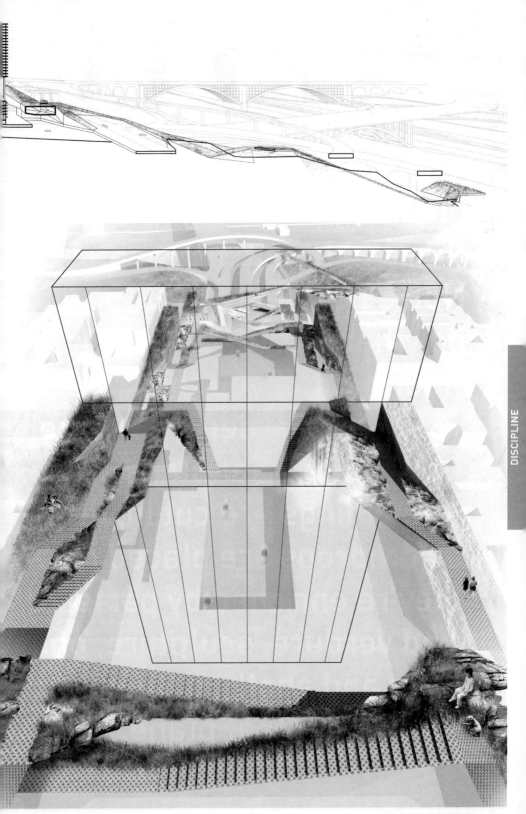

MARION **WEISS**, MICHAEL **MANFREDI** 199

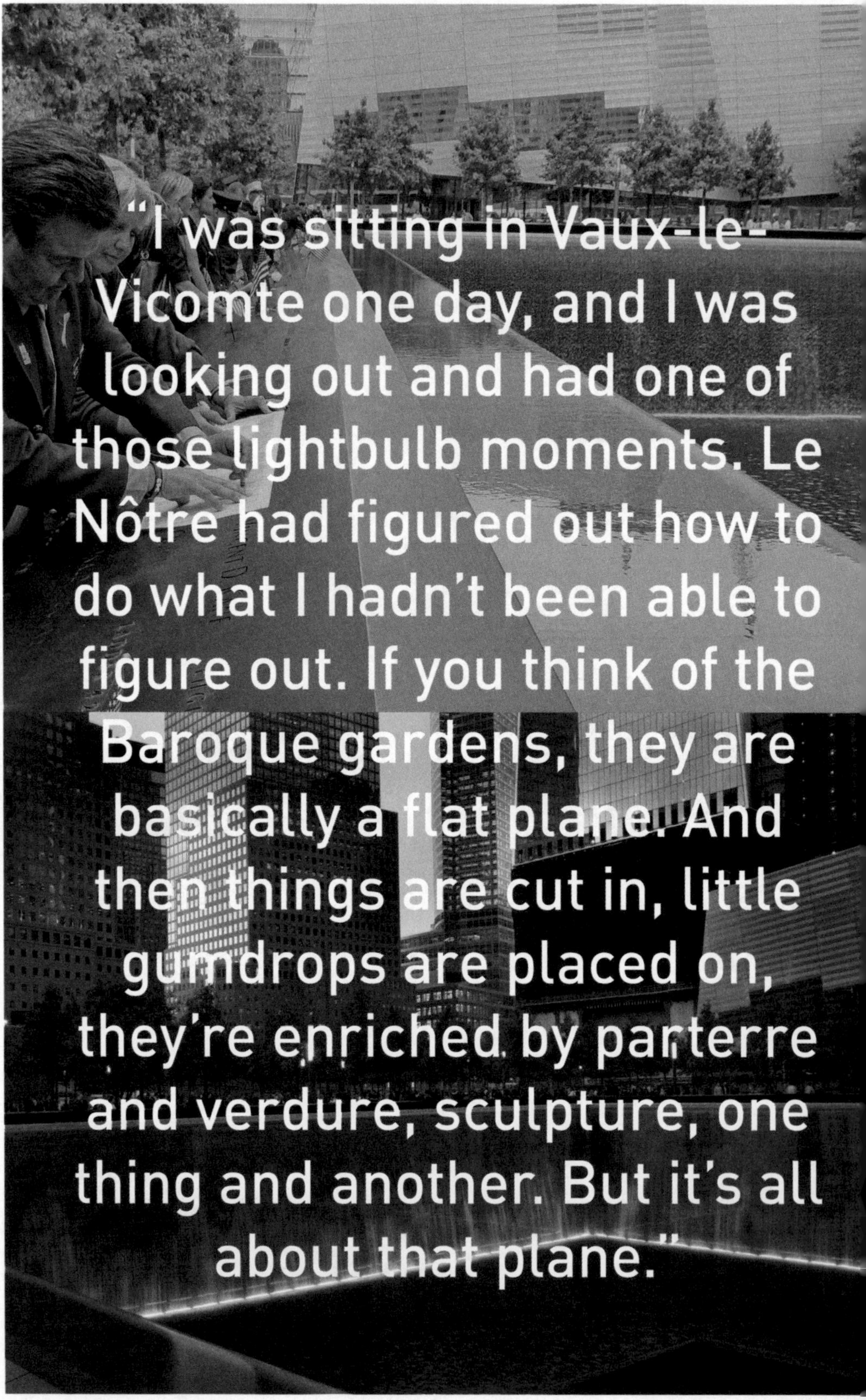

"I was sitting in Vaux-le-Vicomte one day, and I was looking out and had one of those lightbulb moments. Le Nôtre had figured out how to do what I hadn't been able to figure out. If you think of the Baroque gardens, they are basically a flat plane. And then things are cut in, little gumdrops are placed on, they're enriched by parterre and verdure, sculpture, one thing and another. But it's all about that plane."

PW: The first thing you have to say about the World Trade Center Memorial is that if you can imagine those great plazas, shopping centers, stations, hotels, and towers—these holes are all that was left. The scheme itself—as you know—are these two gray voids centered in the spots where the two towers were. The basic idea of the scheme is that the towers were way up in the sky, and now there's nothing left except a hole. Michael Arad raised the plaza up to the street so that you would come to this plane off the street and then come to the voids, which would just drop away.

I was immediately drawn to this scheme. I follow the work of the series of artists who have been called "minimalists"and what they are doing is trying to pare things down. In one case, Michael Heizer was working with the notion of taking a hole, which is in a sense nothing, and making it something. In a way, that is what Arad was doing too: the World Trade Center Memorial is a big plane of concrete, and the strength of the scheme is the plane and the experience of looking down into the holes. Coming right up to the edge is the high point of the drama.

Another reference from the art world is Carl Andre, whose sculptures are a plane, a flat surface, commanding the space above it. This seems almost like a metaphor for landscape. We know the Earth is round, but actually we look at it and think of it as flat. Think of the sea, think of the desert: that's the way we look at the Earth. And the reason this is so powerful is that all other things— architecture, sculpture, people, a tree—stand against and stand vertically on this plane. The drama of landscape architecture is to command that plane. At the start of the project, Arad said, "Here's the trouble I have: the jury loves the

CHARLES WALDHEIM

Waldheim is the John E. Irving Professor of Landscape Architecture and Chair of the Department of Landscape Architecture. He teaches design studios at the intersection of landscape and contemporary urbanism. Waldheim's research focuses on landscape architecture in relation to contemporary urbanism. He coined the term landscape urbanism to describe emerging landscape design practices in the context of North American urbanism. He has written extensively on the topic and edited The Landscape Urbanism Reader *(Princeton Architectural Press, 2006).*

PETER WALKER ON LANDSCAPE ARCHITECTURE

"For me landscape architecture is about picking ideas—ideas of all sorts, and an almost infinite range of ideas, and then developing the skill and the craft to turn those into physical things."

PETER WALKER
In Conversation with Charles Waldheim

idea of these holes, but they hate the 7 acres of stone plaza required to frame them."This is in one of the densest neighborhoods in New York, and they are desperately in need of open space. The mayor's goal was that this could be both a memorial and a park—which poses a problem if you are a purist, because if you started sticking stuff around, you take away that drama.

Many architects like the idea of the tabula rasa because they want to display their building as a piece of sculpture. But they often don't make that tabula rasa something. They think of it as the absence of something, but it isn't empty. And that is foreign to their thinking. Now, by the same token, these architects are teaching me all the time. They are teaching me other things, and that is the joy of my practice. Like the mayor's question: How do you keep this proposal working and make it into something that people would recognize as a park, without destroying the purity of the project that you were trying to do in the first place? You get into that area where you are doing something that either they could not imagine or they think is impossible.

CW: In many ways, both in the earlier projects and also in the memorial, you made particular mention of the value, experience, phenomenon of flatness, as opposed to literal fullness. And much of what you've shared with us had to do with techniques, technologies, embodied wisdom over years of practice about how to achieve certain desirable outcomes vis-à-vis the experience of flatness. And I find myself implicitly thinking that there is something about the sensibilities of the landscape architect that gives this discipline, this profession, a particular purchase on not just the ground plane but flatness as a particular set of objectives.

PW: Le Nôtre was the greatest landscape architect who ever lived, and the discovery of what he was doing—not what the garden looked like—was fundamental. He used the idea of flatness over and over again. I was looking at things carefully and critically; I was trying to get to the point where I actually saw flatness as something, rather than as nothing.

PETER WALKER

Cofounder of the firm Sasaki, Walker and Associates in 1957, Walker opened its West Coast office, which became The SWA Group in 1976. As principal, consulting principal, and chairman of the board, he helped to shape The SWA Group as a multidisciplinary office with an international reputation for excellence in environmental design. In 1983, he formed Peter Walker and Partners, now known as PWP Landscape Architecture.

NATIONAL 9/11 MEMORIAL

of "Reflecting Absence" by Michael Arad and Peter Walker.

DISCIPLINE

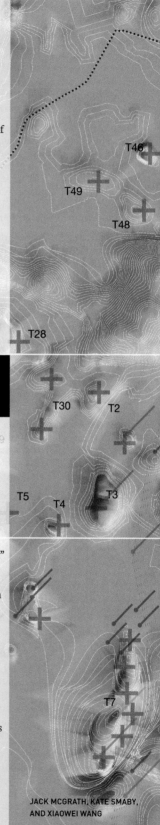

Addressing the inertia of urban planning and the overexertion of civil engineering in the twentieth century, this course focused on the design of large, complex, contaminated brownfield sites with a regional, ecological and infrastructural outlook. Employing the agency of regional ecology and landscape infrastructure as the dominant drivers of design, the studio involved the development of biodynamic and biophysical systems that provided flexible yet directive patterns for future urbanization. Through a series of contemporary mapping methods, field measures, case studies, readings and design investigations, the course resulted in a series of collaborative exercises that lead to a large scale design project and future scenarios. Drawing from canonical case studies on regional reclamation strategies from across the world, the studio was further enhanced by a robust, regional representation program. Focusing on the metrics of geospatial representation and remote sensing, two intensive workshops throughout the term of the studio didactically dealt with the interrelated subjects of regional cartography and site topography as operative and telescopic instruments of design across scales.

MASSACHUSETTS MILITARY RESERVATION

Pierre Bélanger (Coordinator), Niall Kirkwood,
Kelly Shannon, Julia Watson
Landscape Architecture Core Studio III, Fall 2011

Contributing to a complex, multi-layered profiling of the site as "system" and the reformulation of program as "process," the studio established a base platform for engaging an array of complex issues related to site contamination, biophysical systems, regional ecology, land cover, urban infrastructure and economic geography. Precluding conventional forms of urban development such as housing or retail development, the penultimate objective of the course was to explore and articulate the potential effectiveness of broader and longer range strategies, where biophysical systems prefigure as the denominator for re-envisioning public infrastructures and regional urban economies in the future.

The intentionwas to purposely avoid classic remediation efforts that typically favor a bucolic return to an imagined historical state. The project demonstrated how the deployment of proto-ecological strategies at large scales can lead to tactical design maneuvers and spatial interventions at smaller scales, with long term spin-offs that gradually affect one of the most important legacies in the history of America.

JACK MCGRATH, KATE SMABY, AND XIAOWEI WANG

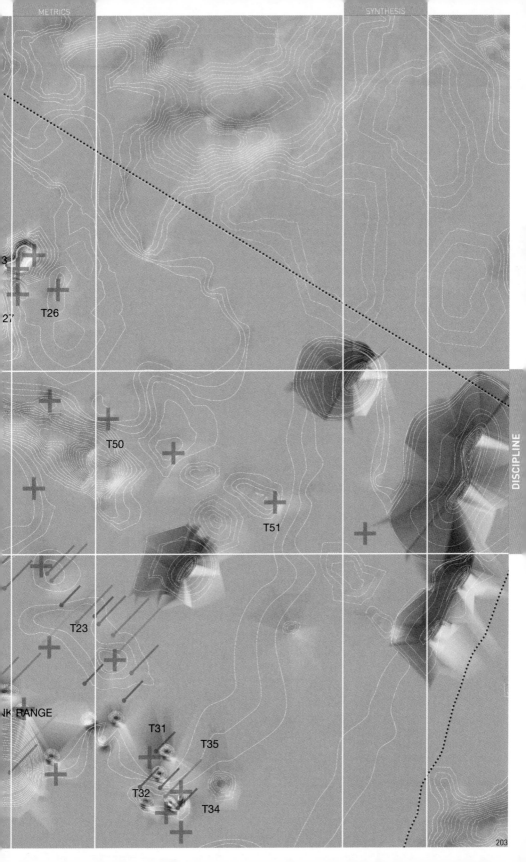

3

27

T26

T50

T51

DISCIPLINE

T23

JK RANGE

T31

T35

T32

T34

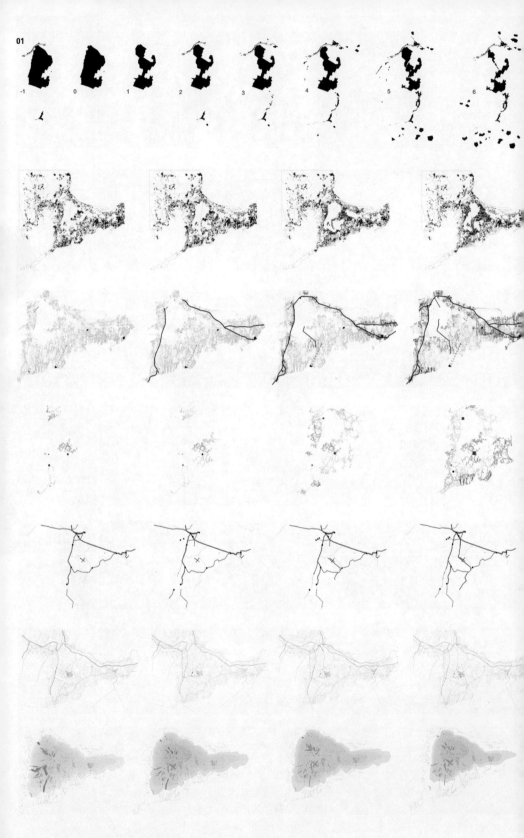

01

01 PHASING STRATEGY
*for Research Urbanism at the
Massachusetts Military Reservation;
urban densities, fiber optic networks,
wastewater and sewage, accessibility,
Sagamore Lens with contamination and
monitoring wells, and electricity and
transmission*

**02 FLOWS AND ZONES OF
INTERVENTION** *for the Massachusetts
Military Reservation*

03 ESTUARY RESEARCH
depicting productive aquaculture

ALL IMAGES JACK MCGRATH,
KATE SMABY, AND XIAOWEI WANG

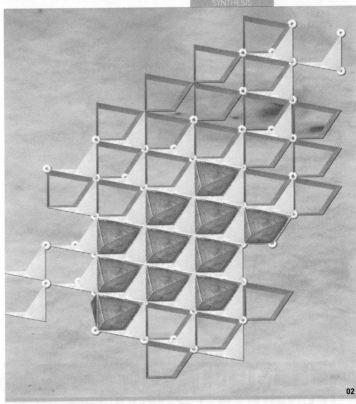

02

03

DISCIPLINE

NIALL **KIRKWOOD**, KELLY **SHANNON**, JULIA **WATSON**, PIERRE **BÉLANGER**   205

ELEMENTS OF URBAN DESIGN

Felipe Correa (Coordinator), Anita Berrizbeitia,
Gabriel Duarte
Urban Design Core Studio, Fall 2011

Elements of Urban Design was an advanced core studio for the post-professional programs in urban design. The studio introduced a wide host of ideas, strategies, and technical skills associated with current thinking on urbanism, and speculated on the designer's projective role in analyzing and shaping complex metropolitan systems. Rigorous research informs a series of interrelated exercises that constructed diverse hypotheses about new formal and experiential urban identities across multiple scales of intervention and development.

FARIDA FARAG,
WILLIAM WEBSTER

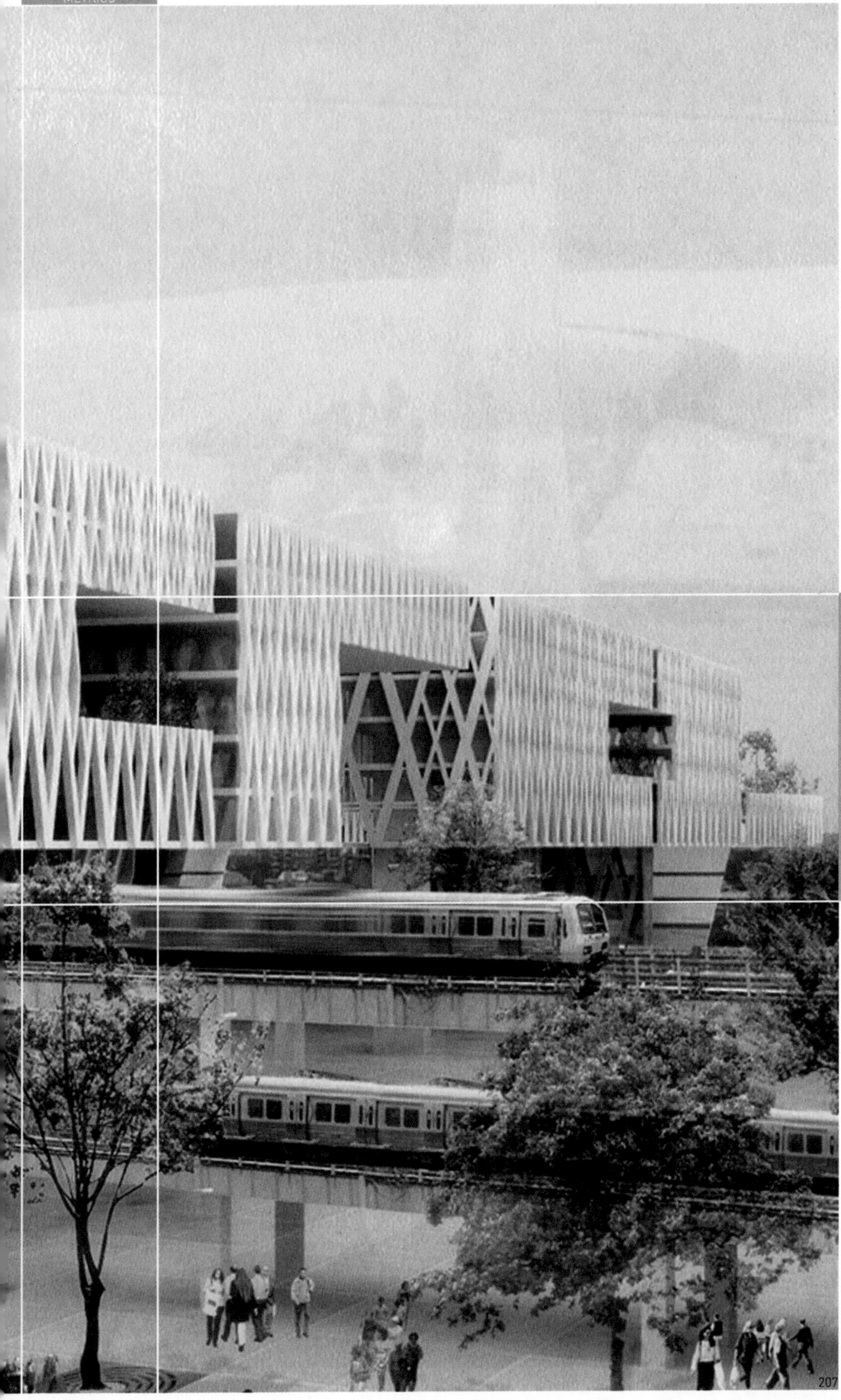

01 TRAX FLY-AROUND

02 JUNCTURES AT THE
BROOKLYN PARK PARKWAY

03 TRAX COMPOSITION

ALL IMAGES FARIDA FARAG,
WILLIAM WEBSTER

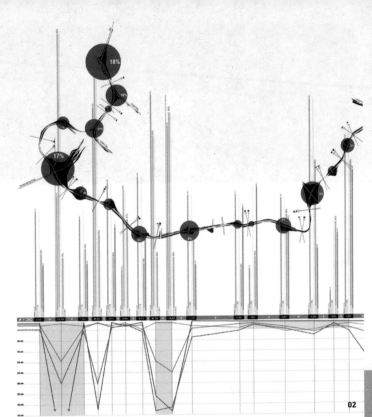

02

03

ANITA **BERRIZBEITIA**, GABRIEL **DUARTE**, FELIPE **CORREA**

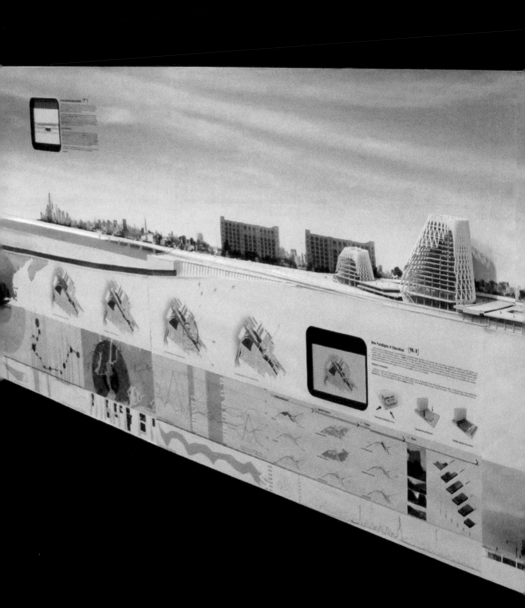

Lightfall was not only an exhibition design and a presentation of the Tel Aviv Museum of Art's new Amir Building; it was an architectural intervention in the Harvard Graduate School of Design that embodied the deeply interiorized concept of the Amir Building's "Lightfall"(an 87-foot-tall spiraling atrium), by inserting a model of it in what appears to be a space that exceeded the limit of the Gund Hall Gallery. The exhibition explored the relationship between pedagogy and practice by including spatial concepts that many GSD students remembered from three foundational projects in the first-year core curriculum of architecture: the "Hidden Room," the "Lodged House," and the "Lock Building."

Located at the center of Tel Aviv's cultural complex, the Amir Building posed an extraordinary architectural challenge: to resolve the tension between the tight, idiosyncratic triangular site and the museum's need for a series of large, neutral rectangular galleries. The solution: the twisting geometric surfaces of the Lightfall that connect the disparate angles between the galleries and the context while refracting natural light into the deepest recesses of the half-buried building.

The Amir Building embodies the tension between two prevailing models: the museum of neutral white boxes that allow for maximum curatorial freedom and the museum of architectural specificity that intensifies the experience of public spectacle. An antidote to the Bilbao phenomenon, the

ALL IMAGES *Justin Knight*

DISCIPLINE

LIGHTFALL:
Herta & Paul Amir Building, Tel Aviv Museum of Art

Amir building signals a new synthesis—deeply interiorized and socially choreographed space, as opposed to the tendency in the 1990s to display the museum as a sculptural object to the city. The complexity of the public spaces and richness of materials—including pre-cast and poured-in-place concrete, stone, wood, and glass—foster the production of site-specific interventions. On display currently are works by Michal Rovner, Anselm Kiefer, and Locomotion.

SEE ALSO

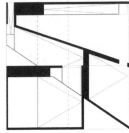

BEN BURDICK
Hidden Room Project,
Architecture Core I, pages 306-309

DISCUSSIONS IN ARCHITECTURE
Preston Scott Cohen in Conversation

MOHSEN MOSTAFAVI: I must admit that I feel very unprepared for introducing Scott Cohen. Those of you who know Scott are fully aware of the fact that he begins his introductions, which are generally written, very beautifully written, very precise, and quite long... and often more precise than some of the lectures that follow. I will tell you that it was a great opportunity for me only a couple of weeks ago to be in Tel Aviv and see Scott's museum. It was part of an important and interesting trip that we took with a number of people from Harvard—the Deans of the Business School, the Law School, the Education School, and a number of faculty from the Business School—to Israel, among other things, to see buildings. It was a special moment because I had seen the drawings of the building, but I was not quite prepared for seeing the building in the way you experience it. It is not a building that is an object, completely visible. From a distance, you arrive into a plaza and then you walk along the side of the building and see all the things that Scott is interested in and we're interested in about the outside, about its geometry and so on—it is very engaging when you see it close up. You are next to the building, you see the window, you see through the window, you see the relationship between the window and the panel. You walk along it and then you enter and come into the building. The main element of the building is this central space that you have seen, and it's very important the way this central space deals with the phenomenon of compression that we all know Scott is interested in—phenomenal distortion.

PRESTON SCOTT COHEN
Cohen is the Gerald M. McCue Professor in Architecture and Chair of the Department of Architecture at the Harvard University Graduate School of Design. He is the coordinator of the first-year design studios and teaches the foundation course in projective and topological geometry, advanced studios, and design thesis. His firm's recent commissions include a Student Center for Nanjing University in Xianlin, China; a public arcade in Battery Park City in New York; and the Fahmy residence in Los Gatos, California. Cohen has received first prizes in the international competitions for the Taiyuan Art Museum, Taiyuan, China; the Robbins Elementary School, Trenton, New Jersey; and the Amir Building, Tel Aviv Museum of Art.

Stan Allen with Preston Scott Cohen

COHEN: In *Field Conditions*, you basically divide the world of architecture— specifically the way it brings things together—according to two principles: the first you call algebraic, constituted by quantifiable units set one upon another; and the second, the geometric, which originates in the rudiments of forms—lines, planes, volumes—organized to submit to the authority of a larger whole. Clearly you are an adder. You are algebraic.

ALLEN: I think it's quite true. I accept the taxonomy. I will happily own up to being an adder in the algebraic camp, and you are the geometrician par excellence. So I think the distinction is a very clear one and a very important one. I did a field condition studio at Columbia in 1994 and the first "Field Conditions"article was published in '96 or '97, so this is awhile ago. Although we were working in very different directions, what we shared was the rethinking of the part-to-whole problem. I think the important piece of context there was that we were all reacting to deconstructivism. The model of deconstructivism was that you started with a whole figure, and you broke it apart. Think of Tschumi, disjunction, and discontinuity. Peter Eisenman, starting with whole figures and fracturing them in different ways. In that sense, dividing was contaminated by the logic of deconstruction and fragmentation. For me, part of the early attraction to the field condition notion was that instead of starting with a whole and breaking it down into parts, you started with small elements—many, many small elements—and, through repetition, began to produce a different sense of the whole.

STAN ALLEN
Allen is the Dean of Princeton University School of Architecture and Principal of SAA/Stan Allen Architect.

Steven Holl with Preston Scott Cohen

STEVEN HOLL

Holl was born in 1947 in Bremerton, Washington. He graduated from the University of Washington and pursued architecture studies in Rome in 1970. In 1976 he attended the Architectural Association in London and established STEVEN HOLL ARCHITECTS in New York City. Steven Holl has realized cultural, civic, academic, and residential projects both in the United States and internationally.

COHEN: There are two directions of your work, scale and type, and I wanted to see if you could talk and narrate how you move between, back and forth, because they are the main, canonic way many people see Steven Holl, and it is through the lens of the memory of your research, which is so significant. The whole idea of going back to the irreducible type, the fundamentals of architecture, and looking for something we hadn't understood before, which is the way it intersected with the city. It isn't the Rossi approach—utterly reduced to pure conditions—it is something that through the hybrid becomes made conscious and changed by that condition.

HOLL: Going back to "Alphabetical City" for a moment: this was a kind of crisis moment in my development, because I was trying to find a way into architecture. It was the height of Post-Modernism, which I was doing war against in 1980. I was trying to find a way to argue: not sure of myself, what was going to be my position, which I never came to until nine years later. In 1984 I had "Alphabetical City." This to me was interesting. I still believe in the fabric of the city and how important it is, but it was a dead end. You can't get a different way into architecture from just typology and urban morphology. It wasn't enough—it didn't have enough poetry. I did this research—it was enormously interesting—but it brought me to a conclusion where I left this research. There has to be an idea, a poetic idea that is stronger than the typological frame. You can't go just to the typological frame. It's not enough. However, the knowledge of the type brings you scale. If I was to do it again, I would still do that research, because then you would intuitively have the nature of the scale.

Nicolai Ouroussoff with Preston Scott Cohen

NICOLAI OUROUSSOFF

Born in Boston, Nicolai Ourous-soff received his Bachelor's degree in Russian from Georgetown University and holds a Master's degree from the Columbia University Graduate School of Architecture. He was the architecture critic at the New York Times from 2004 to 2011 and previously, he was the architecture critic for the Los Angeles Times. In 2004, 2006, and 2011, he was a finalist for the Pulitzer Prize in Criticism.

SEE ALSO

This lecture and discussion accompanies the exhibition Lightfall: the Tel Aviv Museum of Art.

OUROUSSOFF: In the Guggenheim Bilbao, which is also a commentary on the Guggenheim in New York, obviously, one of the ways that Gehry breaks up the narrative, and one of the ways that he deals with the relationship of architects and art and showing art is by coming up with three different types of space: the orthogonal galleries, for smaller paintings; the big whale's belly, which is an interpretation of a warehouse space; and, those smaller spaces. You constrained yourself to rectangular galleries, but distort them by ripping them open as you torque the building and allow for certain views in and out of them. Why do you decide to restrain yourself to rectangular galleries? Does that have to do with the curator, or was that something you thought was important for showing art? Or were you told rectangular, rectangular, rectangular.

COHEN: He did say that, and he gleefully said, "I'm hoping for a miracle that you can make rectangular galleries in this site with this shape." He knew it was a problem. Of course it is a delicious game to play to put rectangles in a shape like that—that's what leads to the Lightfall. It acts to reconcile the many contesting geometries. It is a wonderful problem. If you don't hold on to this rigid requirement, everything falls apart. If the constraint isn't in play, the opposite of the voice of the architect isn't there—you don't have the force of architecture acting on you. Having those rectangles is basically to reckon with architecture, for me. And that is what it did, it forced things to happen.

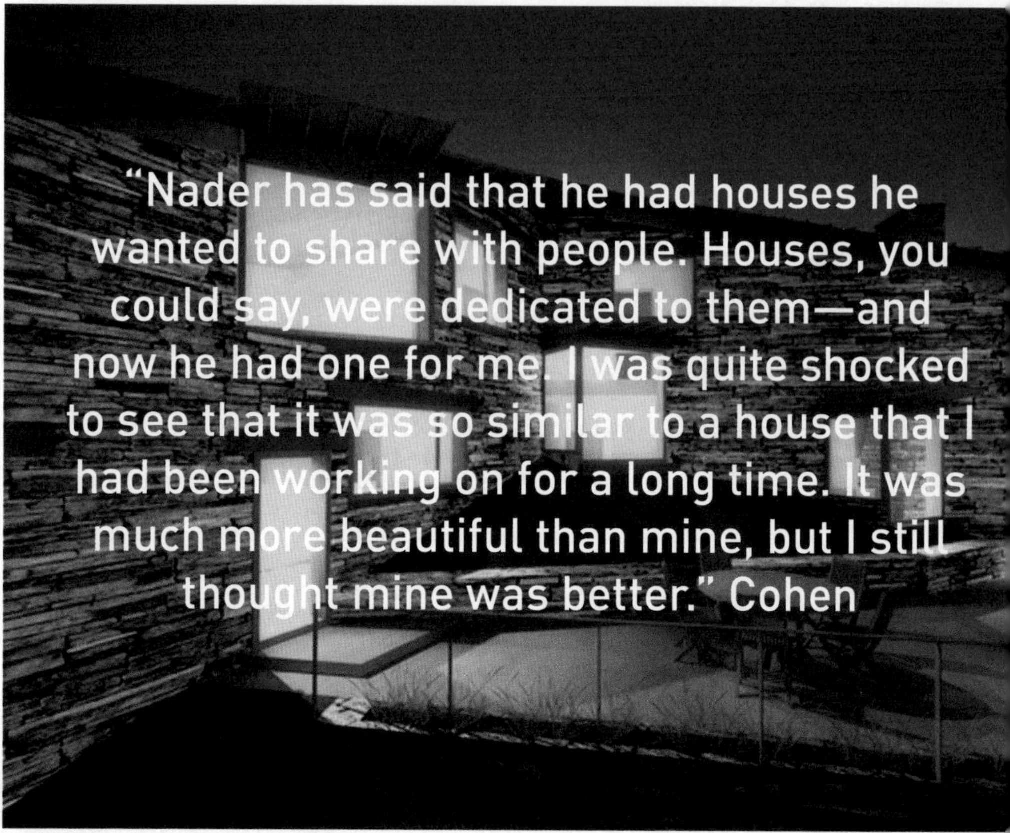

"Nader has said that he had houses he wanted to share with people. Houses, you could say, were dedicated to them—and now he had one for me. I was quite shocked to see that it was so similar to a house that I had been working on for a long time. It was much more beautiful than mine, but I still thought mine was better." Cohen

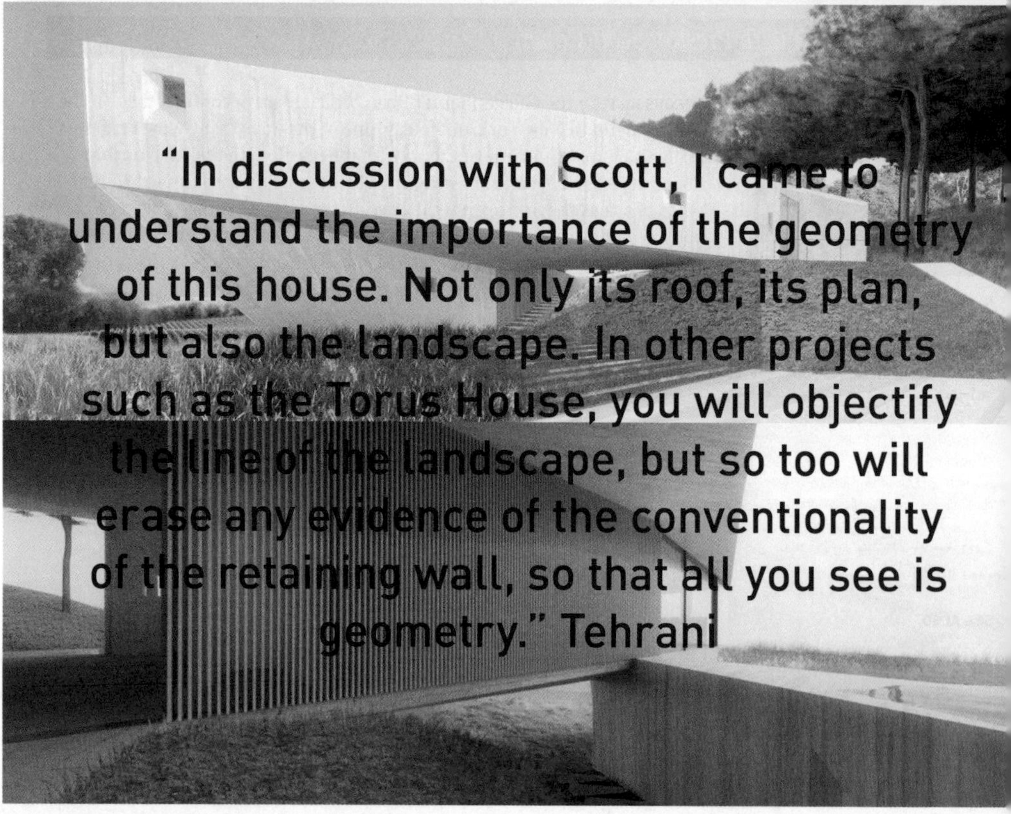

"In discussion with Scott, I came to understand the importance of the geometry of this house. Not only its roof, its plan, but also the landscape. In other projects such as the Torus House, you will objectify the line of the landscape, but so too will erase any evidence of the conventionality of the retaining wall, so that all you see is geometry." Tehrani

NT: The house is very much dedicated to Scott. I was thinking about the trajectory of his work, as in the Torus House and the Wu House, which are reflections on geography's confrontation with typology. In Los Gatos, because of the topography, you could not place the house just anywhere. The connection to the road is critical, but the relationship with the trees is also important, which is why the views privilege the downhill, and you also fold the plan. Like in the Torus House when you objectify the landscape, it no longer functions as a base, but acquires an iconographic status.

The roof geometry that Scott creates is significant because it compounds certain aspects of offsetting the slope of the landscape, which is quite important to its ultimate form. These geometries operate on the ridge, giving you a hip, triangulated roof. But what is interesting is that you get into other geometric predicaments where a ridge centered on the geometry hits an edge condition, which means that the purity of that line is violated by virtue of the contingencies of drainage, the tectonics of roof materials, et cetera. All of those things—the stuff of conventional architecture—which you found ways of erasing, now become its very problems.

PSC: In Dortoir Familial, Nader creates a projected parallelogram—the tectonic implication is that of two bars resting one on top of another. The parallelogram transforms where it needs to make entrances, let in light, and allow views to happen.

Nader is very committed to finding the reasons to invent these remarkable forms. He combines representation—what he calls a figure of architecture—with the idea of performance or function. He tries to merge these two in his

PRESTON SCOTT COHEN: *Nader and I share many interests. He will tell me what's wrong with what I'm doing and I will tell him what I think is wrong with what he is doing. Some would say our differences are of no consequence, but I believe that they exponentially open up interesting issues. This is a time for us to openly lay out some of our disputes.*

MY HOUSE IS BETTER THAN YOUR HOUSE
Nader Tehrani and Preston Scott Cohen

own style, a very refined development at all scales. His work is far more artful than mine, and it is designed through and through. I don't think he adopts the banal elements that I do. This raises a question around the issue of the artful, which is the imposition of art in life. It takes us back to the debate between Loos and the Secessionists. Loos did not believe that architecture should involve the total, integrative design of all things in the domestic spheres of life. The art of the architect is applied to the exterior in a manner that recalls the Renaissance theory of *sprezzatura*, the idea of concealment, a mask of anonymity or inconspicuousness versus the personal space, which might be elaborated in a different way on the inside.

Nader is more interested in expressing the will of the artist by designing everything. I find this the most troubling moment ideologically, because the "artisticness" of it is too hubristic, particularly for private houses. In every way, you make explicit the artifice of signification. I think architecture, in its basic way of being in the world, requires no attention from anyone. There is a situation in which architecture could be attended to, but it is a different kind of project, not a house. You don't have to bear on everyone so heavily with a hand of artistry, to make architecture be remarkable.

NT: I think that architecture does need to radicalize itself—its forms, protocols, and its organizations. It needs to provide the framework for producing new forms of knowledge, not for the sake of artfulness, but to lay bare the devices of the medium. Some of it is technical and technological—about the science of building— and some of it has to do with the way it engages society, perception, and so forth. It is the tension between the image of things versus the actuality of how they perform which causes friction.

PSC: I like thinking about what happens in people's houses. When the architecture of a house is contorted and yet remains, in so many ways, ordinary, it helps me to think about what happened to it spatially, how it became strange.

NADER TEHRANI
Tehrani is a Professor and Head of the Department of Architecture at MIT SA+P. He is the Principal and Founder of NADAAA, a practice dedicated to the advancement of design innovation, interdisciplinary collaboration, and an intensive dialogue with the construction industry.

PRESTON SCOTT COHEN
Cohen is the Gerald M. McCue Professor in Architecture and Chair of the Department of Architecture at the Harvard University Graduate School of Design. He is the Principal and Founder of Preston Scott Cohen Inc.

IMAGES *Top: Preston Scott Cohen, Los Gatos House. Bottom two: Nader Tehrani, Dortoir Familial.*

Despite the intense public role and its symbolic potential, Piazzale Roma is a mere by-product of use, strict and attentive to its role—the arrival and departure of public buses that connect to terra firma, the waiting of users, and the ultimate limit for cars approaching Venice. It is a mechanical tool predicated in the geometry of the turning radius of buses. Private cars can enter the loop and stay up to 20 minutes, after which they must leave, while the public buses occupy the central dock from which to fetch and carry Venetians to and from terra firma.

For the Venetians, as for many tourists, it constitutes, along with the train station, the main entry to the city, the gateway to Venice, the transition point.

We addressed the needs derived from the key infrastructural role of Piazzale Roma by covering the bus station, as it currently is. Simultaneously, we suggested taking advantage of its strategic condition building a public facility of symbolic character—the public facilities of the Historical Archive of the City of Venice.

URBAN SUPERIMPOSITIONS

HISTORICAL ARCHIVE | NEGOTIATING PUBLIC ROLES IN PIAZZALE ROMA
Architecture Option Studio, Fall 2011
Luis Rojo de Castro

The activity of Piazzale Roma is essential for the functioning of the city: twenty-four hours a day, 365 days a year, Piazzale Roma sustains a constant movement of people, buses, and cars to and from Venice. But the large dock of buses remains in the open, unprotected, and the Venetians wait for the arrival and departure of buses in the cold and rain.

Covering the outdoor bus station allowed for the location of the public rooms of the Historical Archive of the City of Venice to be superimposed on the site. The Archive of the City is already divided between Venice and Mestre, keeping most of its content away from the lagoon and from its historical location, for reasons of conservation.

While traditional archives have been built around the notion of the original, its preservation and display, both public institutions and communities of scholars are searching for ways to take advantage of digital technologies to mobilize its content for larger audiences and open up new forms of knowledge creation.

HIBA SHAHZADA

PROGRAM

*Building the Historical Archive of
the City of Venice in Piazzale Roma
mobilizes the relationship between the
city and the history of the city, between
history and the experience of history.*

*Already at a literal level, the mere
programmatic superposition of the
Historical Archive and the bus station is
a typical contemporary operation that
is foreign to Venice techniques.
But at a deeper level, the homogeneity
of the image of Venice veils a whole
series of social and historical processes,
such as its rapidly declining population,
and its increasing museum-ification.
Our project addressed these different
processes in both its site and its
program.*

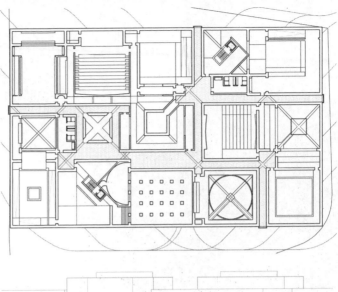

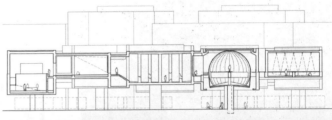

ALL IMAGES HIBA SHAHZADA

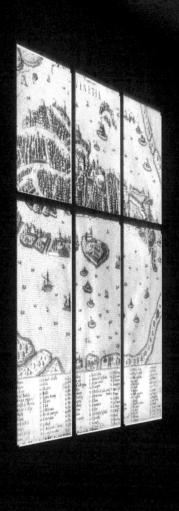

I S

31	232	233	234	235	236	237	238	239	240	241	242	243
58	259	260	261	262	263	264	265	266	267	268	269	270

SYNTHESIS looks at work that maintains a disciplinary tradition of communication and representation, while forming a vehicle within which complex or difficult information is made manageable. The ambition to produce a synthetic design allows for disparate and perhaps competing parts to find a neutral or homeostatic condition given a tempering process or a regulated environment. The scales for this production can range from massive interventions that may require collaborative methods and teams to smaller works where various disciplines may play out a network of influences and types dependent on corresponding design factors, tools, and expertise.

The School hosts many forms of exchange among its varied members. This synthetic approach also branches out to other schools and departments at Harvard University, as well as to peer institutions, creating alliances among experts and their facilities to produce and promote original solutions and provocations.

Our local specialization in design moves beyond a single authority to multiple agents with settings and protocols that can generate robust designs and communicate them to a global audience. The projects included in this section engage with diverse issues, yet they are all linked by the ambition to produce elegant proposals to address complex problems. In these scenarios, various expertise might be necessary to fully gauge and respond to the multiplicity of questions that these projects generate.

The studio explored how an architectural project could relate to the city through the manipulation of the ground line and the skyline.

The aim was to propose a series of autonomous but related architectural interventions around the Suleymaniye in Istanbul in order to connect it physically and programmatically to the surrounding quarters of the old peninsula, while partaking in the definition of the city's skyline.

The Suleymaniye (1551–1557) is named after its patron, Suleyman the Magnificent. It was designed and built by the court architect, Sinan. In addition to the mosque, the complex consisted of a madrassa, a library, a hospice, a hospital, and a hammam. These buildings also carefully mediate between the mosque's skyline and the panorama of the city, and between the constructed ground of the complex and the topography of the hill.

Contour and Silhouette: The site and the complex fall between two formal strategies. On the one hand, the relationship between the ground plane of the complex and the topography of the hill exemplifies contouring as a method of extracting planar succession from three-dimensional form. On the other, the skyline of the complex masterfully shows how a building's silhouette can capture, in its intense articulations, the three-dimensional identity of a building or city.

The studio proposed to recast architecture between these two geometries of extraction, an incremental iteration from contour to form and an intense inscription from skyline to full volume.

ISTANBUL
BETWEEN CONTOUR AND SILHOUETTE
Urban Design / Architecture Option Studio, Fall 2011
Hashim Sarkis

ROLA IDRIS

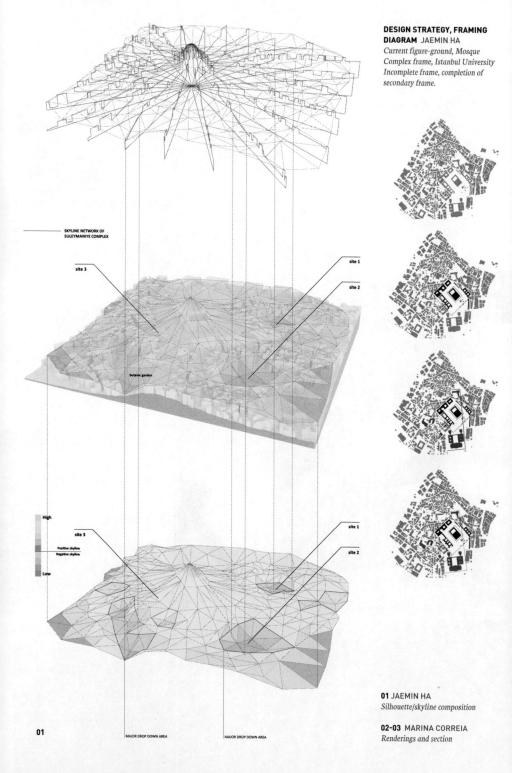

SKYLINE DIAGRAM

SECTIONAL NETWORK OF
SULEYMANIYE COMPLEX

**DESIGN STRATEGY, FRAMING
DIAGRAM** JAEMIN HA
*Current figure-ground, Mosque
Complex frame, Istanbul University
Incomplete frame, completion of
secondary frame.*

SKYLINE NETWORK OF
SULEYMANIYE COMPLEX

site 3

site 1

site 2

botanic garden

High

site 3

Positive skyline
Negative skyline

Low

site 1

site 2

01 JAEMIN HA
Silhouette/skyline composition

02-03 MARINA CORREIA
Renderings and section

01

MAJOR DROP DOWN AREA

MAJOR DROP DOWN AREA

02

03

Gothenburg is a water city, but it no longer has any connection to the water. Once a bustling port and industrial corridor, Gothenburg's Göta älv river is now dominated by hyper-scaled transportation infrastructure. Seas of parking lots, roadways, railway lines, ferry terminals, port infrastructure, and defunct industrial land now completely cut off the city from the river, visually, physically, and mentally. Once described as "The Los Angeles of Scandinavia," Gothenburg is a fragmented archipelago—all of its incredible assets (distinct historic neighborhoods, diverse population, natural resources, and enviable green-space network) are hidden by its sprawling, disconnected layout and massive swatches of vacant land. Even the river itself divides the historic city center on the south bank and the industrial/suburban area on the North. Gothenburg is growing. Nearing its 400-year anniversary in 2021, the city continues to grow with immigration from Europe and North Africa and will continue to be a draw as warming global temperatures open up new shipping routes through the North, potentially reactivating Gothenburg's port. Without a central focus, the city will continue to spread outward, further diluting its population, culture, and tourist draw.

The Rivercity Gothenburg studio explored the ability of the designed landscape to provide an identity, a sense of place, and a physical connection for a growing twenty-first-century city.

RIVERCITY GOTHENBURG

Landscape Architecture Option Studio, Fall 2011
Martha Schwartz and Emily Waugh

EMILY GORDON

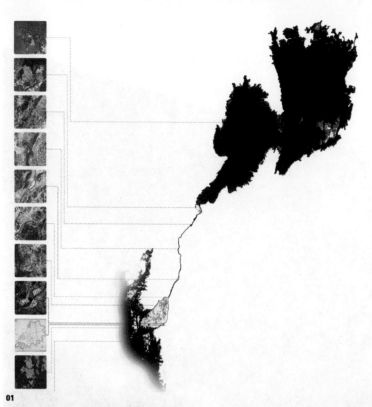

01 MORPHOSIS OF THE GÖTA ÄLV

Geologic history and landrise processes shaped the formation of the post-aquatic region of the Göta älv waterway and islands. Responding to climate change, correlations at the urban scale between transitional post-industrial land, overbuilt infrastructure, and flood prone areas provide the framework for proposing the strategic return of aquasity to Gothenburg, Sweden.

02 SITE PLAN

The site plan illustrates the new park islands and developed waterfront that result on the studio's Frihammen site with the introduction of the new aquatic landscape at an urban scale. Experiences are defined by the dramatic juxtaposition of the new inhabitable water landscape that exists on the islands, embedded within the still active ship-based industry of the major river channel.

01

ALL IMAGES EMILY GORDON

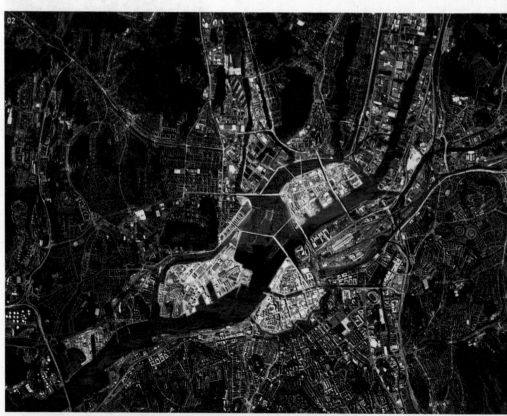

02

03 HYDROLOGIC STRATEGY FOR A NEW URBAN ORGANIZATION

Strategy for the reintroduction of water into the city as a means of organization and of maximizing the economic, social, and ecologic health of future urban growth.

FLOODED VS. DRY CONDITIONS

Flooded condition

Dry condition

04 PERSPECTIVE VIEW

Illustrated moments describe some of the various ways users engage water on the site, and view their city from this new experiential context.

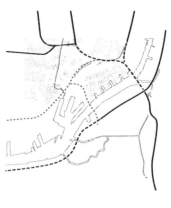
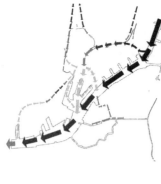

03

04

SYNTHESIS

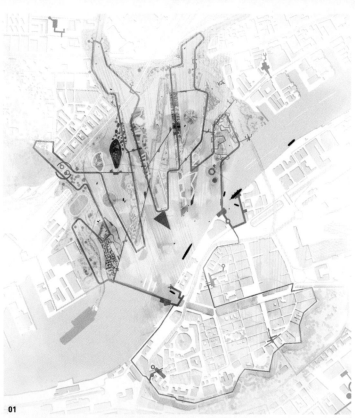

01 **KIDSTOPIA** *City-scale map shows the proposed kids' adventure route, which connects playground nodes in the central parts of Gothenburg .*

02 *Sections illustrate the small-scale adventure islands in the kidstopia archipelago.*

01

Regional kids' adventure path

Recreational space along old canal

Lilla bommen

Göta älv North Bank Linear Park

Göta älv

Ringen

This option studio examined how the introduction of a new metro transit system can serve as the backbone for the development of more comprehensive urban interventions within the context of a mid-size, South American capital city. The studio explored how the stations of a new mass transit system, soon to be implemented in Quito (Ecuador), can become epicenters of a much richer and varied programmatic brief.

The new "metro" project, conceived as a 15 station / 23 kilometer long line, will serve as a central spine further complemented by existing and new rapid bus lines along the east-west corridors in the city. Such an unprecedented project in the context of a topographically complex geography presents the current administration with an immense logistical challenge. More importantly, the project opened up a significant opportunity to rethink portions of the city beyond the basic requirements of the metro in order to capitalize on the urban opportunities an infrastructural project of this scope and ambition can bring to the city. This joint Architecture and Urban Design Studio took the surface footprints of the sub-surface network (the metro stations) as focal points for new centralities in the city that established a spatial framework for a more ambitious transformative process in the city. The studio considered how an expanded programmatic toolkit, one that goes beyond the mono-functional objective of simply solving a transportation deficiency in the city, may incorporate into the system a larger set of cultural, educational and recreational facilities synthesized in precise design projects. The armature of the new metro system resulted in a far more ambitious and comprehensive network of collective spaces with diverse scales and areas of influence. The research and pedagogical bearings of the studio focused on how small and intermediate scale interventions, heavily driven by sectional articulations, took advantage of the "metro" system in order to establish a constellation of projects that, through accretion, can exercise substantial change at a metropolitan scale.

A LINE IN THE ANDES
RETHINKING QUITO
THROUGH ITS SUB-SURFACE
Urban Design / Architecture Option Studio, Spring 2012

Felipe Correa

WILLIAM WEBSTER

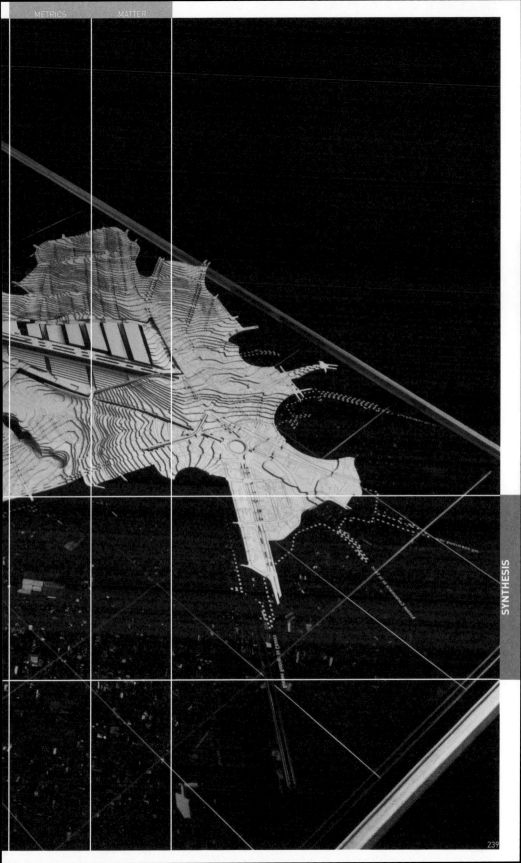

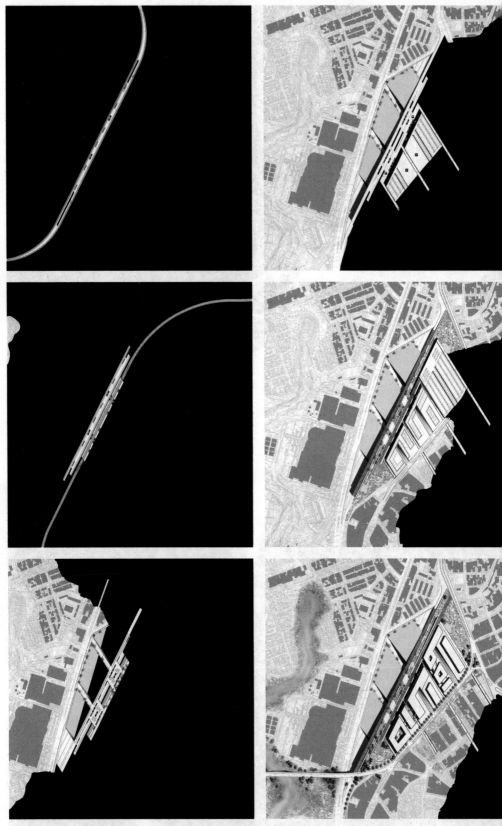

**THE SOUTH AMERICA PROJECT:
HINTERLAND URBANISMS
SYMPOSIUM
CURATED BY FELIPE CORREA**

*This symposium, curated by Felipe
Correa, Associate Professor of Urban
Design and Ana Maria Duran, Loeb
Fellow '11, looked at the Initiative
for the Integration of Regional
Infrastructure in South America
(IIRSA) as a point of departure for an
ample discussion regarding the diverse
models of urbanism that emerge at
the intersection of resource extraction
and regional integration projects
(primarily through mobility corridors).*

SEE *http://www.sap-network.org
for more information*

ALL IMAGES WILLIAM WEBSTER

SYNTHESIS

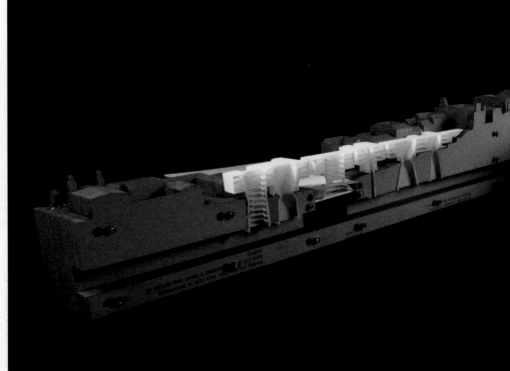

EMMET TRUXES

NATHAN SHOBE

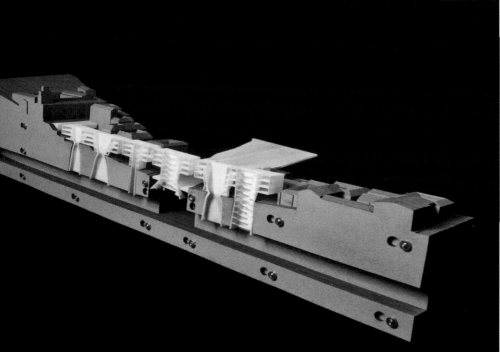

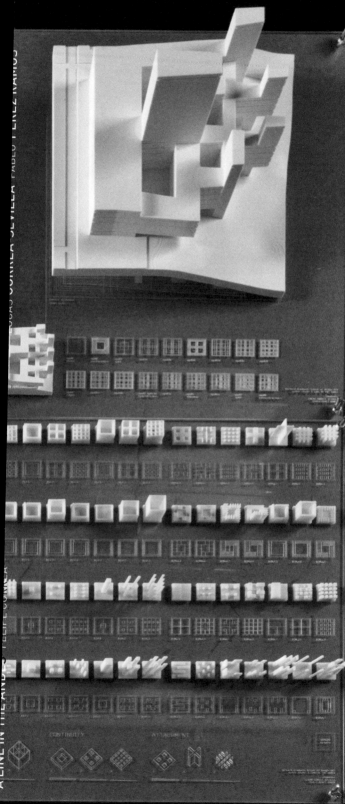

Most traditional Western cities are founded on principles of stability and permanence. Change or uncertainty—often in the form of rich and complex landscape systems—are typically erased, filled, leveled, denuded, marginalized, or stabilized.

This studio took a different approach to city-making—or, in this case, to urban renovation—we assumed change is the norm. In doing so, we built on ecologists' reconceptualization of their field over the past quarter-century, in which classical Newtonian concerns with stability, certainty, and order have given way to more contemporary understandings of dynamic, systemic change. With this reconceptualization comes the related phenomena of adaptability, resilience, and flexibility—phenomena applicable not only to ecological systems (whether native or adapted), but also applicable to city-systems, infrastructures, and urbanism writ large.

In this sense, then, we moved away from traditions of master-planning, which value the comprehensive and fixed vision, in favor of more dynamic and responsive frameworks for small and large-scale civic change. We also explored multiple development scenarios (assemblies/deployments) over time—rather than a singular and totalizing plan. These scenarios were operated according to a set of rules or parameters, and were programmed to respond to a range of differing inputs across time. In this way, our proposals aspired to a level of resiliency with regard to long-term environmental, social, political, and economic shifts—and therefore were made truly sustainable over the long term.

FLUX

Chris Reed (Coordinator), Gary Hilderbrand,
David Mah, Miho Mazereeuw
Landscape Architecture Core Studio IV, Spring 2012

ELLEN GARRETT

0.0

.50

1.0

1.5

2.0

2.5

3.0

3.5

SITE *The site is an urbanized river mouth / filled estuary and adjacent lands on the margins of the Flushing and Corona neighborhoods in Queens, New York. It is a series of industrialized and contaminated properties on the fringes of some vibrant, ethnically diverse communities; adjacent to the New York Mets' home, CitiField, the United States Tennis Center, and Flushing Park, the former home to two World's Fairs; and pierced by extensive transportation infrastructure that connects the boroughs of New York City to Long Island and New England, and all to nearby LaGuardia Airport.*

01 Performative Plan

01 KUNKUOOK BAE

02 TAEHYUNG PARK

03 CHUHAN ZHANG

04 YIZHOU XU

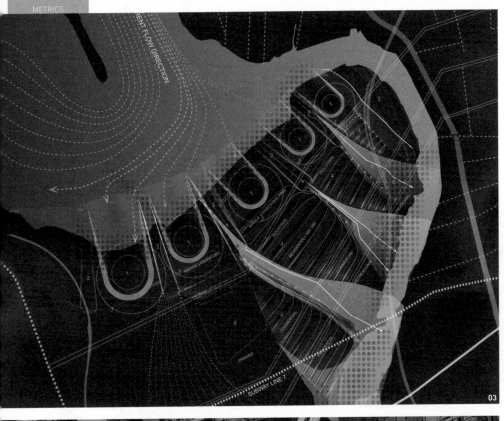

03

04

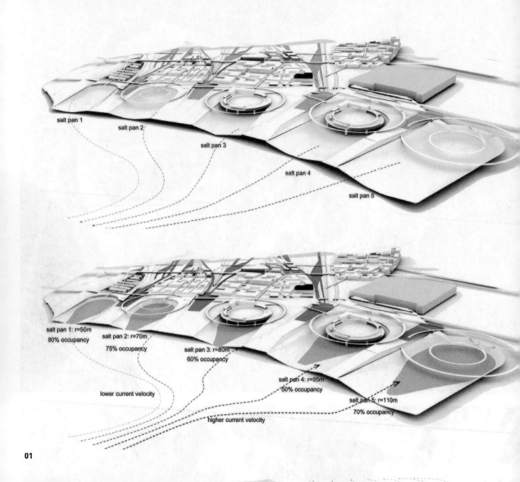

salt pan 1

salt pan 2

salt pan 3

salt pan 4

salt pan 5

salt pan 1: r=50m
80% occupancy

salt pan 2: r=70m
75% occupancy

salt pan 3: r=80m
60% occupancy

salt pan 4: r=95m
50% occupancy

salt pan 5: r=110m
70% occupancy

lower current velocity

higher current velocity

01

02

low salinity

tidal mud sediment grow

salt pan habitat observatory

high salinity

COLLABORATIONS

Two collaborations with students in the fourth-semester architecture core studio allowed for cross disciplinary collaboration on topics of mutual interest. The first was a larger seminar on the question of Urbanism. The second was collaborative and interdisciplinary group discussions focused on a series of important urban case study projects from the last 50 years. Students and faculty from both departments worked together, allowing the disciplinary perspective that each brought to inform one another.

01 CHUHAN ZHANG
Dynamic saltscape: salt pan as landscape machine to accelerate salt marsh succession

02 CHUHAN ZHANG
Dynamic exchange of the urban landscape

03 TAEHYUNG PARK
Detail designs for integrating ponds types and urban system

04 TAEHYUNG PARK
Serene marsh fields

03

04

SYNTHESIS

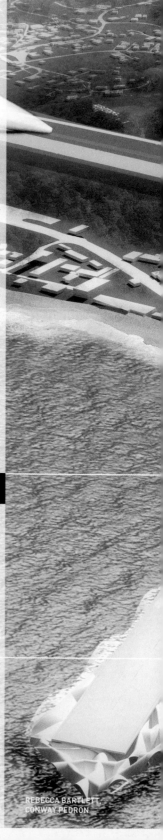

This studio was dedicated to reimagining the future of Gabon's capital, Libreville, in the wake of recent developments in the country. Gabon holds a unique position in Africa. Referred to as Africa's "Eden," it has the second-largest rainforest in the world. With the stated goal of becoming the first carbon-neutral country, it recently set aside 11 percent of its land to become national parks, a ratio of protected territory second only to Costa Rica. As it addresses a projected growth in tourism and urban development to accommodate this change, Gabon is confronting the economic viability of environmental action at a scale of global concern. Given this unprecedented opportunity, it is important to ask what will be the shape of Gabon's future. In ecological and urban terms, the answer to this question will serve as a new model for an African nation and capital in the twenty-first century.

Libreville has a small population of less than 1 million inhabitants. To confront the city's growth and development within the surrounding national parks, this studio presented the "Park-City-Boundary" problem as a primary issue to position Libreville as a model capital for the twenty-first century. Libreville is literally a city in a park: to the east is Akanda National Park, to the north are Mondah National Park and The Cap Esterias, and to the east and south by the Waterfront Parks. Six group projects were asked to select a site from these different geographical perspectives of the city's edge. The studio was conceived in association with the real-world objectives established by the forward-thinking group behind Gabon's national parks, the ANPN (Agence Nationale des Parcs Nationaux) and their affiliations.

RETOOLING GABON

Landscape / Architecture Option Studio, Spring 2012
Benjamin Aranda

REBECCA BARTLETT,
CONWAY PEDRON

BENJAMIN ARANDA *"I want...to subtly push [the domicile] beyond what people know, to have some uncanniness that may go completely unnoticed... I would rather the building just look like a normal building as much as it possibly can and to make it as interesting as possible architecturally while maintaining its normality to the greatest degree."*

Quote from lecture given by Benjamin Aranda at the Harvard GSD. See GSD YouTube Channel for more.

ALL IMAGES
REBECCA BARTLETT,
CONWAY PEDRON

A code is a systematic arrangement of relationships that specifies the legitimate and illegitimate functions of the objects, images, behaviors, or processes that are contained within its purview. Codes may be statutory or customary; preventative or exhortatory; formal or informal; artificial or biological. Codes may be expressed textually or graphically or with gestures, colors, or sounds. The contemporary city is a dense mesh of codes, overlapping one another in complementary and contradictory ways. To undertake an act of design in the city is to enter into this frantic dialogue of codes. For whether that act of design begins from the perspective of economics and finance, or politics and communities, or forms and images, the codes exist in advance, as property rights, real estate pro forma, mass transit capacities, closing times, marriage laws, traffic signals, or historic overlay districts. In addition, even as it becomes the corollary of these external codes, architecture carries along its own embedded codes—conventions that regulate forms and representations, parametric scripts that define the conditional logics of design, standards that govern the behavior of architects or the sequences of fabrications. The density of these external and internal codes and the fluidity of their presence have only increased in the digital restructuring of the contemporary city, and this in turn has only increased the urgency of a new architectural fluency in, and a new architectural attention to the medium of codes.

CITY/CODE

Timothy Hyde (Coordinator), Danielle Etzler, Eric Höweler, Florian Idenburg, Michael Piper, Rafi Segal
Architecture Core Studio IV, Spring 2012

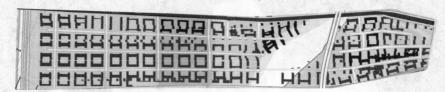

01 LAUREN GERDEMAN, REN TIAN, MOLLY GAZZA

02 JIELU LU, DOROTHY XU, HANKYU KIM, BONGJAI SHIN

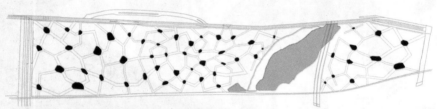

03 JIELU LU, DOROTHY XU, HANKYU KIM, BONGJAI SHIN

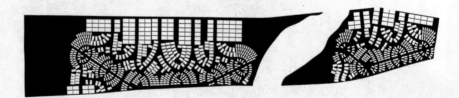

04 KATHERINE CHIN, WAQAS JAWAID, MARIANNE KOCH, JUAN YACTAYO

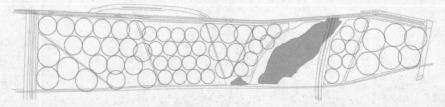

05 JIELU LU, DOROTHY XU, HANKYU KIM, BONGJAI SHIN

LAUREN GERDEMAN, REN TIAN, MOLLY GAZZA **06**

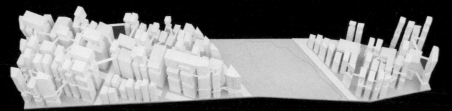

CHARLENE CHAI, MINA NISHIO, ZUNHENG LAI **07**

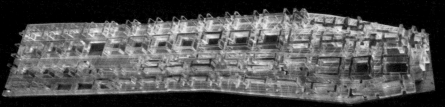

LAUREN GERDEMAN, REN TIAN, MOLLY GAZZA **08**

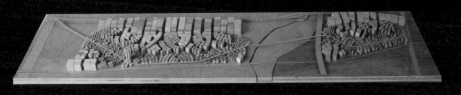

KATHERINE CHIN, WAQAS JAWAID, MARIANNE KOCH, JUAN YACTAYO **09**

SYNTHESIS

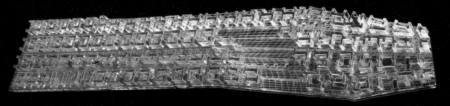

LAUREN GERDEMAN, REN TIAN, MOLLY GAZZA **10**

VOXEL SUBDIVISION
IF THE MINIMUM BUILDING VOLUME REQUIREMENT CANNOT BE MET, THE VOXEL MUST BE SUBDIVIDED AND SOLD

VOXEL PURCASING REQUIRMENTS
ONLY VOXELS WHICH HAVE ATLEAST 4 BUT LESS THAN 9 NEIGHBOURS ARE AVAILABLE FOR SALE

VOXEL PURCASING REQUIRMENTS
HOUSING TERRASES, TRANSPORTATION IS LINEAR, COMMERICAL IS VERTICLE & RETIAL IS HORIZONTAL

CIRCULATION CORE REQUIREMENTS
A 40' x 40' CIRCULATION CORE, AS SHOWN SHARED BETWEEN A) FOUR VOXELS, B) THREE VOXELS OR C) TWO VOXELS

CIRCULATION CORE REQUIREMENTS
A LINEAR AGGREGATION OF VOXELS MAY SHARE A CIRCULATION CORE ALONG A SINGLE EDGE MEAUSING A MAX OF 30' x (80' x (TOTAL # VOXELS - 1))

CIRCULATION CORE REQUIREMENTS
AN L SHAPED ARRGEMENT OF VOXELS MAY SHARE A CIRCULATION CORE ALONG ITS INTERIOR EDGE, MEASURING A MAX OF 30' x (80'*(TOTAL # VOXELS - 1)

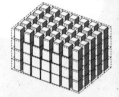

REQUIRMENTS FOR POROSITY
POROSITY INCREASES TOWARDS PERIPHERIES DUE TO DECREASING MAX BUILDING VOLUME ALLOWANCE

MAX BUILDING VOLUME
BUILDINGS MAY BE SET BACK AGAINST ANY SIDE BUT MUST MAINTAIN A MINIMUM ATTACHMENT TO THE UPPER MOST FACE TO INSURE STRUCTURAL INTEGRITY

MAX BUILDING VOLUME
SET BACK VOLUMES CAN BE FULFILLED THROUGH CLOSED COURT YARDS

MAX BUILDING VOLUME
BUILDING VOLUME DECREASES NOT ONLY TOWARDS THE EXTERIOR BUT ALSO VERTICALLY

01

02

RESEARCH The studio commenced with research and analysis of selected urban systems and their architectural elements. These precedents were interpreted and understood through code, with relational structures as the knowledge deciphered and instrumentalized.

DECODING The first systems to be decoded and encoded were a set of urban "slices" — fragments cut from existing cities in a scale or proportion commensurate to the project site. These slices were understood as condensations of multiple differentiated codings that are the substance of the contemporary city. The task was to reverse engineer these slices not only as formal objects but as coded situations, a process that entailed not the discovery of existing codes but the speculative design of codes capable of producing the situations that the slices reveal.

01 LINDA ZHANG, JENNY LEE, CHLOE PARK, DAVID THIESZ
Voxity: An Owner's Manual to Developing and Purchasing Voxels

02 LINDA ZHANG
Voxity housing: neighborhood section showing porosity

03-04 WAQAS JAWAID

03

04

SYNTHESIS

ARCHITECTURE CODE: *The second part of the studio which extended for the rest of the semester was the development of a code that regulates the position, form, use, scale, material, and image of a subset of urban elements. This Architecture Code had to have a defined and coordinated relationship to the Urban Code and not only a scalar relationship, though it also included aspects and details not covered by the Urban Code. Aspects of urban life and urban fabric that are not necessarily constituted in architectural form such as park space, lighting of public areas, the river that cuts through the site, etc. were also taken into account at this scale.*

ROUNDTABLE DISCUSSIONS
The studio participated in a roundtable discussion with Keller Easterling, an American architect, urbanist, writer, and teacher.

01-02 MARY STUCKERT, REBECCA ESAU, MICHAEL PEGUERO, SARA TAVAKOLI

03 MARY STUCKERT
Interior rendering

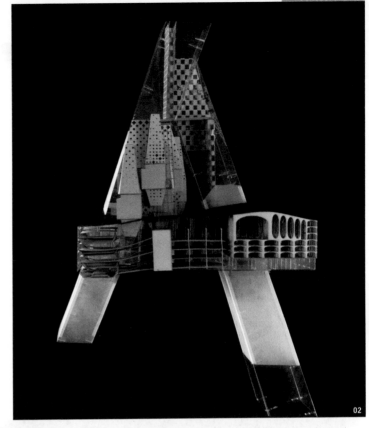

02

03

SYNTHESIS

DANIELLE **ETZLER**, ERIC **HÖWELER**, FLORIAN **IDENBURG**, MICHAEL **PIPER**, RAFI **SEGAL**, TIMOTHY **HYDE**   265

CREATIVE PROCESSES

Krzysztof Wodiczko: September 11, Memory, Vision, Practice

The context of the recent September Eleventh commemoration—the opening of the World Trade Center Memorial—as well as memorials in other U. S. cities, asks for analytical and critical reflection, as well as design imagination, regarding the past, the present, and the future of memorials. The word memorial—a monument—is an important thing to bring back here to our discussion. The monument in Latin derives from the verb *monēre*: to remind, to warn, with regard to future conduct of events. The word memorial refers to memento—precisely a command to the mind to beware or remind. How is it possible to see a memorial function as this kind of warning—an admonishing device, or event? In what way could this create a dynamic, inspired, discursive, or critical dialogue with the past toward a better future? In thinking about this—and also on the basis of my own experience of my own work, and I work with people on my projects—I believe that for larger, social, commemorative projects, we can learn a great deal from individuals and groups, who, in order to survive—to survive their own survival and survive the survival of their causes—could become memorials themselves. To leave monuments to their own trauma: warn, admonish, advise. To heal themselves, they strive to create their own capacity to express their emotions, speaking in public, elaborating their loss, testifying to their own loss, to the unspeakable. They become philosophers, judges, theologians, testimonial and interventionist artists. For them, the memory is an action of telling their story. By doing so, they may challenge the melancholic silence of building memorials and demonstrate there, on their grounds, the truth of their countermemory.

KRZYSZTOF WODICZKO *is Professor in Residence of Art, Design, and the Public Domain at the GSD. He is renowned for his large-scale slide and video projections on architectural façades and monuments. He has realized more than eighty such public projections in Australia, Austria, Canada, England, Germany, Holland, Ireland, Israel, Italy, Mexico, Poland, Spain, Switzerland, and the United States. Since the late 1980s, his projections have involved the active participation of marginalized and estranged city residents.*

Hélène Binet: Composing Space

In my book, *Composing Space,* I decided not to focus on individual architects because this is already in many books, but to reorganize the work that I've photographed by topics. So we have Memory, Light and Shadows, Materiality, and the Ground. Together with these subjects, I brought together architects that might either have some relation or no relation at all. This was a difficult task—graphically—to make sure their work could stand together.

HÉLÈNE BINET *was born in 1959 in Sorengo and is of both Swiss and French background. She currently lives in London with her husband, Raoul Bunschoten, and their two children. She studied photography at the Instituto Europeo di Design in Rome, where she grew up, and soon developed an interest in architectural photography. Over a period of twenty-five years, Binet has photographed both contemporary and historical architecture.*

I will start with this first chapter, which is entitled "memory." I want to talk about what it is for me to photograph architecture or to photograph space. I'm not in a position to make a lecture about space—I'm sure you know much more than me—I just want to point out some of the big issues that we have when we are visiting a space, and what I do with my camera—what the experience that a camera, a very, very simple tool—can do? There is a quote from John Hejduk that I always like to mention, which is, "When we visit a building, compared to all other experiences of art, we are digested by the building." So we have a complete body experience of the space because the space transforms us. That is an experience where all our senses are working together. We can know the building already—have a memory, have an intellectual knowledge of the plan, we remember the room we have seen before, we can smell, we can hear the noise. We are faced with this very simple and complex idea: what can I do with my camera? This is the main dilemma. I don't want to represent architecture. I don't want to compete with this complex experience. It is not the space—it is a photograph. That is why I look at the space with very simple interventions.

***COMPOSING SPACE* BY HÉLÈNE BINET,** *forthcoming 2012.*

Marjetica Potrč: A Vision of the Future City and the Artist's Role as Mediator

MARJETICA POTRČ *is an artist and architect based in Ljubljana and Berlin. Her work has been featured in exhibitions throughout Europe and the Americas, including the São Paulo Biennial in Brazil (1996 and 2006), the Venice Bienniale (1993, 2003, and 2009), and Skulptur Projekte Münster (1997); and she has had solo shows at the Barbican Art Gallery in London (2007), Kunsthalle Fridericianum Kassel (2004), and the Guggenheim Museum in New York (2001).*

What will the future city look like? It will be a city of strong, small neighborhoods, not a metropolis. Here, shared space—community space—is more important than public space. New allegiances are forged as local communities connect with the world and with each other on their own terms. In an age of local collaborations, sharing ideas and practices with the world is essential.

Today, after the financial crisis of 2008 and the Occupy movements of 2011, the vision of the future city matters more than ever. In 2007, I saw the exhibition "Design for the Other 90 Percent" at the Cooper-Hewitt National Design Museum in New York. The cover of the catalog showed an African woman drinking from a puddle of muddy water a using a specially designed filter that looked like a simple straw. The title of the exhibition implied that I, as a visitor to the show, was part of the 10 percent. I was reminded of this last year when I came across a photo of an Occupy Wall Street protester holding a poster saying "We are the 99 percent." And I was surprised at how rapidly our sense of which world we belong to had changed—in only four years.

That said, I believe that people who live in stressed conditions can develop the tools they need for transforming their communities and their environment for the better. By doing so, places of crisis become places of hope. For me, the communities I worked with in Caracas and in Amsterdam are just that. They articulate a new culture of living that other communities, in seemingly more stable environments, can learn from in the search for a sustainable existence.

Marina Abramović: Personal Views on the Past, Present, and Future of Performance Art

MARINA ABRAMOVIĆ, *born in 1946 in Belgrade, Yugoslavia, is one of the seminal artists of our time. Since the beginning of her career during the early 1970s when she attended the Academy of Fine Arts in Belgrade, Abramović has pioneered the use of performance as a visual art form. The body has always been both her subject and medium. Exploring the physical and mental limits of her work, she has withstood pain, exhaustion, and danger in the quest for emotional and spiritual transformation. Abramović's concern is with creating works that ritualize the simple actions of everyday life like lying, sitting, dreaming, and thinking—in effect, the manifestation of a unique mental state.*

The people the same age as I am, they stopped performing in the 1970s, for many different reasons. One reason is economics. You could not live just doing performances. The second is because it is too demanding. You have to always be involved. You can't just pick the painting to go to the exhibition, you are the painting. So, you have to send yourself. You have to become a gypsy moving from space to space. I've developed an entire system, titled In-between, which I think is an incredibly important space. I live constantly in this in-between space. This is when you leave one situation and you are intransit to go to another situation. You are away from your habits, you are away from the things you do normally, you are away from your friends. And this is the moment when you are in a bus station, in a train station, in an airport, when you are most open to destiny. This is when you are actually the most alert—where things are happening. So I start living in that kind of space. I believe that performance for me is the only way that I can work as an artist. That is my medium. I can't do anything else.

Performance art has been—for such a long time—an alternative form of art. I was fed up with this. Alternative forms of art were also video and photography, which have stopped being alternative and have become really the mainstream art—but not performance. So you always get these little invitations that say, "oh, we are doing an opening at the museum, can you do a little performance?" With everyone standing around, everyone looking at you, and you are performing. Performance art is serious business and cannot be treated in this manner. It took me many years of working to create situations where performance could become mainstream art—to get into this category.

SYNTHESIS

The beginning of the twentieth century promised a paradigm shift in human life and community as industry and innovation in engineering and science brought about great of technological change. These changes promised to undermine the social stratification in a new age of Modernity. For architects, this future would be manifested in the transformation of our homes and cities.

If there is a paradigm shift in how we think, and with how we design, there must also be a theory or a course of evaluation in which to gauge its consequence.

As architecture incorporates emerging media and technologies, new design processes and new conditions of inhabitation are produced. With the current rate of circuit speed and capacity, and electromechanical components now available—where formerly access was only available to industry and institutions—electronics and mechanisms can be made and quickly tested as never before. The implications of this prototyping require a measured and structured historiography to temper the exuberance that comes with only fascination for the medium.

COFLEXIONS *A responsive inflatable attempts to create a system that investigates the relationship between the individual and collective. We will achieve this through the creation of an inflatable with a mirrored skin which exists within a greater, controlled environment. The "smart" skin of the inflatable is designed to receive haptic input in the form of flexure and pressure, creating a dynamic interplay between the individual within the inflatable and those without. While the individual within the inflatable is impaired from point of view, his senses are amplified as the group affects his environment through haptic actions. The surface of the inflatable is the membrane through which inputs are received and processed. It is a reactive surface that produces a specific interiority for the individual and at the same time impacts the greater environment of the collective.*

MECHATRONIC SPACE

Mariana Ibañez and Simon Kim, Spring 2012

As responsive technologies become easily accessible to architects and designers, they provide greater opportunity for users to have agency over their spatial environment. By embedding actuators into the fabric of our architecture, it begins to have the ability to regulate form as a direct output from users. This enables architects and designers to reconsider the way in which space can adapt in real time using intelligent technologies to enhance user desires.

COFLEXIONS *A responsive inflatable is an attempt to understand how this connection between user and architecture can occur by embedding sensors into the skin of the inflatable. Since an inflatable relies on the malleability of its surface, flex sensors are a way to amplify this affirmation by allowing the inflatable skin to comply to its user's desires. As the outside group manipulates the inflatable skin, sensors detect the distortion and immediately respond by redefining the form and affecting the interior environment.*

ALL IMAGES BRANDON CUFFY, JUDY FULTON, STACY MORTON

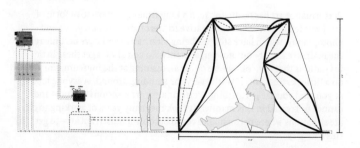

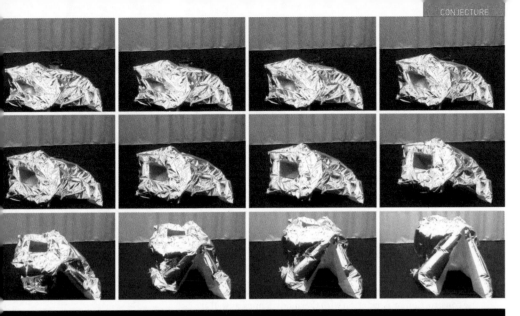

The studio consolidated an advanced understanding of high-rise construction in association with thermodynamics, as well as experimented with various somatic aspects of human behavior.

The studio developed a spatial grammar and syntax associated with thermodynamics, through the definition of an operative topology, experimentation with energy-balanced open and closed systems, the analysis of significant case studies, and a proposal for a vertical campus in two climatic and economically differentiated locations.

The initial identification of spatial and aggregational principles defined the methodological and instrumental base for the subsequent design of mixed vertical entities, developed in two different sets of site-specific conditions. The objective of the studio was to test the methodology in real scenarios in technical and cultural terms.

THERMODYNAMIC SOMATISMS

VERTICALSCAPES II
Urban Planning and Design Option Studio, Spring 2012
Iñaki Ábalos

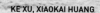

KE XU, XIAOKAI HUANG

SYNTHESIS

DATABASE *Students were provid[ed] with the following databases to in[itiate] research:*

1. Thermodynamic definition of programs:
-The interval of time over twenty-f[our] hours (when the program is active)
-Heating/cooling demands (heat absorption/emission) in two differ[ent] climates (winter and summer)
-General data and diagrams that r[elate] time/watts in summer and winter w[ill] be provided, as well as a color-code[d] template for everyone.

2. A booklet with examples of optimized minimum units, taking into special consideration the energy transmission by convection[,] conduction, and radiation.

3. Information about the two clim[ate] conditions: Givoni Diagram, Com[pass] Rose, Solar Chart. Other example[s] of diagrams: Givoni Diagram (196[9]), Givoni.Milne (1981), UCLA (199[9]).

4. Chart with architectural design strategies according to its climatic condition (passive measures, M.Wieser chart).

01 *Optimization of heat transmiss[ion] Radiation*

02 *Optimization of heat transmiss[ion] Conduction*

03 *Optimization of heat transmiss[ion] Convection*

04 *Wind convection: pressure and velocity*

ALL IMAGES
CHENXING LI, WEILUN XU

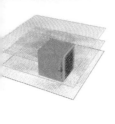
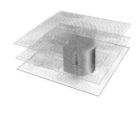
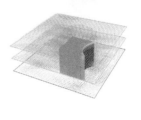

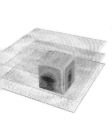
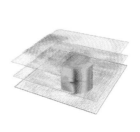

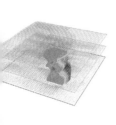
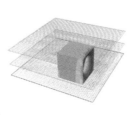
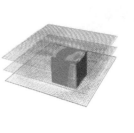

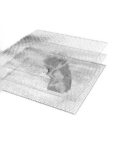
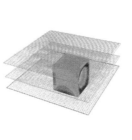
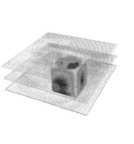

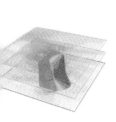
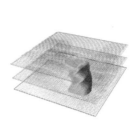
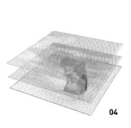

SYNTHESIS

04

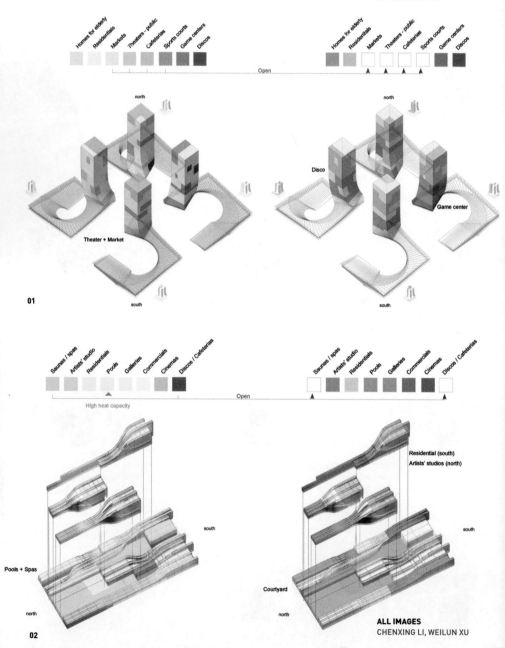

01 *Barcelona: seasonal programming (left: winter, right: summer)*

02 *Barcelona: seasonal facades (left: summer, right: winter)*

03 *Madrid: seasonal programming (left: winter, right: summer)*

04 *Madrid: overview*

ALL IMAGES
CHENXING LI, WEILUN XU

sun protection keeps building
from being over heated

open the sun protection
warm up the interior

get the air go up
and go into the building

open the glass wall dissipation

seal the glass wall
to contain heat inside
the building

03

04

SYNTHESIS

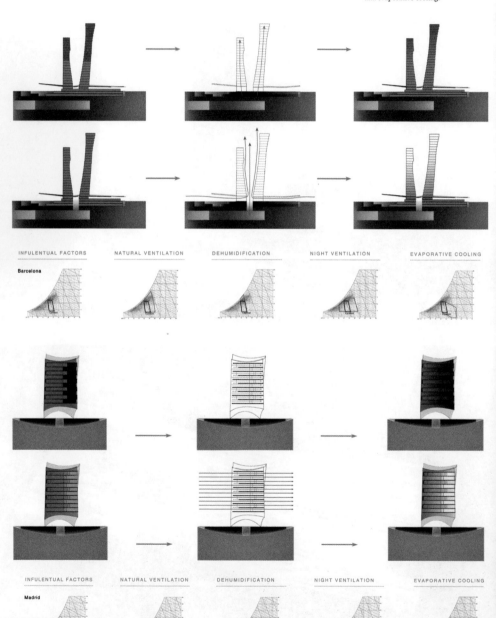

THERMODYNAMIC PERFORMANCE
The diagrams depict the thermodynamic conditions during winter and summer in both Barcelona (left page) and Madrid (right page) in relationship to the proposal. Various factors were considered during design, including natural ventilation, dehumidification, night ventilation, and evaporative cooling.

INFULENTUAL FACTORS   NATURAL VENTILATION   DEHUMIDIFICATION   NIGHT VENTILATION   EVAPORATIVE COOLING

Barcelona

INFULENTUAL FACTORS   NATURAL VENTILATION   DEHUMIDIFICATION   NIGHT VENTILATION   EVAPORATIVE COOLING

Madrid

ALL IMAGES
CHENCHEN HU, SHUANG BAO

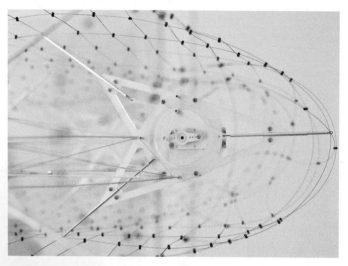

WEATHER VISUALIZATION *The nuances of weather's continuously shifting states are largely oversimplified as the information is transmitted into our daily experience. Our various home and mobile devices most likely distill a forecast into static representations, such as numeric values or simple infographics. There is a deep discrepancy between the flatness of the visualizations we are accustomed to and the rich mixture of tactility and perceptibility of our immediate physical experience. Point Cloud emerged as a sculptural form defined by a thin wire mesh, driven asynchronously by eight individual servos controlled via Arduino. As the whiteness of the hanging structure begins to disappear into the background, the viewer is treated to a constantly morphing swarm of black points dancing through midair.*

Point Cloud attempts to reimagine our daily interaction with weather data. Weather has always had a unique place in our lives, because it has a multiplicity that encompasses both the concrete and the indeterminate. It is the intangible context within which we build our lives and our cities, but it is also the physical element against which we create protective shelter. Most of the time it is an invisible network that we can see but are not aware of; yet it can manifest in a spectacle or disaster, come forward and activate our senses, make us forget our rationality in delight or fear. With modern scientific and technological developments, we can now deploy sophisticated monitoring devices to document and observe weather. Despite these advances, our analysis and understanding of meteorology is still largely approximate, and in many cases, inaccurate. Weather continues to surprise us and elude our best attempts to predict, control, and harness the various elements.

PROJECT AMBITIONS First and foremost it sought to meditate on the transmutation of digital data back into analog movement. In the prototype, the speed, smoothness, and direction of rotation were modulated to interpret a live feed of weather data. Instead of displaying static values of temperature, humidity, or precipitation, Point Cloud performed the data, dynamically shifting between stability and turbulence, expansion and contraction. It reintroduced weather conditions as a permanently variable state, and created a visceral experience in our interactions with weather.

POINT CLOUD

Independent Study Advisor: Eric Höweler   *James Leng*

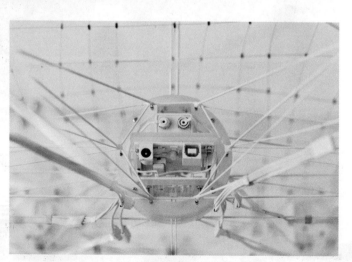

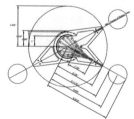

MODULE *Modular dimensions of system within Point Cloud*

ALL IMAGES JAMES LENG

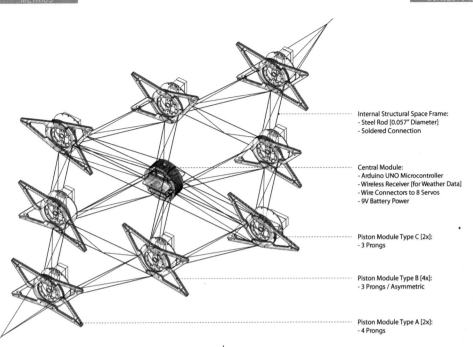

Internal Structural Space Frame:
- Steel Rod [0.057" Diameter]
- Soldered Connection

Central Module:
- Arduino UNO Microcontroller
- Wireless Receiver [for Weather Data]
- Wire Connectors to 8 Servos
- 9V Battery Power

Piston Module Type C [2x]:
- 3 Prongs

Piston Module Type B [4x]:
- 3 Prongs / Asymmetric

Piston Module Type A [2x]:
- 4 Prongs

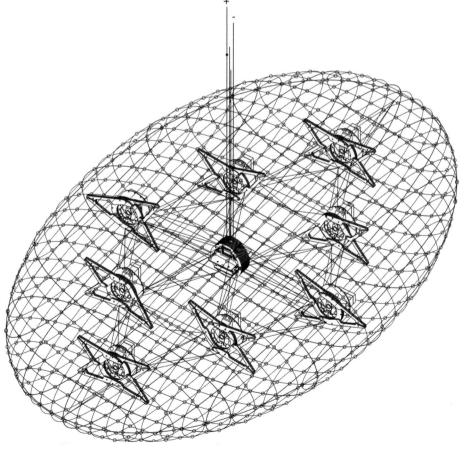

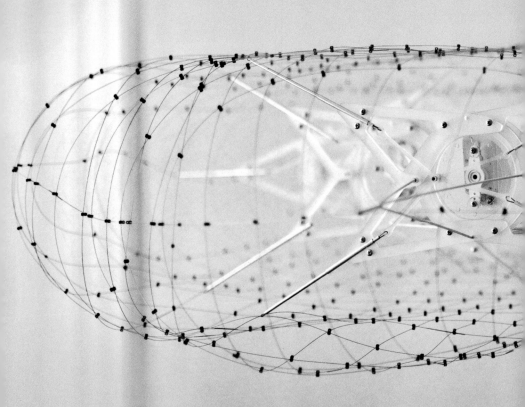

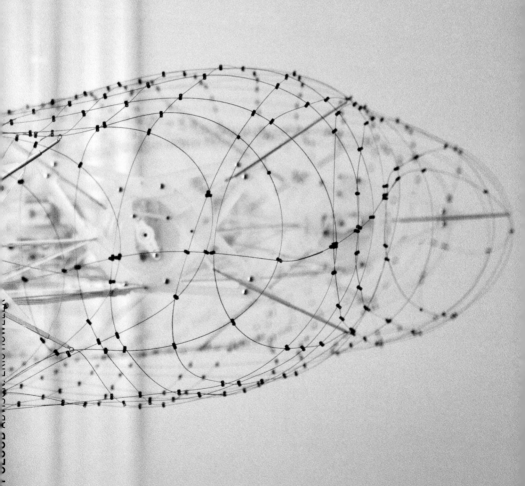

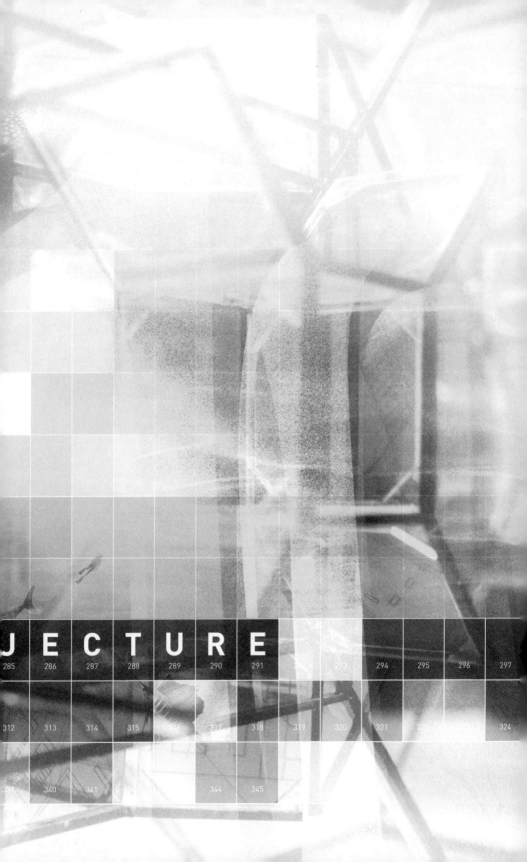

JECTURE

CONJECTURE

CONJECTURE produces speculations and experimentation that perhaps have no preceding domains, or cut across the accepted norms of existing ones. At the School, this is found in an environment that encourages students and researchers to assume risk, coupled with a design sensibility to suspend premature judgment that may curtail innovation.

The work that takes on conjecture does not rely on totalizing answers but sustains open questions. These questions can be the subject matter of design and its precedents—its types and typologies—and it can be about the forms of representation themselves.

The projects included in this section explore the opportunity to investigate and perhaps extend the known boundaries of the design disciplines. The innovations that come out of this investigation may represent incremental steps from existing work or may establish novel means to produce or to inhabit. All of them then come under scrutiny, with the understanding that new formats of intellectual inquiry may be required, or that some challenging ideas are left open for future development.

Situated between 59th Street and 110th Street, in the heart of New York City, Central Park is the prototype vision of the metropolitan park as "green machine." Described by Rem Koolhaas in *Delirious New York* as "a taxidermic preservation of nature that exhibits forever the drama of culture outdistancing nature — a synthetic Arcadian carpet, grafted onto a grid,"it is now time to reconsider the validity of the park's original intent. The Central Park Revisited studio acted as a laboratory to develop new ideas, programs, and concepts for the park in the twenty-first century. After a forensic autopsy, students were invited to produce a new manifesto for Central Park and select a site-specific project to act as a catalyst for change. The intent of the studio was to reactivate the park as a cultural manifestation and provide an expression of emerging concepts of nature.

CENTRAL PARK REVISITED

Landscape Architecture Option Studio, Fall 2012
Eelco Hooftman and Bridget Baines

YUNSUN SHIM

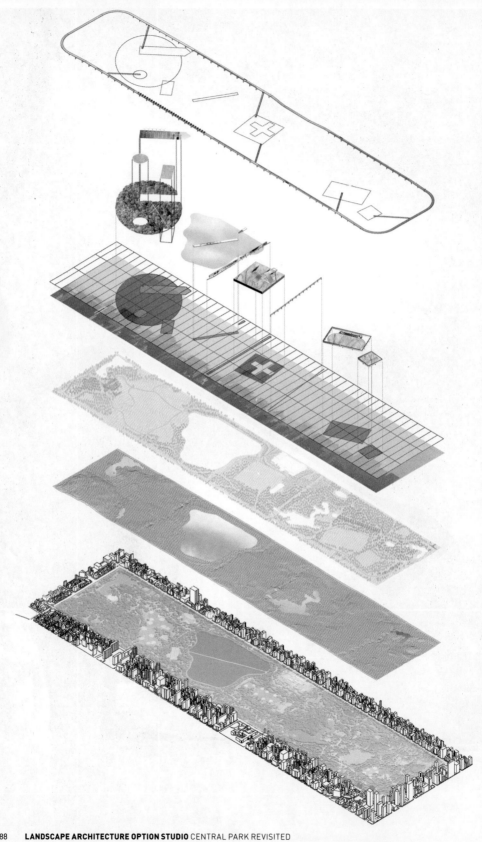

IVAN CHTCHEGLOV *"All cities are geographical; you cannot take three steps without encountering ghosts bearing all the prestige of their legend. We move within a closed landscape whose landmarks constantly draw us toward the past. Certain shifting angles, certain receding perspectives, allow us to glimpse original conceptions of space, but this vision remains fragmentary."*

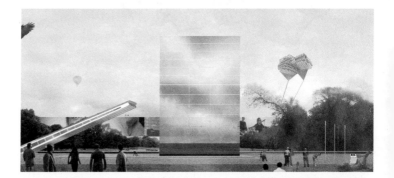

ALL IMAGES
MARIANO GOMEZ LUQUE

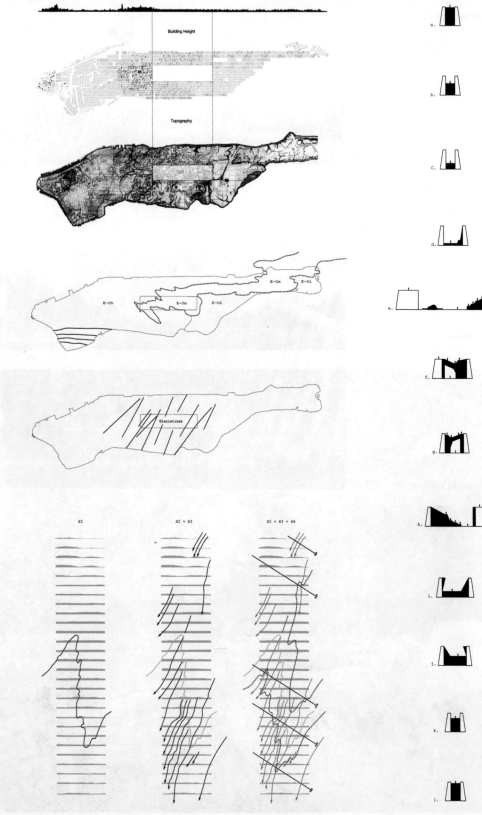

The path follows the Cameron's Line, which is an Ordovician suture fault in the northeast United States which formed as part of the continental collision known as the Taconic orogeny around 450 million years ago. The manifestation of the immense along the geological line reveals the old geological history of Manhattan as well as introduces new spatial program, recreating the meaning of sublime and picturesque in an urban context. Central Park will be revisited by "walking on the bedrock."

ALL IMAGES YUNSUN SHIM

CONJECTURE

By 2015, it is predicted that the quality of information on the internet will reach a zettabyte — more information than produced in the history of recorded civilization. Citizens will be surrounded by a data atmosphere manipulated and spun with mobile devices. Yet, the divide between those with and without technological augmentation is in flux. The more important divide for architects, however, is the one of meaningful information in the digital miasma, and the relevance of embedded information within the physical objects of our buildings and cities. We are in real danger of witnessing the loss of the role of design to others. More non-architect specialists and experts are now designing— interfaces, tools, devices, vehicles, buildings. What was once the province of a designer, from branding to product to production plant, is now a reduced package.

But what more can a well-crafted building—beyond light and mass—hold as information within its collection of elements and occupancy? What can be added to increase its information by several orders of magnitude that still retains meaningful knowledge and experience beyond the digital noise of most internet media?

We addressed this challenge through inversion, a function whereby elements in a closed field became transposed. We strove to make Architecture Machines again.

The familiar program of live/work was reconsidered within a research and design environment and was reformulated by each part and their relationships—a Domicile/Office/Lab. Research and Development is the industry's heroic laboratory outside of academic institutions where invention need not immediately answer to the market. Research and Development of Architecture Machines is similarly not bound only by program and form but can be linked with other speculations—garments, robotics, material, interaction, reconfiguration.

ARCHITECTURE 2.0
PENDING FUTURES
Architecture Option Studio, Spring 2012
Mariana Ibañez and Simon Kim

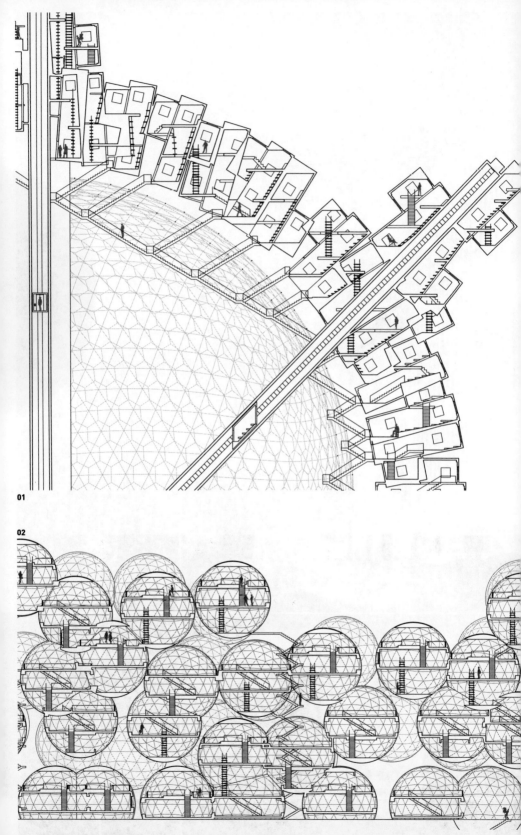

01

02

PROJECT REFERENCES

These two projects shown below (Habitat '67 by Moshe Safdie and Buckminster Fuller's Dome) served as the base model to which the functions (right) were applied.

01 *Section showing Habitat '67 units aggregated around one Buckminster Fuller dome*

02 *Section showing Buckminster Fuller dome aggregation around Habitat '67*

03 *Diagrams showing various scenarios for logic handling*

01-03 FREDERICK WES THOMAS

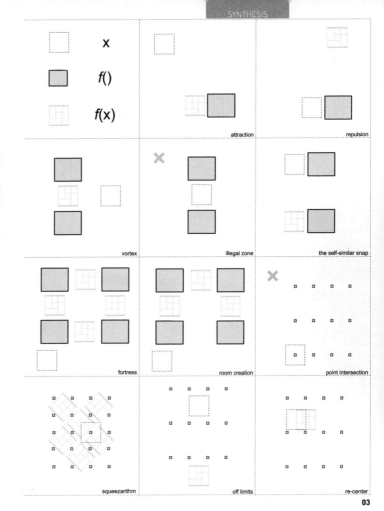

x   *f*()

f(x)

attraction   repulsion

vortex   illegal zone   the self-similar snap

fortress   room creation   point intersection

squeezarithm   off limits   re-center

03

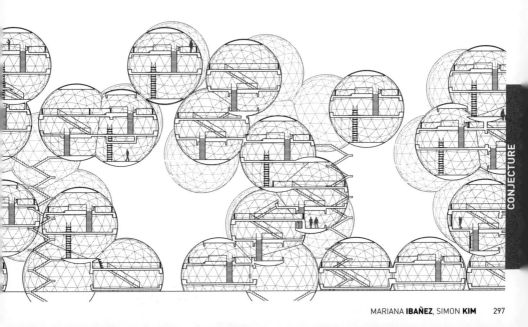

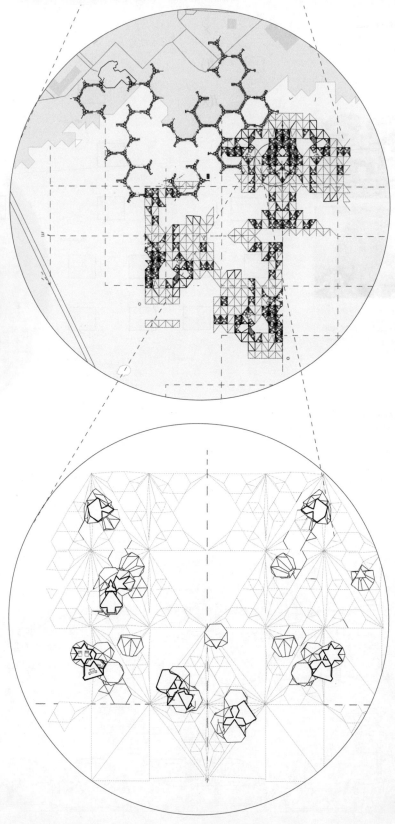

Truncated
Tetrahedron

Vertices: 12
Edges: 18
Faces: 4 triangles
4 hexagons

Tetrahedron

Vertices: 4
Edges: 6
Faces: 4
Dihedral Angle: 70.53

AGGREGATIVE UNITS

Fl 6 : Scenario 1 Fl 6 : Scenario 2 Fl 6 : Scenario 3

Fl 5: Scenario 1 Fl 5: Scenario 2 Fl 5: Scenario 3

Fl 3: Scenario 1 Fl 3: Scenario 2 Fl 3: Scenario 3

Model of Crawlers

ALL IMAGES LAUREN KIM

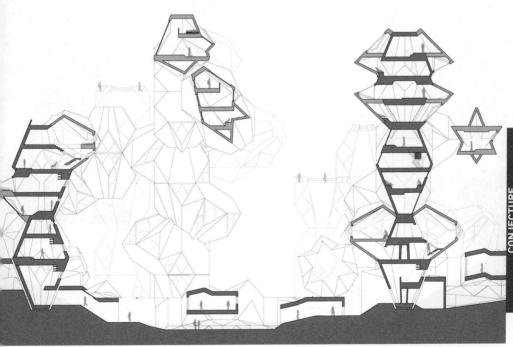

CONJECTURE

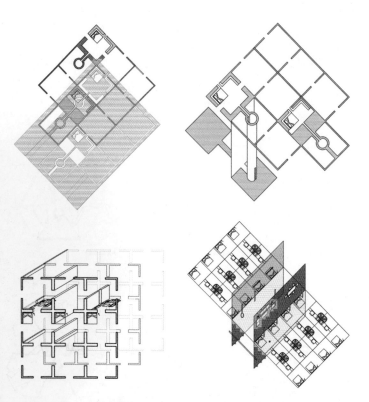

ALL IMAGES HAL WUERTZ

SITE

Our siting of the Research and Development Domicile/Office/Lab is in the old industry of Montreal, with its layering and its past promises of future life (Expo '67 and the 1976 Olympics). Bounded by the Vieux Port, its adjacent Quais, and the Cité-du-Havre, the project recognizes its industrial past and the harbingers from the Expo.

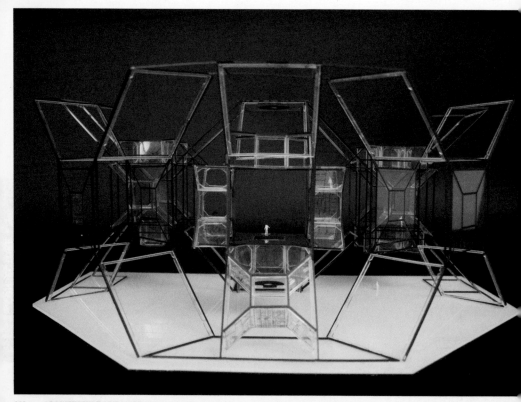

PROGRAM

The new programmatic conditions will interrupt established patterns of usage, or rhythms of civic life; patterns that may become transformed with an anomaly not easily discarded due to its intrinsic links within the design discipline. Connecting known architectural types and devices for the unknown or the recently lost through inversion will create a methodology to engage a synthetic world of nature and machine and architecture, where the machine is not reduced to a technological filter or interface. The inversion of nature and the uncanny agent-to-agent relationship is then highly compelling as Machine will come to mean an autonomous agent, a player or author—as the architect is also a player or author—engaged in conversation.

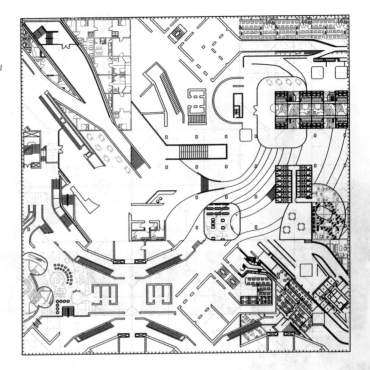

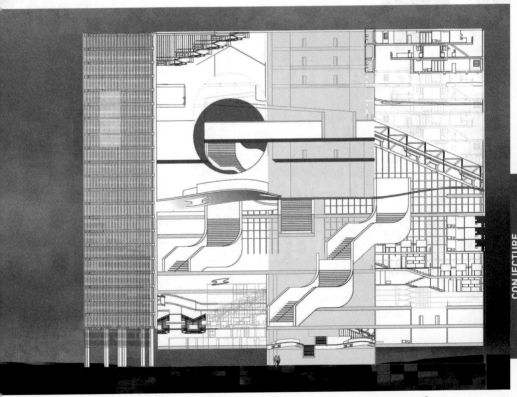

CONJECTURE

"I think doing something that is playful is always of great help when developing ideas."

MOHSEN MOSTAFAVI: We are at the beginning of the 75th anniversary celebrations of the GSD, and who better to start us off than Anne Tyng? Anne has always been a pioneer. She was here at Harvard in the early 1940s. She was part of the first class at the GSD that admitted women. Needless to say, there weren't a lot of women at that time doing the kinds of things that she was doing.

It is very interesting to see how, early on, she was drawn to issues related to geometry, the role of the body, consciousness, the subconscious—she was thinking about architecture in a very holistic fashion. The way in which geometry, specifically, and triangulation in geometry was developed was something unique, and was of course explored in her own work and also in the work that she did together with Louis Kahn in subsequent years.

When Kahn received the adulation and recognition that he deserved, it was also due to a lot of things that they had done together. I hope that tonight is at least a tiny moment of true recognition for all the things that she has achieved.

ANNE TYNG: There has been a tremendous amount of change in architecture, which should be very exciting and challenging right now. Geometry is available for any kind of building at any scale. It is just three-dimensional form. But I think there is—as you relate the infinitely small to the very large—that potential of achieving some kind of breakthrough in terms of expressing a more active architecture. I think we may be getting to a point where the shift in architecture may be toward animate form, as opposed to inanimate.

The geometries that Louis had me doing were done in an office that was very informal. If there were no projects to do, you could come in and produce your own work. The Bucks County School was the first attempt to use geometry in layers. The three pieces come to a tetrahedral column where it travels to the ground to a point. These layers diminish as they travel from the center of the overall triangle where each of them would form one building made of three classrooms. It grows its own support out of the same geometry. Usually these geometries would have been considered separate.

The City Tower Project was never a job. It was just something that I think needed to be explored. In it, each level is identical, but they rotate in plan as you go up, so it seems to animate the structure to some degree. It appears as though the building might be in motion, if you have enough imagination for that.

CITY TOWER
An unbuilt project by Louis Kahn and Anne Tyng for a futurist City Tower in the late 1950s, later exhibited at MoMA.

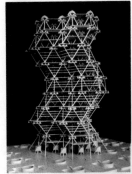

IMAGES
Top: Anne Tyng sitting in her furniture design in 1945.
Left: Mohsen Mostafavi and Anne Tyng in conversation at the GSD.

ANNE TYNG (1920–2011)
Known for her collaboration with Louis Kahn, Anne Tyng was an architect and professor. She studied under Walter Gropius and Marcel Breuer as one of the first women to graduate from the GSD ('44). Furthermore, she was the only woman to undertake the architecture licensing exam in 1949. She earned her Ph.D. and taught at the University of Pennsylvania.

ANNE TYNG IN CONVERSATION WITH MOHSEN MOSTAFAVI
Beaux Arts Complexity to Bauhaus Simplicity

The Museum of Modern Art was going to have an exhibit, and I never got an invitation to the opening, so I asked around, and the secretary said, "Well maybe you'd better speak to Louis [Kahn]." He actually took my name off. So I went into his office and I said, "Wouldn't it be better if you called them, than if I called them?" and he did and straightened it out. But I think we are getting past that. I think we are in a phase where the feminine principle is more dominant, and there are many women doing things that they never did before, or given positions that they were never given before. They had earned it before, but never got it.

CONJECTURE

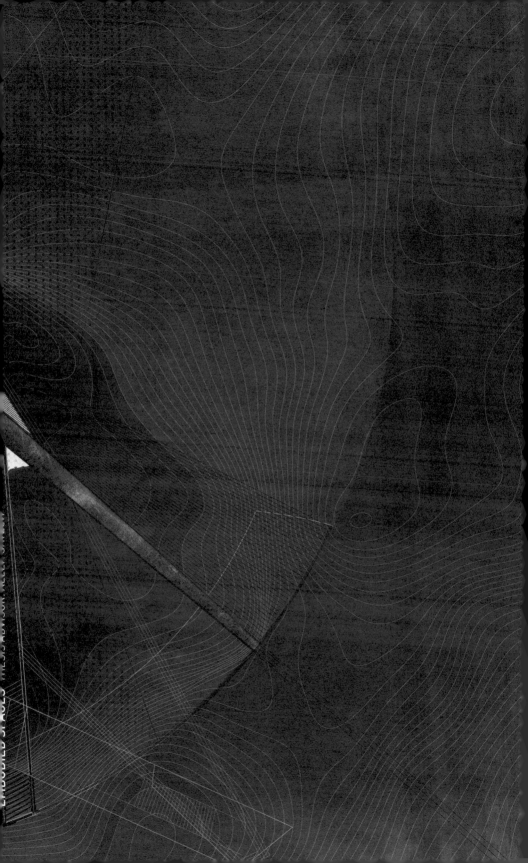

This project involved designing a group of five rooms, one of which seemed to be hidden from the other four. The program required providing a means of access to the hidden room, while controlling the degree to which the room became vulnerable to a disclosure. On the one hand, the hypothesis of concealment required consideration of the relationship between the visual, experiential, and conceptual bases of architecture.

On the other hand, it elicited the interpretation of a specific idea and the processes by which it was given three-dimensional form and represented in architectural drawings, namely the plan.

The project focused on four distinct concepts of the hidden in architecture: visual concealment, that is, optical obfuscation; hermetically sealed space that was, to a certain degree, physically inaccessible from without; spaces presumed absent, according to conventions or expectations that would exclude them, but which were in fact present; and the hierarchical representation of objects, spaces, or relationships.

The hidden involves the art of camouflage and surreptitious passage. To effectively conceal a room, knowledge of the entire building is likely to be deferred for both the inhabitants of the building and for the audiences of its representations, that is, the architectural critics. In other words, it was unlikely that there would be a single plan or section that is capable of describing the entirety of the proposal. The dualities of the project (open/closed, public/private, exposed/hidden, transparent/opaque) were played out as a result of the hybrid nature of the project and its programmatic coupling. Duality and tension were subtly manifested or negated—masked not only through modes of spatial communication but also by the apparent exterior massing and fenestration.

HIDDEN ROOM

Preston Scott Cohen (Coordinator), Yael Erel,
Mariana Ibañez, Kiel Moe, Ingeborg Rocker,
Elizabeth Whittaker, Cameron Wu
Architecture Core I Studio, Fall 2012

01

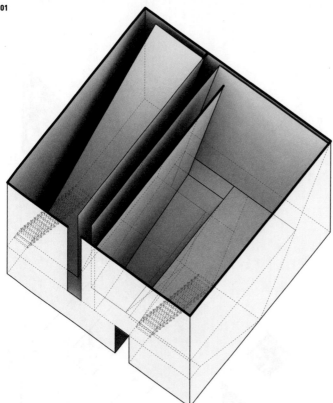

THE PIN-WHEEL *in which the hidden room is embedded in the center.*

THE PLAN OF GROWTH *and change in which the four principal rooms transform progressively and exclude sufficient space to contain the Hidden Room .*

THE LABYRINTH, *which establishes a coherent and complex system of communication between the rooms such that one of the five is logically excluded.*

THE UNFOLDING *of the room in actual time involving a mechanism or constructed affect that allows it to dynamically emerge from an otherwise static context.*

POCHE *the construction of dense versus open space and the establishment of hierarchy.*

01 WESLEY HO

02 BEN BURDICK

03 CHEN LU

04 DUNCAN SCOVIL

02

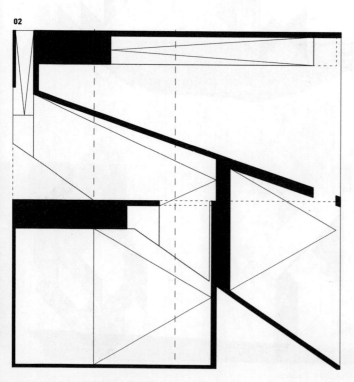

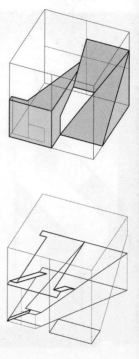

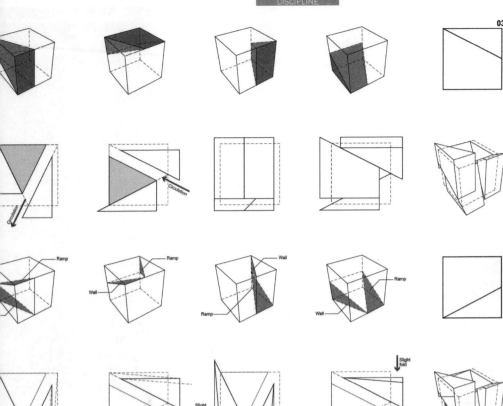

03

04

YAEL **EREL**, MARIANA **IBAÑEZ**, KIEL **MOE**, ELIZABETH **WHITTAKER**, CAMERON **WU**, PRESTON SCOTT **COHEN**   309

short the'sis, n [AS. scort, scort, short; O.H.G. scurz, short, cut off; ON. skort, short piece of clothing. L thesis; Gr. thesis, a position, from lithenai, to put, place.]

1. a kind of thesis varying widely in length but shorter than the dissertation; characteristically it develops a single central theme or impression and is limited in scope and number of characters.

rad'i-căl, a [Fr., from LL. radicalis, having roots, from L. radix, root.]

1. of or from the root or roots; going to the center, foundation, or source of something; fundamental; basic; as, a radical principle.

2. (a) favoring fundamental or extreme change; specifically, favoring such change of the social structure.

This studio explored design possibilities for radical interior spaces—radical interiors that are at once from the root and favoring extreme change. Each student's project began in the space of personal memory, which became a kinetic site with unquestionable origins—a site whose spatial character and embodied meaning was fundamentally transformed through the individualized lens of a personal thesis and provocative program.

WHITE NAPKINS
A COLLECTION OF SHORT THESES ON RADICAL INTERIORS

Architecture Option Studio, Spring 2012
Mack Scogin

ALBERTO MONTESINOS

CONJECTURE

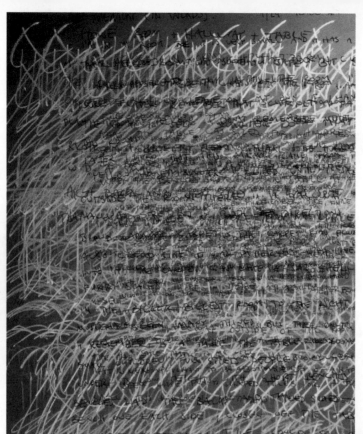

THESIS

Content's displacement by Formation privileges the active invention of reality.

PROGRAM

A place that affords the transformation of context and production as a result of an individual's design, free of institutional control. It is a place to exercise this transformation as a critique and creative act in the contemporary American art world. That is to say, it is the training ground for the demolition of the art institution and its influence.

TRIPTYCH

A non-narrative object whose rhythms and relationships are themselves a subject of the work. The construction existing between the panels is ultimately the prime subject of the work.

ALL IMAGES TAYLOR DOVER

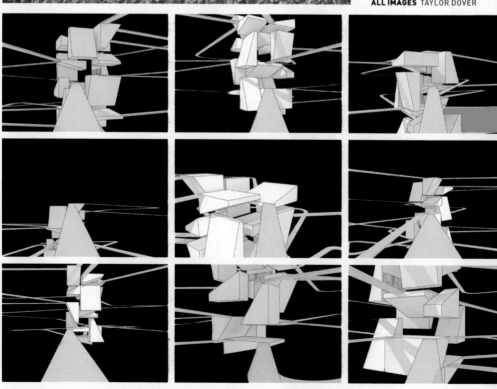

Level 6

Level 4

Level 5

Level 3

Level 7

Level 2

Level 1

Level 9

CONJECTURE

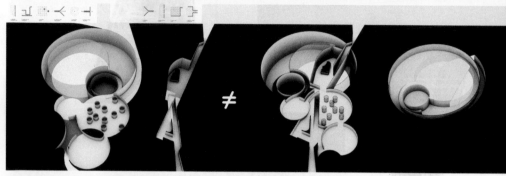

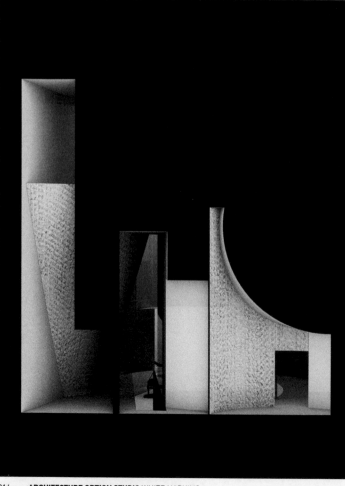

SHORT THESIS

The exercise was a dressing room for Lady Gaga and Jerry Lee Lewis. The idea was to define two spatial sequences informed by each artist's transition between reality and the stage. Then, since the artists had to share one space, those sequences would be juxtaposed, intertwined, like in a Twister game. At least in theory, the result would be more than the simple addition of two different sequences —a variation of the usual methods of juxtaposition. Architecture has the ability to articulate uncompromising differences, consolidating incongruous juxtapositions.

ALL IMAGES
ALBERTO MONTESINOS

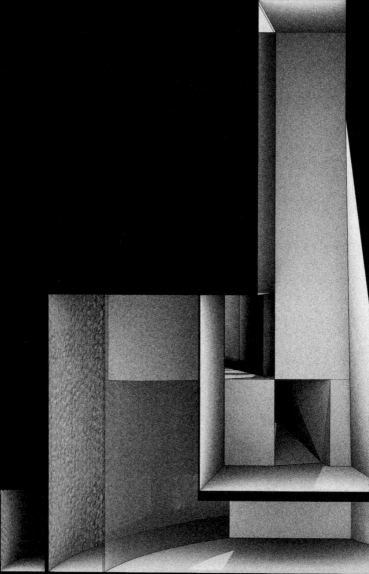

We are at a moment where information and communication are instantaneous. What was once a fantastical impossibility (i.e., the constant flow of data and the immediate quashing of questioning and wonderment) is now the accepted and expected norm. The "unknown" is no longer; the spectacular is harder to come by and acts less and less as a source of amazement. This thesis was a reaction to the question of how architecture can respond to the shifting nature of our built environment and the unknowns of the natural world while still adhering to the faith and curiosity we have in both.

This project explored the liminality of a place, the simultaneous growth and decay of nature and architecture, inhabitation, and time-based phenomena. The installation of the Reservatory Observatory atop the Venice Salt Dome in the Mississippi Delta would allow for a desired and spe-

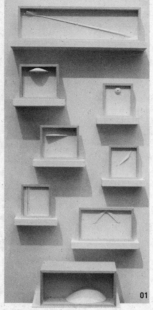

01

cific pilgrimage on a site of undesired uncertainty. The journey of arriving at the observatory is a 22 kilometer walk into the depths of the earth and bedrock, mingling with allowed atmospheric and shifting conditions of air, water, sound, earth, and light.

02

01 *1:100 Sectional models with protruding atmospheric "rooms"*

02 *Found objects (below the earth); geological foundations, prehistoric salt phenomena, and dramatic shifts over time*

THE RESERVATORY OBSERVATORY
Faith in Nature, Time, and Architecture

Thesis Advisor: Mack Scogin

Natalya Egon

Terminating at the Observatory and literally stepping out on the top of the Venice Salt Dome—a geologic object hidden and physically untouched—the viewer is faced with the full responsibility of observing time, the earth, and the unknown. People have been defined by origins; entire cultures were built off of inexplicable phenomena. In turn, innate curiosity of these constructed cultures unearthed the truth behind phenomena, and the extent to which we have discovered and quantified the spectacle is the base of the modern persistence of society, cities, and architecture.

RESEARCH BASED ON *T.S. Eliot, Four Quartets*

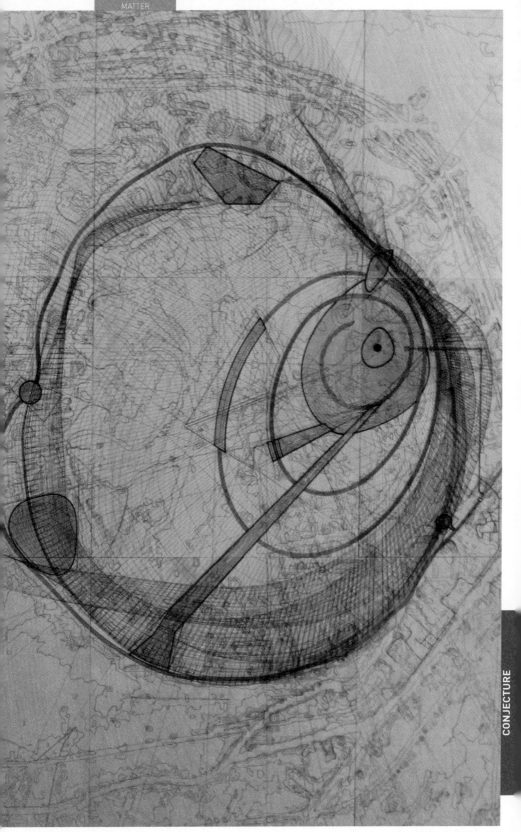

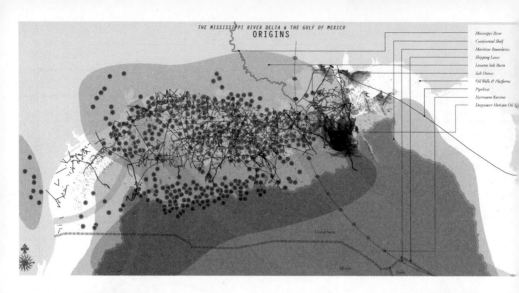

THE MISSISSIPPI RIVER DELTA & THE GULF OF MEXICO
ORIGINS

Mississippi River
Continental Shelf
Maritime Boundaries
Shipping Lanes
Louann Salt Basin
Salt Domes
Oil Wells & Platforms
Pipelines
Hurricane Katrina
Deepwater Horizon Oil Spill

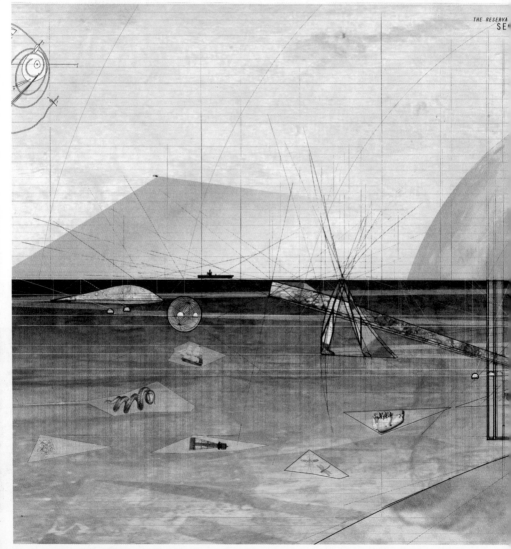

THE RESERVA
SE

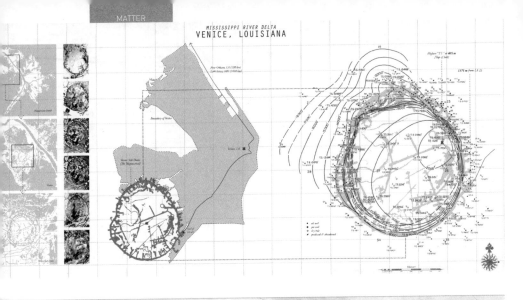

MISSISSIPPI RIVER DELTA
VENICE, LOUISIANA

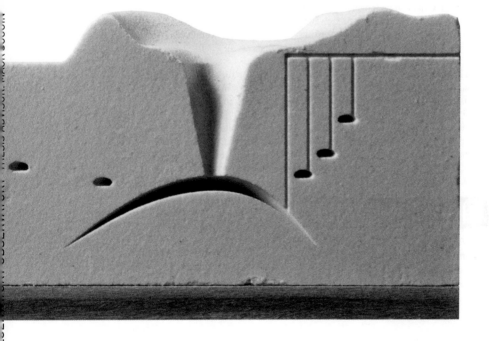

How can we define the concept of monumentality in contemporary architectural terms? To what power structure(s) does the condition of monumentality belong? How does programmatic content align with symbolic intent? Can the social context of monumental architecture shift, or does it in some way remain aligned to its historical origins? We have intentionally juxtaposed the concept of lightness and monumentality to put the terms into question. We all understand the preconception that the monumental connotes a certain gravity, a staid materiality, a relationship to particular ideologies. However, lightness conveys different conceptual streams that are central to contemporary urbanism—lightness of ecological and energy footprints, lightness of tectonics that can no longer rely upon unlimited human labor, lightness of compressed construction timeframes required by modern urbanization, lightness of rapidly shifting cultural and social contexts, and of course the phenomenological qualities of light itself.

The Korean context is an especially significant backdrop for addressing these current issues. With the creation (and recreation) of new urban areas, architecture has become not only the vehicle through which these territories compete for a sense of international identity; it has also become the catalyst through which the concept of the public domain is defined within a climate of dynamic social change. A site in Seoul, pivotal to its future development and identity, acted as the framework through which each studio member questioned, invented, and defined the terms of "Light Monumentality."

LIGHT MONUMENTALITY

Architecture Option Studio, Fall 2011
John Hong and Jinhee Park

GLEN SANTAYANA

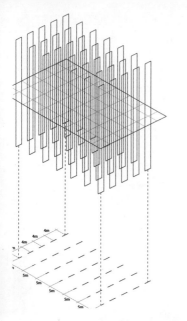 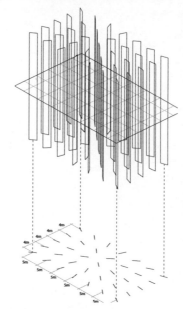

VANISHING THRESHOLDS

The train station is made up of 2,549 0.5m x 2 m rectangular columns arrayed in a gridded pattern with each column specifically rotated to accommodate a programmatic, visual, or circulatory necessity. The rotation of each column creates a sense of enclosure by limiting and opening views, through which space becomes inherent in its macro organization. The columns and program respond to each other in the sense that the rotation of the column determines program and vice-versa.

ALL IMAGES GLEN SANTAYANA

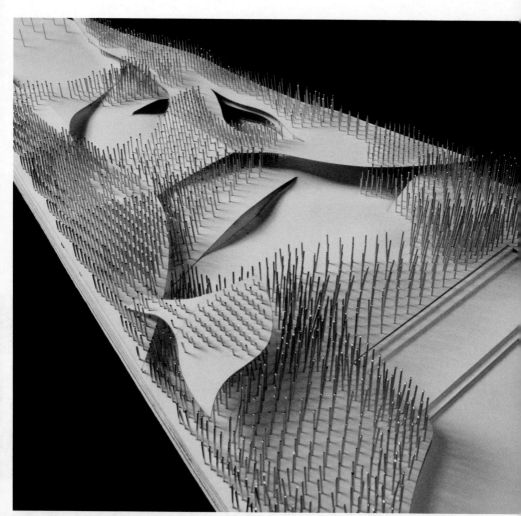

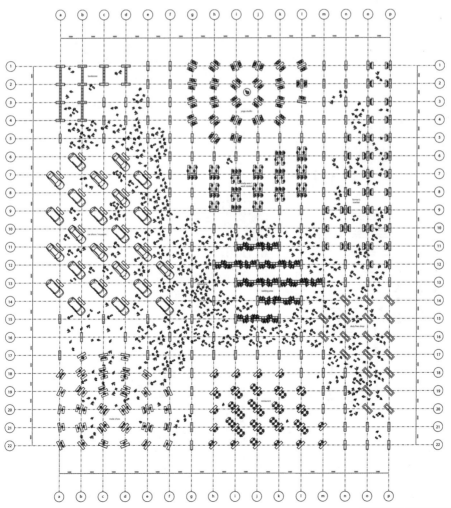

CONJECTURE

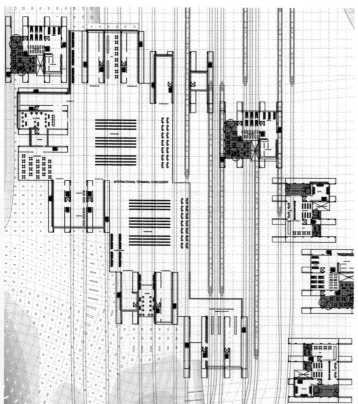

EMERGENT MONUMENTALITY

The monument refers to the object. The monumental refers to the subjective experience of that object. Monumentality emerges through this notion of the subjective, allowing for the experience of a singular, overwhelming, and all-encompassing moment. A moment of presence. Light monumentality creates the opportunity to mask this presence, revealing it within a transformative, subjective experience. By manipulating the notion of an emergent figure within a field, this project attempted to mask the presence of a large-void public space within a field of program. The project, then, sought to evoke light monumentality by the emergence of a presence through the animation of an absence.

ALL IMAGES FAREEZ GIGA

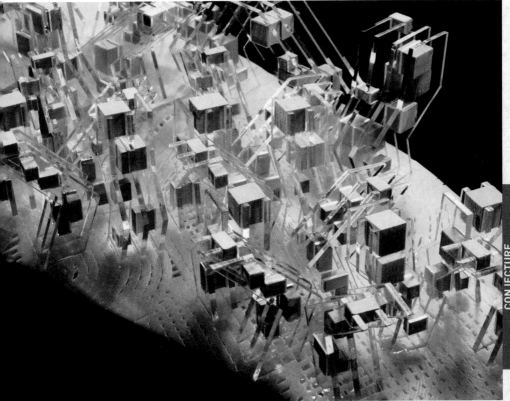

JOHN **HONG**, JINHEE **PARK**   329

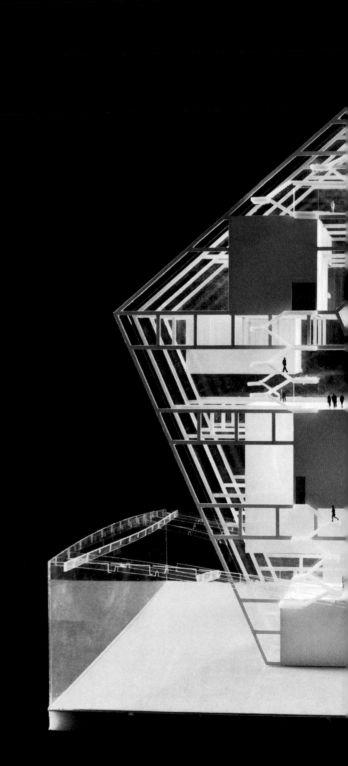

Skyscraper collectives, tower agglomerations, mixed-use developments, high-rise housing developments, marinas and luxury condominiums; airport hubs, office enclaves, industrial parks, hotel complexes, conference centers, financial centers; satellite cities, theme parks, thematic cities, branded cities, central districts, gated communities—what is the potential latent in extraordinarily large urban typologies currently restricted by the typological tradition of urbanism and by the predominant segregation of disciplinary domains? What is the reach of such potential to think aggressively about the contemporary metropolitan condition and to imagine future developmental models?

Following on the previous experiences of Neonatures (2010) and Overurbanism (2011), The Generic Sublime Series undertook the project of radical typological integration in a single, post-urban cybernetic universe; large-scale machines that nurture unpredictable organizations through paradoxical programmatic coexistence, radical systemic inclusiveness and through the mutual intensification between architectural events. The Generic Sublime incarnates the ultimate post-systemic megalomania—a territorial organization made of a multitude of systems interacting in the synthetic field of competition and synergy of a single building. The Generic Sublime upgrades the potentials of urbanism after the skyscraper, exploring the self-surmounting form that urbanism takes when assembling anti-urbanisms in a larger collective. Instantaneous cities made of "cities within the city."

Through proliferation, The Generic Sublime magnifies the idea of the skyscraper as a condition that surpasses urbanity by multiplying its logics. The skyscraper is a laboratory for new modes of collective life and explodes the texture of normal life to offer an aggressive alternative reality that discredits all naturalistic urban realities. The Generic Sublime is a laboratory of the potentials of these alternative realities when operating in a condition of multiplicity. Its discipline assumes the challenge of assembling contemporary, large-scale types—whole worlds of their own—in a manifold singularity, a monstrous globalized commune. If the skyscraper incarnates the metropolitan unconscious in a self-evident medium for the thoughtless constitution of theories, architectural theory without representation breeds the fantastic and the irrational out of the pragmatic and the rational. The Generic Sublime consciously develops meta-rational models to amass sublime potentials out of generic types, architectural power beyond ideology.

NEOKOOLHISMS

Urban Planning and Design Option Studio, Spring 2012
Ciro Najle

NICHOLAS POTTS,
PETER ZUROWESTE

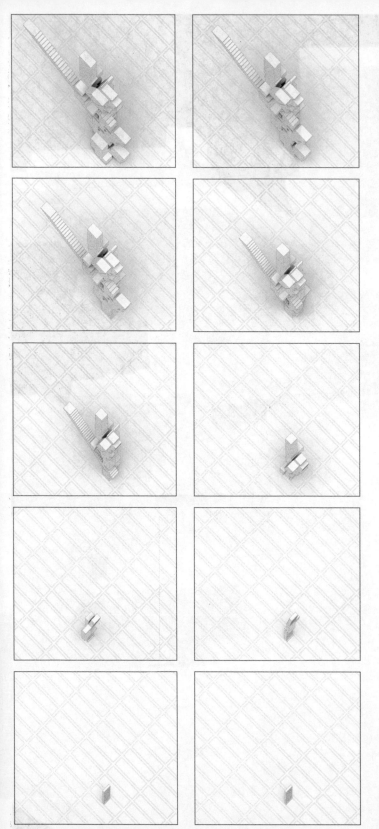

GENERIC MODEL VARIABILITY

LEFT *Degrees of proliferation responding to an increase in floor area ratio, plot coverage, and plot area values.*

RIGHT *Iterations of generic models responding to an increase in floor area ratio, plot coverage, and plot area.*

ALL IMAGES
NICHOLAS POTTS
PETER ZUROWESTE

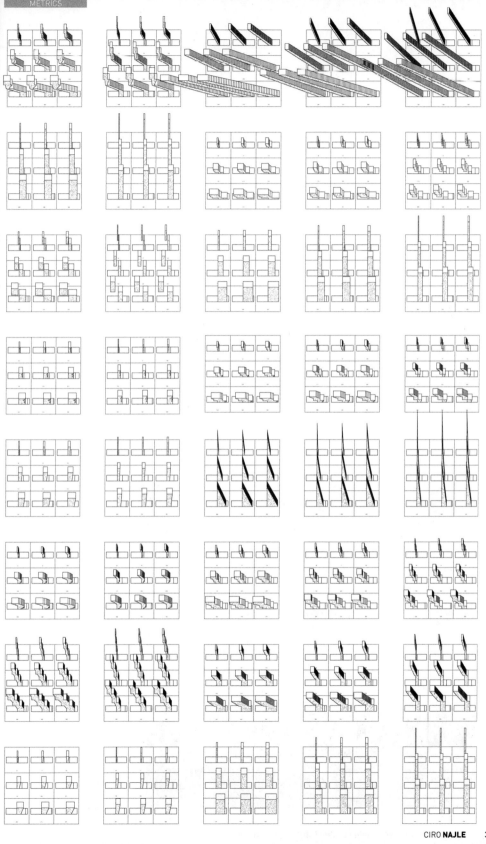

0.000	0.0625	0.1875	0.2500
0.3125	0.3750	0.4375	0.5000
0.5625	0.6250	0.6875	0.7500
0.8125	0.8750	0.9375	1.0000

DIAGRAMS *Catalog of possible variations*

IMAGES *Collages depicting variations implemented within various sites*

ALL IMAGES
MARIANO GOMEZ-LUQUE
PABLO BARRIA-URENDA

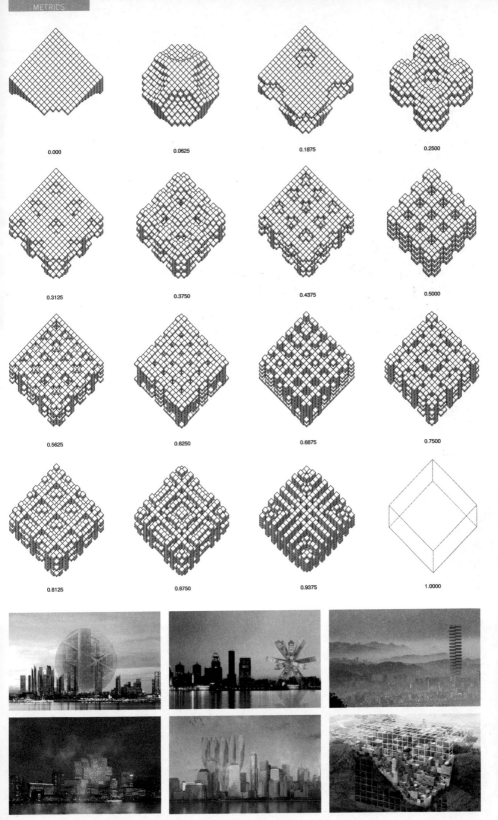

0.000

0.0625

0.1875

0.2500

0.3125

0.3750

0.4375

0.5000

0.5625

0.6250

0.6875

0.7500

0.8125

0.8750

0.9375

1.0000

CONJECTURE

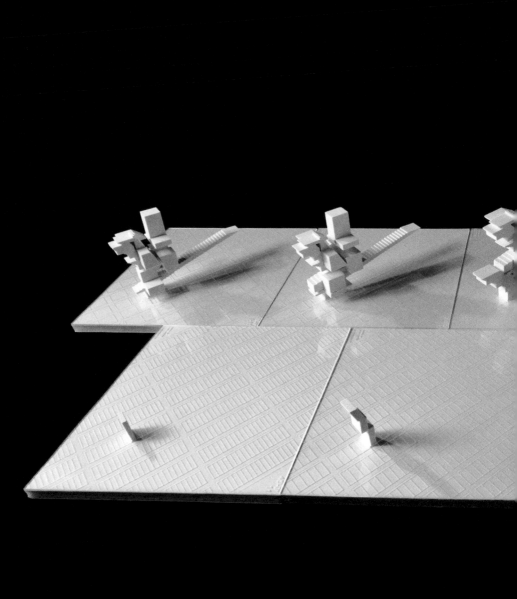

This project begins with a work of literature by Jorge Luis Borges entitled "The Library of Babel." While the thesis itself doesn't pursue the library typology, out of an obsession with this fictional Universe, a series of architectural questions are explored through the production of an analogous architectural Universe.

The beauty of Borges' library lies in its poetic occupation of polar extremes and ability for its components to be both completely real—even banal—and its consequences extreme. The world of Borges' fiction is one in which the reader is caught in a perpetual moment of hesitation between the real and the imaginary, and as a result allows a condition of the fantastic to permeate.

This thesis leverages the fantastic (as defined in literary theory by Todorov) and the genre of metafiction in order to maintain an ambiguous relationship to the known and the real, producing a machine framework in architecture that can straddle the territory between the visionary and the banal, ultimately instrumentalizing fiction, the imaginary and the playful for the grounded and the real.

The program is a menagerie for animals. While the zoological garden is generally oriented around education, research, and conservation, with

PATRICIA WAUGH *"Metafiction is a term given to fictional writing that self-consciously and systematically draws attention to its status as an artifact in order to pose questions about the relationship between fiction and reality...such writings not only examine the fundamental structures of narrative fiction, they also explore the fictional quality of the world outside the literary fictional text...they explore a theory of fiction through the practice of writing fiction."*

BELOW *Roof and ground model of vaulted system*

01

BABEL

Thesis Advisor: Mariana Ibañez   Jeremy Jih

animal exhibits arranged ecologically or zoogeographically, the menagerie is often characterized by structured, taxonomic arrangements that, rather than seeking to reproduce a naturalistic environment, explicate an order of things. The requirements of each animal are singular and specific enough to be distilled into a series of specific sectional and planimetric moves, while allowing for a degree of abstraction in their satisfaction. In this way, variation of the structural and geometric system is able to produce typological differentiation, pairing geometry and typology.

01 *Ground plan*

02 *Underwater render*

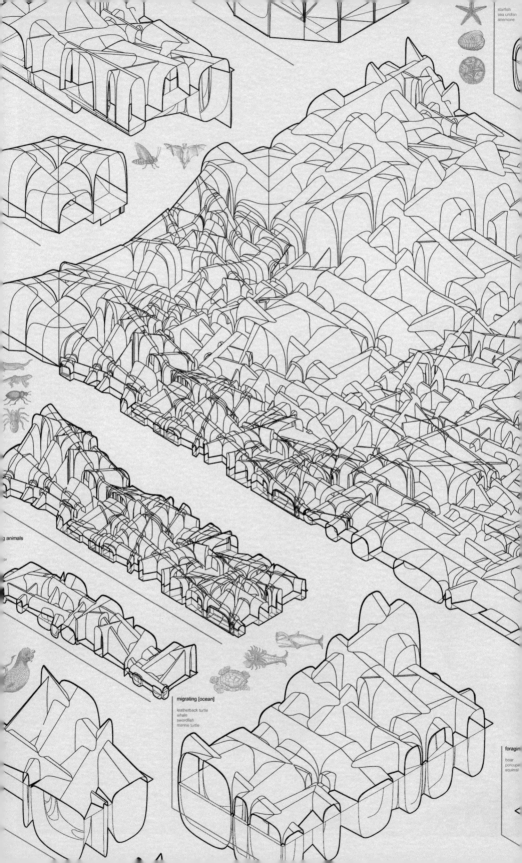

starfish
sea urchin
anemone

animals

migrating [ocean]

leatherback turtle
whale
swordfish
marine turtle

foragin

boar
porcupine
squirrel

climbing

baboon
ape

socializing

getulian dog
hound

swimming [saltwater]

lump fish
sea horse
lamprey
flying fish
ray

grazing
[small]

bactrian camel
antelope
saiga
goat
mouflon
unicorn
ox
llama

stalking
[varied terrain]

wild cat
polecat
lynx

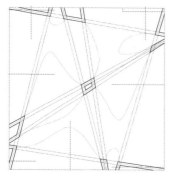

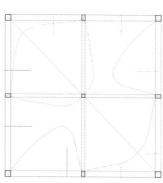

**FRANCIS BACON
GESTA GRAYORUM (1594)**

"Every true gentleman must have...a garden to be built about with rooms to stable in all rare beasts and to cage in all rare birds; with two lakes adjoining, the one of fresh water the other of salt, for like variety of fishes. And so you may have in small compass a model of the universal nature made private."

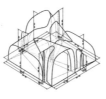

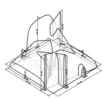

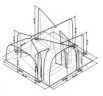

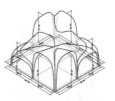

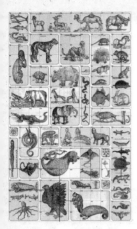

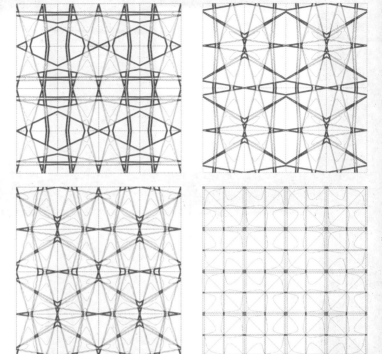

ABOVE *Regarded as the first modern zoological work, Conrad Gesner's seventeenth-century tome,* Historia Animalium, *was the first comprehensive attempt to document all known animals within a single work. Gesner treats familiar animals in unfamiliar ways, indeed doubting the existence of many animals from the New World quite familiar to us, and presents fictional animals in familiar ways.*

CONJECTURE

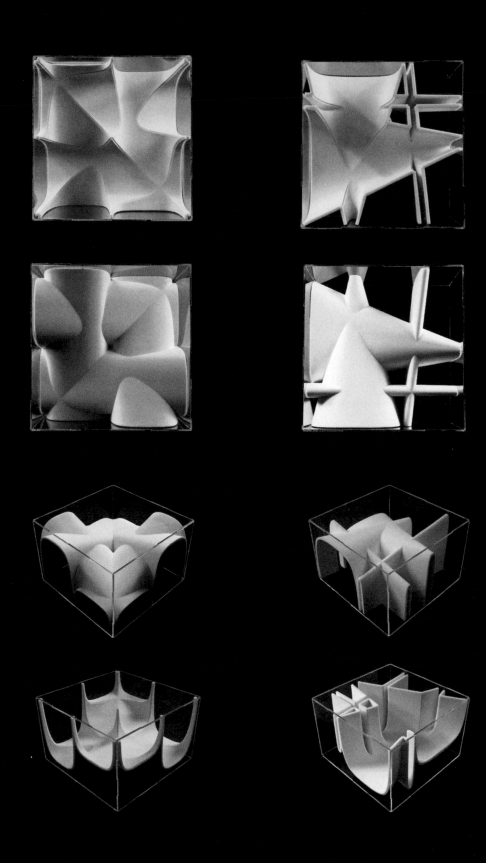

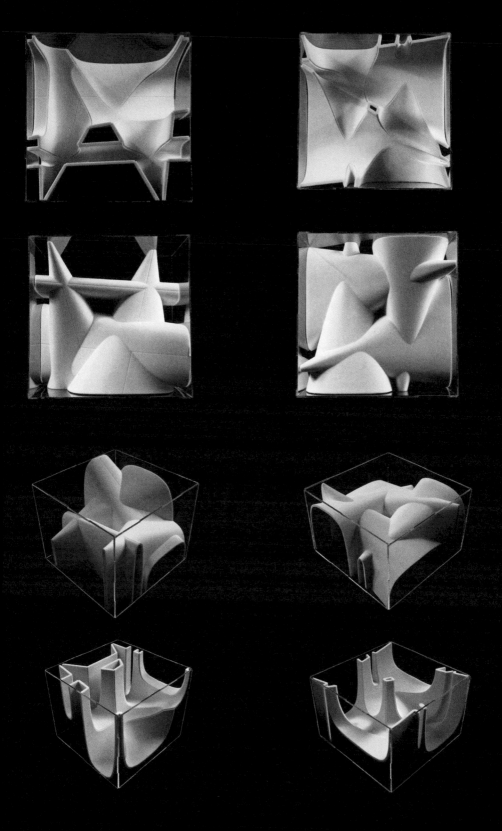

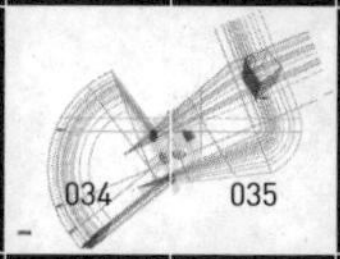

034 035

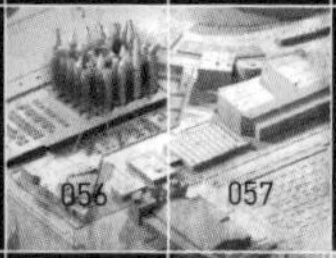

056 057

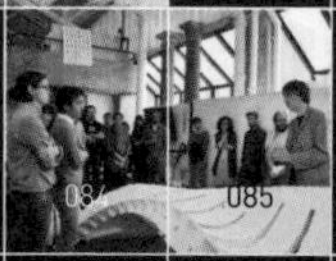

085

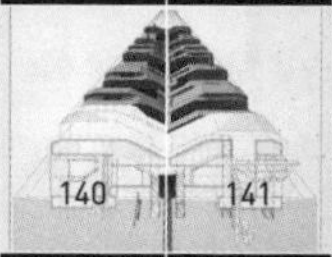

140 141

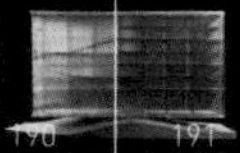

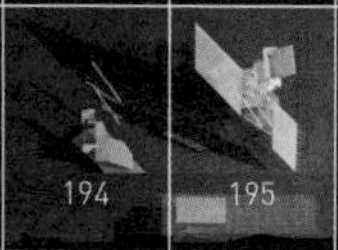

194 195

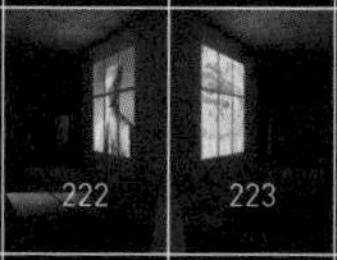

222 223

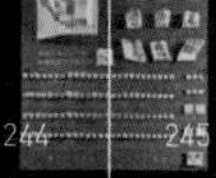

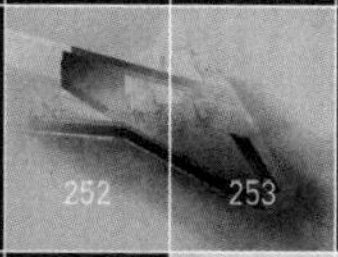

252 253

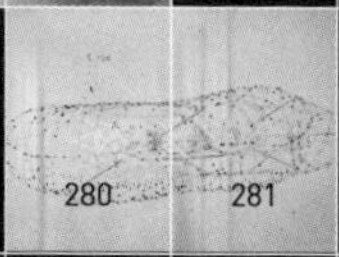

280 281

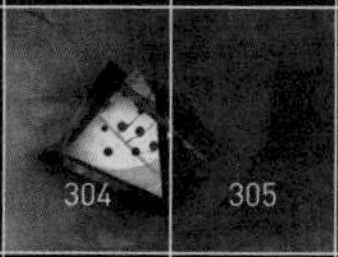

304 305

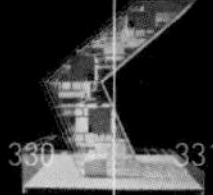

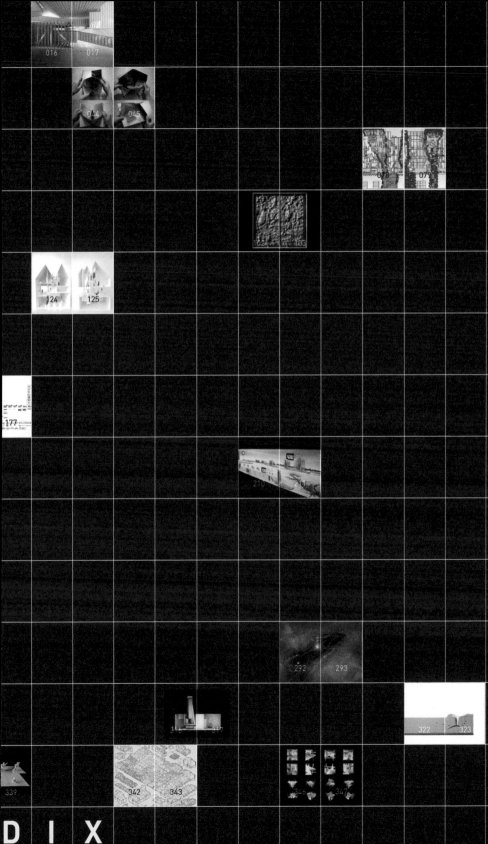

016 017

044 045

078 079

102 103

124 125

177

210 211

292 293

316 317

322 323

339 342 343 346 347

D I X

HARVARD DESIGN MAGAZINE

Harvard University
Graduate School of Design
Architecture
Landscape architecture
Urban planning and design
2011

34

ARCHITECTURES OF LATIN AMERICA

HARVARD DESIGN MAGAZINE 34
Harvard University Graduate School of Design

This issue is dedicated to presenting and analyzing the work and surrounding cultural/political issues of the architectures of Latin America judged to be of most merit and interest by a faculty committee at the Harvard Graduate School of Design. Their sense was that much of this work had not yet received sufficient attention and acclaim. They were adamant that the issue not imply that Latin American architecture and culture were one kind of thing: in fact, a goal of the magazine is to dispel stereotypes and conventional opinion, to seek diversity.

EXTREMEURBANISM

Reimagining Mumbai's Back Bay
a Studio Research Report of the Harvard Graduate School of Design

Edited by Rahul Mehrotra and Victor Muñoz Sanz

EDITED BY RAHUL MEHROTRA AND VICTOR MUÑOZ SANZ
Harvard University Graduate School of Design

The Back Bay of Mumbai—underdeveloped, sandwiched between high rise office and residential blocks, historic buildings, a fishing village, and slums—is perhaps the most contested locality in the city. It's a place where the "Static City" or planned urban environment collides with the "Kinetic City" of temporary materials and constant flux. Beginning in 2011, Rahul Mehrotra, Chair of the department of Urban Planning and Design at the Graduate School of Design, has undertaken the challenge of honoring this duality while imagining a future for the site in the Extreme Urbanism Studio.

SARAH WHITING, JORGE SILVETTI, LUCIA ALLAIS, JAMES CARPENTER, MARK LINDER
Harvard University Graduate School of Design

Two essays and a set of original diagrams consider the parameters of the "something beyond" in James Carpenter's projects. Mark Linder offers a view of Carpenter's work, placing his early career as an installation artist and experimental filmmaker in the context of contemporary art practices. Architectural critic Sarah Whiting examines the sensibilities and constituencies that emerge from Carpenter's practice.

DESERT TOURISM
TRACING THE FRAGILE EDGES OF DEVELOPMENT

VIRGINIE PICON-LEFEBVRE WITH AZIZA CHAOUNI
Harvard University Graduate School of Design

Deserts are becoming increasingly popular tourist destinations. However, the growth of this tourism niche raises particular challenges, jeopardizing their fragile ecosystems and straining scarce resources. Paradoxically, the increasing popularity of desert tourism is undermining the very essence of the allure of these places.

DAN WEISMAN, ANYA BRICKMAN RAREDON, CHRISTIAN WERTHMANN, PHIL THOMPSON
Harvard University Graduate School of Design

Sustainable long-term urbanization of the Port au Prince Region cannot be created solely through the construction of houses. This document proposes an exemplary development process for a community at Zoranje in the Plain Cul de Sac—a process that defines sustainable land-use and building construction through the integral creation of jobs, infrastructures, and social services. Through analysis and recommendations at four scales from the Port au Prince region down to a neighborhood, this proposal seeks to create long-term replicable solutions that may be employed across the Port au Prince region and throughout Haiti.

TONI GRIFFIN, ANDREA HANSEN
Harvard University Graduate School of Design

It goes without saying that unprecedented levels of vacancy have taken a social and economic toll on Detroit. However, the proliferation of unmaintained vacant lots also has potentially transformative repercussions in the form of emergent landscapes that can be collectively harnessed into a new open-space system to improve Detroit's ecological performance and its communities. But first, a change in perception and ideals is required. We must let go of what we know as Detroit, unthink it, interrupt it, and reexamine the pieces to build a better, healthier city.

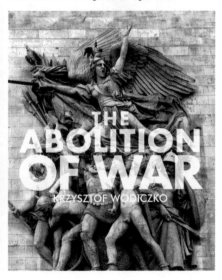

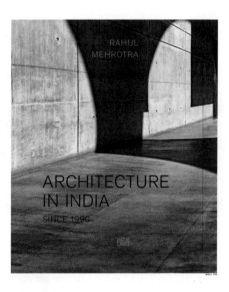

KRZYSZTOF WODICZKO
Black Dog Publishing

The Abolition of War *explores the ideas that inform Krzysztof Wodiczko's project, The World Institute for the Abolition of War, and is a manifesto for the dismantling of what Wodiczko sees as the ubiquitous, unconscious, and ultimately perilous "Culture of War," which is embedded within and constantly reaffirmed by our monuments and our historical narratives.*

RAHUL MEHROTRA
Hatje Cantz

Pluralism, fusion, and hybridity are the dominant traits of cultural change in twenty-first-century India. The resultant architecture reflects this fabric of one of the world's largest and most populous nation states. Architect, educator, and author, Rahul Mehrotra has been at the forefront of the Indian contemporary architecture scene for more than two decades, and Architecture in India *is his unique take on the topic.*

HARVARD UNIVERSITY GRADUATE SCHOOL OF DESIGN

Drew Gilpin Faust, President of Harvard University
Mohsen Mostafavi, Dean of the Graduate School of Design
Martin Bechthold, Co-Director of the Master in Design Studies Programs
Anita Berrizbeitia, Director of the Master in Landscape Architecture Degree Program
Preston Scott Cohen, Chair of the Department of Architecture
Felipe Correa, Director of the Master of Architecture in Urban Design and the Master of Landscape Architecture in Urban Design Programs
K. Michael Hays, Associate Dean for Academic Affairs and Co-Director of Doctoral Programs
Jerold Kayden, Director of the Master in Urban Planning Degree Program
Sanford Kwinter, Co-Director of the Master in Design Studies Programs
Rahul Mehrotra, Chair of the Department of Urban Planning and Design
Mark Mulligan, Director of the Master in Architecture Programs
Antoine Picon, Co-Director of Doctoral Programs
Charles Waldheim, Chair of the Department of Landscape Architecture

FACULTY OF DESIGN

Iñaki Ábalos, Design Critic in Architecture and Urban Planning and Design
Alan Altshuler, Ruth and Frank Stanton Professor in Urban Policy and Planning and Harvard University Distinguished Service Professor
John Beardsley, Adjunct Professor of Landscape Architecture
Martin Bechthold, Professor of Architectural Technology
Pierre Bélanger, Associate Professor of Landscape Architecture
Anita Berrizbeitia, Professor of Landscape Architecture
Eve Blau, Adjunct Professor of the History of Urban Form
Neil Brenner, Professor of Urban Theory
Joan Busquets, Martin Bucksbaum Professor in Practice of Urban Planning and Design
Preston Scott Cohen, Gerald M. McCue Professor in Architecture and Chair of the Department of Architecture
Felipe Correa, Assistant Professor of Urban Design
Diane Davis, Professor of Urbanism and Development
Peter Del Tredici, Adjunct Associate Professor of Landscape Architecture
Jill Desimini, Assistant Professor of Landscape Architecture
Danielle Etzler, Assistant Professor of Architecture
Susan Fainstein, Professor of Urban Planning
Richard T.T. Forman, Professor of Advanced Environmental Studies in the Field of Landscape Ecology
Jose Gomez-Ibañez, Derek Bok Professor of Urban Planning and Public Policy
Toni Griffin, Adjunct Associate Professor of Urban Planning
K. Michael Hays, Eliot Noyes Professor of Architectural Theory
Gary Hilderbrand, Adjunct Professor of Landscape Architectural History
John Hong, Adjunct Associate Professor of Architecture
Michael Hooper, Assistant Professor of Urban Planning
Eric Höweler, Assistant Professor of Architecture
Jane Hutton, Assistant Professor of Landscape Architecture
Timothy Hyde, Associate Professor of Architecture
Mariana Ibañez, Assistant Professor of Architecture
Jerold Kayden, Frank Backus Williams Professor of Urban Planning and Design
Niall Kirkwood, Professor of Landscape Architecture and Technology
Remment Koolhaas, Professor in Practice of Architecture and Urban Design
Alex Krieger, Professor in Practice of Urban Design
Sanford Kwinter, Professor of Architectural Theory and Criticism
Mark Laird, Adjunct Professor of Landscape Architecture
Andrea Leers, Adjunct Professor of Architecture and Urban Design
George L. Legendre, Adjunct Associate Professor of Architecture
Jonathan Levi, Adjunct Professor of Architecture
Judith Grant Long, Associate Professor of Urban Planning
Rahul Mehrotra, Professor of Urban Design and Planning and Chair of the Department of Urban Planning and Design
Kiel Moe, Assistant Professor of Architectural Technology
Rafael Moneo, Josep Lluís Sert Professor in Architecture
Toshiko Mori, Robert P. Hubbard Professor in the Practice of Architecture
Mohsen Mostafavi, Dean of the Faculty of Design and Alexander and Victoria Wiley Professor of Design
Farshid Moussavi, Professor in Practice of Architecture
Mark Mulligan, Adjunct Associate Professor of Architecture
Erika Naginski, Associate Professor of Architectural History
Richard Peiser, Michael D. Spear Professor of Real Estate Development

FACULTY OF DESIGN, CONTINUED

Antoine Picon, G. Ware Travelstead Professor of the History of Architecture and Technology
Spiro Pollalis, Professor of Design Technology and Management
Chris Reed, Adjunct Associate Professor of Landscape Architecture
Christoph Reinhart, Associate Professor of Architectural Technology
Ingeborg Rocker, Associate Professor of Architecture
Joyce Klein Rosenthal, Assistant Professor of Urban Planning
Peter Rowe, Raymond Garbe Professor of Architecture and Urban Design and Harvard University Distinguished Service Professor
A. Hashim Sarkis, Aga Khan Professor of Landscape Architecture and Urbanism in Muslim Societies
Allen Sayegh, Adjunct Associate Professor of Architectural Technology
Daniel Schodek, Kumagai Professor of Architectural Technology
Matthias Schuler, Adjunct Professor of Environmental Technology
Martha Schwartz, Professor in Practice of Landscape Architecture
Mack Scogin, Kajima Professor in Practice of Architecture
Jorge Silvetti, Nelson Robinson Jr. Professor of Architecture
Christine Smith, Robert C. and Marian K. Weinberg Professor of Architectural History
Carl Steinitz, Professor of Landscape Architecture and Planning
John Stilgoe, Robert and Lois Orchard Professor in the History of Landscape Development
Maryann Thompson, Adjunct Professor of Architecture
Michael Van Valkenburgh, Charles Eliot Professor in Practice of Landscape Architecture
Charles Waldheim, John E. Irving Professor of Landscape Architecture and Chair of the Department of Landscape Architecture
Christian Werthmann, Associate Professor of Landscape Architecture
Krzysztof Wodiczko, Professor in Residence of Art, Design, and the Public Domain
Cameron Wu, Assistant Professor of Architecture

VISITING FACULTY

Steven Apfelbaum, Lecturer in Landscape Architecture
William Apgar, Lecturer in Urban Planning and Design
Benjamin Aranda, Design Critic in Landscape Architecture
Leire Asensio Villoria, Lecturer in Architecture and Landscape Architecture
Bridget Baines, Design Critic in Landscape Architecture
Vincent Bandy, Design Critic in Architecture
David Barron, Honorable William S. Green Professor of Public Law, HLS
Henri Bava, Design Critic in Landscape Architecture
Michael Bell, Visiting Professor in Urban Planning and Design
Eric Belsky, Lecturer in Urban Planning and Design
Silvia Benedito, Lecturer in Landscape Architecture
Adrian Blackwell, Visiting Assistant Professor of Landscape Architecture
Sibel Bozdoğan, Lecturer in Architectural History
Giuliana Bruno, Professor of Visual and Environmental Studies, FAS
Jeffry Burchard, Design Critic in Architecture
Jose Castillo, Design Critic in Urban Planning and Design
Steven Caton, Visiting Professor in Urban Planning and Design
Jana Cephas, Instructor in Urban Planning and Design
Shane Coen, Design Critic in Landscape Architecture
Betsy Colburn, Lecturer in Landscape Architecture
Jürg Conzett, Lecturer in Architecture
Janne Corneil, Design Critic in Urban Planning and Design
Paul Cote, Lecturer in Urban Planning and Design
Pierre de Meuron, Arthur Rotch Design Critic in Architecture
Timothy Dekker, Lecturer in Landscape Architecture
Richard Dimino, Lecturer in Urban Planning and Design
Daniel D'Oca, Design Critic in Urban Planning and Design
Gareth Doherty, Lecturer in Landscape Architecture and Urban Planning and Design
Gabriel Duarte, Design Critic in Urban Planning and Design
Sonja Duempelmann, Visiting Assistant Professor of Landscape Architecture
Farès el-Dahdah, Lecturer in Urban Planning and Design
Rosetta Elkin, Lecturer in Landscape Architecture
Philip Enquist, Design Critic in Urban Planning and Design
Yael Erel, Design Critic in Architecture
Stephen Ervin, Lecturer in Landscape Architecture and Urban Planning and Design
Michael Flynn, Lecturer in Landscape Architecture
Gerald Frug, Affiliated Professor to the Department of Urban Planning and Design; Louis D. Brandeis Professor of Law, HLS

David Gamble, Lecturer in Urban Planning and Design
Ana Gelabert-Sanchez, Design Critic in Urban Planning and Design
Andreas Georgoulias, Lecturer in Architecture
Shauna Gillies-Smith, Lecturer in Landscape Architecture
Jeff Goldenson, Instructor in Architecture
Joana Goncalves, Visiting Professor in Architecture
Gregory Halpern, Lecturer in Landscape Architecture
Steven Handel, Visiting Professor in Landscape Architecture
Andrea Hansen, Daniel Urban Kiley Fellow and Lecturer in Landscape Architecture
Ewa Harabasz, Visiting Assistant Professor in Landscape Architecture
Romy Hecht, Visiting Associate Professor of Landscape Architecture
Roisin Heneghan, Design Critic in Architecture
Jacques Herzog, Arthur Rotch Design Critic in Architecture
Eelco Hooftman, Design Critic in Landscape Architecture
Michel Hossler, Design Critic in Landscape Architecture
Christopher Hoxie, Lecturer in Architecture
John Hunt, Visiting Professor of Landscape Architecture
Florian Idenburg, Design Critic in Architecture
Toyo Ito, Design Critic in Architecture
Michael Jakob, Visiting Professor of Landscape Architecture
Richard Jennings, Lecturer in Architecture
Wes Jones, Design Critic in Architecture
Hanif Kara, Pierce Anderson Lecturer in Creative Engineering
Stephanie Kayden, Visiting Professor in Urban Planning and Design
Brian Kenet, Lecturer in Landscape Architecture
Kathryn Kennen, Instructor in Landscape Architecture
James Khamsi, Design Critic in Architecture
Matthew Kiefer, Lecturer in Urban Planning and Design
Nico Kienzl, Lecturer in Architecture
Simon Kim, Visiting Assistant Professor in Architecture
Eugene Kohn, Lecturer in Architecture
Anne Lacaton, Kenzo Tange Design Critic
Christopher Lee, Design Critic in Architecture
Nina-Marie Lister, Visiting Associate Professor of Landscape Architecture
Karen Lohrmann, Lecturer in Landscape Architecture
Wenyu Lu, Design Critic in Architecture
Peter Lynch, Lecturer in Architecture
Clare Lyster, Visiting Assistant Professor of Landscape Architecture
John Macomber, Senior Lecturer in Real Estate, HBS
Kathryn Madden, Design Critic in Urban Planning and Design
David Mah, Lecturer in Landscape Architecture
Michael Manfredi, Design Critic in Architecture and Urban Planning and Design
Edward Marchant, Lecturer in Urban Planning and Design
Sébastien Marot, Lecturer in Architecture
Wilson Martin, Lecturer in Landscape Architecture
Christopher Matthews, Lecturer in Landscape Architecture
Miho Mazereeuw, Lecturer in Landscape Architecture
Patrick McCafferty, Lecturer in Architecture
Anne McGhee, Lecturer in Landscape Architecture
Panagiotis Michalatos, Lecturer in Architecture
Lars Müller, Lecturer in Architecture
Nashid Nabian, Lecturer in Urban Planning and Design
Ciro Najle, Design Critic in Urban Planning and Design
Paul Nakazawa, Lecturer in Architecture
John Nastasi, Lecturer in Architecture
Yusuke Obuchi, Instructor in Architecture
Ken Tadashi Oshima, Visiting Associate Professor of Architecture
Peter Osler, Visiting Assistant Professor of Landscape Architecture
Erkin Ozay, Lecturer in Urban Planning and Design
John Palfrey, Visiting Henry N. Ess III Professor of Law
Jinhee Park, Design Critic in Architecture
Katharine Parsons, Lecturer in Landscape Architecture
Shih-Fu Peng, Design Critic in Architecture
Emmanuel Petit, Visiting Associate Professor of Architecture

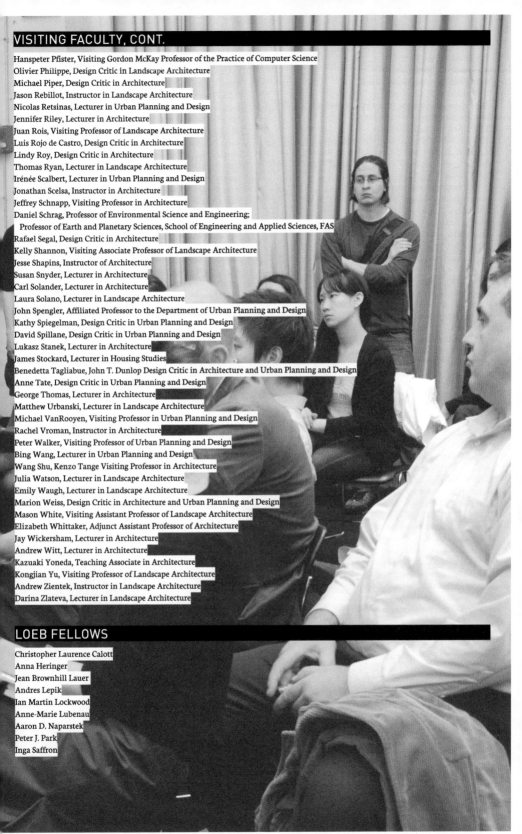

VISITING FACULTY, CONT.

Hanspeter Pfister, Visiting Gordon McKay Professor of the Practice of Computer Science
Olivier Philippe, Design Critic in Landscape Architecture
Michael Piper, Design Critic in Architecture
Jason Rebillot, Instructor in Landscape Architecture
Nicolas Retsinas, Lecturer in Urban Planning and Design
Jennifer Riley, Lecturer in Architecture
Juan Rois, Visiting Professor of Landscape Architecture
Luis Rojo de Castro, Design Critic in Architecture
Lindy Roy, Design Critic in Architecture
Thomas Ryan, Lecturer in Landscape Architecture
Irénée Scalbert, Lecturer in Urban Planning and Design
Jonathan Scelsa, Instructor in Architecture
Jeffrey Schnapp, Visiting Professor in Architecture
Daniel Schrag, Professor of Environmental Science and Engineering;
  Professor of Earth and Planetary Sciences, School of Engineering and Applied Sciences, FAS
Rafael Segal, Design Critic in Architecture
Kelly Shannon, Visiting Associate Professor of Landscape Architecture
Jesse Shapins, Instructor of Architecture
Susan Snyder, Lecturer in Architecture
Carl Solander, Lecturer in Architecture
Laura Solano, Lecturer in Landscape Architecture
John Spengler, Affiliated Professor to the Department of Urban Planning and Design
Kathy Spiegelman, Design Critic in Urban Planning and Design
David Spillane, Design Critic in Urban Planning and Design
Lukasz Stanek, Lecturer in Architecture
James Stockard, Lecturer in Housing Studies
Benedetta Tagliabue, John T. Dunlop Design Critic in Architecture and Urban Planning and Design
Anne Tate, Design Critic in Urban Planning and Design
George Thomas, Lecturer in Architecture
Matthew Urbanski, Lecturer in Landscape Architecture
Michael VanRooyen, Visiting Professor in Urban Planning and Design
Rachel Vroman, Instructor in Architecture
Peter Walker, Visiting Professor of Urban Planning and Design
Bing Wang, Lecturer in Urban Planning and Design
Wang Shu, Kenzo Tange Visiting Professor in Architecture
Julia Watson, Lecturer in Landscape Architecture
Emily Waugh, Lecturer in Landscape Architecture
Marion Weiss, Design Critic in Architecture and Urban Planning and Design
Mason White, Visiting Assistant Professor of Landscape Architecture
Elizabeth Whittaker, Adjunct Assistant Professor of Architecture
Jay Wickersham, Lecturer in Architecture
Andrew Witt, Lecturer in Architecture
Kazuaki Yoneda, Teaching Associate in Architecture
Kongjian Yu, Visiting Professor of Landscape Architecture
Andrew Zientek, Instructor in Landscape Architecture
Darina Zlateva, Lecturer in Landscape Architecture

LOEB FELLOWS

Christopher Laurence Calott
Anna Heringer
Jean Brownhill Lauer
Andres Lepik
Ian Martin Lockwood
Anne-Marie Lubenau
Aaron D. Naparstek
Peter J. Park
Inga Saffron

Jane Acheson, Dean's Office
Joseph Amato, Building Services
Robert Angilly, Frances Loeb Library
Nader Ardalan, Architecture
Alla Armstrong, Academic Programs Business Office
John Aslanian, Student Services
Lauren Baccus, Human Resources
Kermit F. Baker, Joint Center for Housing Studies
Pamela H. Baldwin, Joint Center for Housing Studies
Lauren L. Beath, Finance Office
Eric S. Belsky, Joint Center for Housing Studies
P. Todd Belton, Computer Resources
Shantel Blakely, Events
Sue Boland, Computer Resources
Dan F. Borelli, Exhibitions
Stacy Buckley, Academic Services
Kevin Cahill, Building Services
Susie Chung, Joint Center for Housing Studies
Bonnie Campbell, External Relations
Anna Cimini, Computer Resources
Douglas F. Cogger, Computer Resources
Ellen Colleran, Landscape Architecture, UPD
Sean Kelliher Conlon, Student Services
Paul Cote, Computer Resources
Anne Creamer, Career Services
Andrea Croteau, Architecture
Maria T. da Rosa, Frances Loeb Library
Mary Daniels, Frances Loeb Library
Zhu Xiao Di, Joint Center for Housing Studies
Sarah Dickinson, Frances Loeb Library
Kerry Donahue, Joint Center for Housing Studies
Barbara Elfman, Advanced Studies Program
Stephen Ervin, Computer Resources
Beth Falkof, Development and Alumni Relations
Angela Flynn, Joint Center for Housing Studies
Rena Fonseca, Executive Education
Jennifer Friedman, Frances Loeb Library
Heather Gallagher, Executive Education
Erica George, Landscape Architecture, UPD
Suneeta Gill, Dean's Office
Keith A. Gnoza, Student Services
Meryl Golden, Career Services
Desiree Goodwin, Frances Loeb Library
Irina Gorstein, Frances Loeb Library
Hal Gould, Computer Resources
Norton Greenfeld, Development and Alumni Relations
Arin Gregorian, Academic Programs Business Office
Deborah Grohe, Building Services
Kim Gulko, Architecture
Gail Gustafson, Admissions
Mark Hagen, Computer Resources
Jennifer Halloran, Development and Alumni Relations
Barry Harper, Building Services
Jill Harrington, Admissions
Amanda Heighes, Publications
Cynthia Henshall, Real Estate Academic Initiative
Christopher Herbert, Joint Center for Housing Studies
Jackie B. Hernandez, Joint Center for Housing Studies
Megan A. Homan, Development and Alumni Relations
Joanna Hurier, Human Resources
Maggie Janik, Computer Resources
Anne Jeffko, Human Resources
Nancy J. Jennings, Executive Education
Pilar Jordan, Academic Programs Business Office
Johanna Kasubowski, Frances Loeb Library

Adam Kellie, Frances Loeb Library
Linda Ruth Kitch, Frances Loeb Library
Karen J. Kittredge, Finance Office
Jeffrey Klug, Career Discovery
Beth Kramer, Development and Alumni Relations
Mary Lancaster, Joint Center for Housing Studies
Ameilia Latham, Finance Office
Kevin Lau, Frances Loeb Library
Elizabeth LaJeunesse, Joint Center for Housing Studies
Sharon Lembo, Real Estate Academic Initiative
Burton LeGeyt, Fabrication Labs
Mary MacLean, Finance Office
Daniel McCue, Joint Center for Housing Studies
Michael A. McGrath, Faculty Planning
Megan McHugh, Human Resources
Jennifer Molinsky, Joint Center for Housing Studies
Margaret Moore De Chicojay, Executive Education
Corlette Moore McCoy, Executive Education
Maria Moran, Advanced Studies Program
Jerry Mui, Computer Resources
Maria Murphy, Student Services
Gerilyn Sue Nederhoff, Admissions
Page Nelson, Francis Loeb Library
Caroline Newton, Landscape Architecture, UPD
Meg Nipson, Joint Center for Housing Studies
Christine O'Brien, Communications
Trevor D. O'Brien, Building Services
Robert Ochshorn, Academic Services
Jackie Piracini, Administration and Academic Programs
Cecily Pollard, Development and Alumni Relations
Benjamin Prosky, Communications
Alix Reiskind, Frances Loeb Library
Ann Renauer, Finance Office
Carlos Reyes, Student Services
Patricia J. Roberts, Administration and Academic Programs
Kate Ryan, External Relations
Meghan Sandberg, Harvard Design Magazine
Rocio Sanchez-Moyano, Joint Center for Housing Studies
Nicole Sander, Landscape Architecture, UPD
Ronee Saroff, Communications
William S. Saunders, Harvard Design Magazine
Paul Scannell, Building Services
Emily Scudder, Frances Loeb Library
Laura Snowdon, Student Services
Vinu Srinivasan, Executive Education
Melinda Starmer, Faculty Planning
Jim Stockard, Loeb Fellowship
Jennifer Swartout, Architecture
Aimee Taberner, Academic Services
Kelly Teixeira, Student Services
Julia Topalian, Development and Alumni Relations
Ashley Torr, Architecture
Jennifer Vallone, Finance Office
Edna Van Saun, Design Labs
Melissa Vaughn, Publications
Rachel Vroman, Fabrication Labs
Ciel Wendel, Student Services
Ann Whiteside, Frances Loeb Library
Sara J. Wilkinson, Human Resources
Abbe H. Will, Joint Center for Housing Studies
Cameron J. Willard, Fabrication Labs
Janet Wysocki, Executive Education
Sally Young, Loeb Fellowship
Inés Maria Zalduendo, Frances Loeb Library
David Zimmerman-Stuart, Exhibitions

STUDENT GROUPS

Africa GSD
ASLA
Asia GSD
Asia Real Estate Association
Beer n' Dogs
Canada GSD
China GSD
The Developing World Forum
DIY (Design Initiative for Youth)
European Design Circle
FLOAT
Greece GSD
Green Design
GSD Christian Community
GSD Real Estate Development Club (RED)
Harvard Urban Planning Organization (HUPO)
India GSD
Inflatables
International Development and Urbanism (IDU)
Italian Society at Harvard Graduate School of Design
Japan GSD

Jewish Students of Design (JewSD)
Korea GSD
Land GSD
Landscape Lunchbox
Latin GSD
MDesS Club
The Mediterranean Society
National Organization of Minority Architecture Students (NOMAS)
New Geographies
Out Design
SoCA (Social Change and Activism)
Student Lecture Series
Student Wall
Symposium for Curating: Art, Design, and the Public Domain
Trays
Urban Mobilities
Women in Design
"YES NO" Student Journal
Yoga GSD

PRESTON SCOTT COHEN

RAHUL MEHROTRA

MICHAEL HAYS AND JORGE SILVETTI

CHARLES WALDHEIM, ANITA BERRIZBEITIA, CHRIS REI

JOAN BUSQUETS, FELIPE CORREA

PRESTON SCOTT COHEN AND CHARLES WALDHEI

SANFORD KWINTER

JORGE SILVETTI, JONATHAN LEVI, ERIKA NAGINSKI, ANTOINE PICON

CHARLES WALDHEIM

MOHSEN MOSTAFAVI

EL MOE AND CAMERON WU

ANTOINE PICON AND TIMOTHY HYDE

HASHIM SARKIS

ARTIN BECHTHOLD

JEROLD KAYDEN

TOSHIKO MORI WITH PHILIP GLASS

JILL DESIMINI

REM KOOLHAAS AND MICHAEL HAYS

NEIL BRENNER

ERIKA NAGINSKI, KRZYSZTOF WODICZ[K]
MICHAEL ARAD, AND ANTOINE PIC[O]

LIGHTFALL RECEPTION

MOSHE SAF[DIE] WITH BENJAMIN PROSKY

THOM MAYNE WITH CHARLES WALDHE[IM]

GSD AUDIENCE

LEX KRIEGER

ANDREW WITT

SANFORD KWINTER WITH MARINA ABRAMOVIĆ

ARK MULLIGAN

INGEBORG ROCKER

AUDIENCE QUESTIONS

JANE HUTTON, ROSETTA ELKIN,
SILVIA BENEDITO, AND JILL DESIMINI

LANDSCAPE INFRASTRUCTURE CONFERENCE

GSD 075 EXHIBITION

PLATFORM 4 EXHIBITION

PRESTON SCOTT COHEN'S LIGHTFALL EXHIBITION

DISPATCHES FROM THE HARVARD GSD: 075 YEARS OF DESIGN

...offer the opportunity to consider the past as an active ...ith the present and the future. For the GSD, this means ...an array of agents—people, events, objects and ...institutional history to bring the collective memory ...years into sharper focus for design practice today ...Conjuring a comprehensive account of the institu... ...its thousands of alumni, hundreds of faculty and ...ments—would run the risk of homogenizing a history ...to consistently by heterogeneity and multiplicity. ...ibition employs an approach that is episodic, reve... ...of the GSD's history that are as singular as they are ...have been conceived of as journalistic dispatches ...with its own narrative and artifacts. Writing ...rent tones, as this exhibition does, is an attempt

...to make the GSD's vitality clear and to claim a future that is at once inherited and projective.

The 130 dispatches in this exhibition begin in 1936 and arrive at the present day to include a handful of contemporary thought-pieces that form a cross section of the School's faculty, each expressing in a single authorial voice a reflection on the state of design today and the challenges of its future. The historical dispatches are organized into six thematic categories: Design as Research, Design as Critique, Design as Process, City as Form, The Continuous Institution, and The Shifting Institution. Each section contains dispatches that speak to a greater set of themes spanning all of the School's programs and departments, various media, and all seventy-five of the School's years. In momentarily stopping the clock, this exhibition hopes to enliven the GSD, and Harvard University at large, with the engagement and propulsion that the past can offer us today and tomorrow.

—Peter Christensen, PhD 2014, Curatorial Director

...'22 – DECEMBER 22, 2011

...ation With Harvard University's 375th Anniversary Celebration.

GSD 075 EXHIBITION

D 075 EXHIBITION

PRESTON SCOTT COHEN'S LIGHTFALL EXHIBITION

GSD 075 EXHIBITION

K-POP BEER AND DOGS

CHAUHA

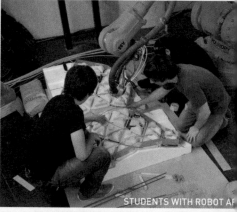

STUDENTS WITH ROBOT A

THE TRAYS AT GUND HALL

LLYWOOD BEER AND DOGS

LLYWOOD BEER AND DOGS

BEAUX-ARTS BALL

THE TRAYS AT GUND HALL

TIMOTHY HYDE AT BEN BRADY'S REVIEW

RACHEL ROBINSON REVIEW

CARL D'APOLITO-DWORKIN REVIEW

STEPHANIE LIN REVIEW

LIE CHEN REVIEW

JEREMY JIH REVIEW

BBY PIETRUSKO REVIEW

QUITO STUDIO FINAL REVIEW

BEN BRADY REVIEW

Harvard Graduate School of Design

Drew Gilpin Faust, President of Harvard University
Mohsen Mostafavi, Dean of the Graduate School of Design
Martin Bechthold, Co-Director of the Master in Design Studies Programs
Anita Berrizbeitia, Director of the Master in Landscape Architecture Degree Program
Preston Scott Cohen, Chair of the Department of Architecture
Felipe Correa, Director of the Master of Architecture in Urban Design and the Master of Landscape Architecture in Urban Design Programs
K. Michael Hays, Associate Dean for Academic Affairs and Co-Director of Doctoral Programs
Jerold Kayden, Director of the Master in Urban Planning Degree Program
Sanford Kwinter, Co-Director of the Master in Design Studies Programs
Rahul Mehrotra, Chair of the Department of Urban Planning and Design
Mark Mulligan, Director of the Master in Architecture Programs
Antoine Picon, Co-Director of Doctoral Programs
Charles Waldheim, Chair of the Department of Landscape Architecture

Pat Roberts, Executive Dean
Beth Kramer, Associate Dean for Development and Alumni Relations
Benjamin Prosky, Assistant Dean for Communications

Platform 5 Editorial Team

Mariana Ibañez - Associate Professor of Architecture and Faculty Editor

Gabrielle Patawaran (M.Arch I 2013) - Editor
Alison Von Glinow (M.Arch I 2013) - Editor
Fareez Giga (M.Arch I 2013) - Editor
Ben Brady (M.Arch I 2012)
Jeremy Jih (M.Arch I 2012)

ACTAR TEAM
Ramon Prat
Anna Tetas
Núria Saban

Melissa Vaughn, Director of Publications
Amanda Heighes, Copyeditor
Jake Starmer, Proofreader

Photo Credits

Anita Kan - Model Photography (unless otherwise noted)
Justin Knight
Maggie Janik
Aaron Orenstein
Sunggi Park
Peter Vanderwalker

Iwan Baan
Julia Xiao
Lv Hengzhong
Hufton and Crow

Imprint

Published by Harvard University Graduate School of Design and Actar

Graphic design and production, ActarPro
Printed at Grafos S.A., Barcelona

GSD Platform 5 represents selected studios, seminars, research, events, and exhibitions from the 2011-2012 academic year.

For additional information and a more comprehensive selection of student work, please visit www.gsd.harvard.edu.

The Harvard Graduate School of Design is a leading center for education, information, and technical expertise on the built environment. Its Departments of Architecture, Landscape Architecture, and Urban Planning and Design offer masters and doctoral degree programs, and provide the foundation for the school's Advanced Studies and Excecutive Education programs.

ISBN: 978-84-15391-28-9
DL: B-28008-12

Distribution

ActarD
Barcelona - New York
www.actar-d.com

Roca i Batlle 2
E-08023 Barcelona
T +34 93 417 49 93
F +34 93 418 67 07
salesbarcelona@actar.com

151 Grand Street, 5th floor
New York, NY 10013, USA
T +1 212 966 2207
F +1 212 966 2214
salesnewyork@actar.com

Special Thanks

We would like to thank the following individuals, for without their efforts this publication would not have been possible:

Mohsen Mostafavi, Benjamin Prosky, Melissa Vaughn, Felipe Correa, Eric Höweler, Dan Borelli, David Zimmerman Stuart, Anita Kan, Maggie Janik, Mark Hagen, Hal Gould, Jackie Piracini, Andrea Croteau, Trevor O'Brien, Drew Cowdrey, and Simon Kim.